THE RESEARCH COMPANION

Social science research has traditionally focused on the historical study of research methods, frequently overlooking the practical skills needed to undertake a research project. *The Research Companion* addresses this need for instruction in the practice of research and offers clear, honest advice to help avoid typical problems and improve standards.

The whole research process is covered in detail, from setting up a study through to presenting findings, with sections on all the basic tasks central to any research project, including:

- Planning research
- Researcher and participant safety
- Monitoring research in progress
- Research ethics.

The structure of the book means it is useful for researchers at all levels of experience. The numerous examples and case histories make it ideal for students just beginning their first research project, while the breadth of coverage and wealth of practical tips will also be highly relevant to experienced researchers.

This book will be invaluable to all researchers in the social or health sciences, whatever their level of experience, making research more accurate, ethical and productive.

Petra M. Boynton is a lecturer in International Primary Care at University College London. She has been awarded *Cosmopolitan* magazine's "Woman of Achievement" award for her educational work and was named one of Britain's "women to watch" by *The Guardian* for being the UK's first evidence-based agony aunt.

The Research Companion

A practical guide for the social and health sciences

Petra M. Boynton

Psychology Press
Taylor & Francis Group

HOVE AND NEW YORK

First published 2005
by Psychology Press
27 Church Road, Hove, East Sussex BN3 2FA

Simultaneously published in the USA and Canada
by Psychology Press
270 Madison Avenue, New York NY 10016

Psychology Press is part of the Taylor & Francis Group

Typeset in Palatino by RefineCatch Ltd., Bungay, Suffolk
Printed and bound in Great Britain by TJ International Ltd., Padstow, Cornwall
Cover design by Hybert Design

This publication has been produced with paper manufactured to strict
environmental standards and with pulp derived from sustainable forests.

British Library Cataloguing in Publication Data
A catalogue record for this book is available from the British Library

Library of Congress Cataloging-in-Publication Data
Data Boynton, Petra M.
The research companion : a guide for the social and health sciences / Petra M.
Boynton. – 1st ed.
       p. cm.
   Includes bibliographical references and index.
   ISBN 1-84169-304-9 (hardcover) – ISBN 1-84169-305-7 (pbk.)
   1. Social sciences—Research. 2. Social sciences—Methodology. I. Title.
   H62.B6284 2005
   300′.72–dc22
                                                                    2004027139

ISBN 1-84169-304-9 (hbk)
ISBN 1-84169-305-7 (pbk)

For B.B.—for everything

Contents

Acknowledgements   viii

1. Introduction   1

2. Planning research   19

3. Starting out   39

4. Completing research   61

5. Participants   71

6. Researcher well-being   119

7. Once a study's underway   139

8. End results and reporting findings   153

9. Endnote   179

References   183

Author index   189

Subject index   191

Acknowledgements

This book would never have been written without the positive and negative experiences I've encountered as a researcher. I would particularly like to thank the many participants, students, and colleagues I've worked with over the years, who have shown me where things don't work—and how research can be done better.

My grateful thanks as ever to my family—Patricia, Gerard, Leah, and Sylvester. I am indebted to my grandparents Nina Mary and Harry Hannaford, who serve as the inspiration for much of this book. Both were practical people who, when something needed to be done, got on and did it. I'd like to think this work represents a small step in this direction within research. To Gary Wood, Susan Catt, and Chris Carter, who are wonderful friends, and also have shared in the many discussions about how to improve research that underpin this book. I would also like to thank Jane Morton and Narrice Bucknor, who showed me how the research lessons we learn in "the lab" do not automatically transfer to a wider community context.

To the initial reviewers who approved the idea of this book: Jane Ussher, Alan Carr, Nigel Hunt and the anonymous contributor whose comments provided helpful advice and direction. To Caroline Osborne of Taylor & Francis, who, thanks to a fortuitous flight delay, had to endure my ideas about this book—and who luckily thought they were worth pursuing; and Lucy Farr and Claire Lipscomb for their support and prompt feedback. A warm "thank you" to David Wilson, Trish Greenhalgh and Dennis Howitt for their positive feedback on the final draft of this text. Particular gratitude is due to the following people who helped with reading drafts of this book: Will Callaghan (Chapters 1 to 4), Jill Russell (Chapter 2), Geoff Wong (Chapter 3), Julia Langham (Chapter 4), Sue Catt (Chapter 5), Gary Wood (Chapters 6 and 8), and Natalie Boston and Angela Crook (Chapter 7). With thanks to colleagues and students at the Open Learning Unit, Department of Primary Care & Population Sciences, University College London, for putting up with me while I was writing this book, and Will Callaghan for his unending support and interest.

Introduction 1

I wonder what you're thinking as you hold this book in your hand. Chances are it might be something like *not another book on research methods!* And you wouldn't be alone. When I proposed this book that was precisely the reaction of one of the reviewers, although luckily for me they went on to say they realised this text didn't fit that category. It's true, though; hundreds of books are available about methodologies for the social and health sciences, and the varied ways in which research "data" can be analysed. This one is different. Rather than focusing on how to choose or carry out methodological approaches, my aim is to give you skills to make research easier, less stressful, and more efficient. I've done this through using existing research examples, by reflecting on my own experience, and through feedback from other researchers, which you'll see throughout.

I really enjoy completing research, and find that working from a study idea through to a finished report, paper or intervention can be an amazing experience. One of the reviewers of this book pointed out that there is a tremendous amount of joy and pleasure to be gained from learning new skills, making research discoveries, solving tricky problems, or getting a significant result. And they are right. Research is a journey—one that can sometimes be tiring, but is equally likely to be exciting. It's the aim of this book to share that journey of research with you, to give you skills to get the most from your studies, and the opportunity to make your research story as positive as possible.

Why use this book?

You may have chosen this book because you are an undergraduate or postgraduate student who needs to learn more about the practical aspects of carrying out research. You may be a member of a community or patient group—a consumer who wants to commission or carry out some research—or maybe you've been approached to work on a study. Some of you will be graduates working as research

unwelcome yet not uncommon. Chen (1997) suggests that a conceptual boundary may take root in the difference between different content areas, if two constructs cannot maintain their distinctiveness in sharing the same content area simply because the quantitative and qualitative bounds will be ruined by reversible codings. This viable approach to clarification is based on the specific purposes of a study, and therefore certain flexibility in operationalization is indispensable and some variability in conceptualization should be envisioned. This perspective supplements the traditional notion of validity in psychometrics by removing the rigidity of the construct to be measured. If the researcher allows some degree of overlapping of the constructs in a relational analysis, he must acknowledge this and interpret his results on that particular basis. On the other hand, if his constructs are mutually exclusive, then all kinds of scaling procedures could be used and the multiple measurement results as a whole indicate the "true" relationship among the constructs.

Owing to the impact of the interrelations among theoretical constructs on their respective content areas and structures, theoretical formulations in empirical research will always be considered as flexible and specific. The price for avoiding confounding will be the modification of the definitions of various constructs. It seems unlikely that one must possess a theory valid enough to predict how test data should appear (Meier, 1994), but that the theory is to be finally specified in the validation process in which data could also be predicted. The viewpoint of relativity is important, and the role of research purpose need be stressed. With a sound, prerequisite logical basis, our scaling efforts could center on vigorous exploration and systematic development of multiple measurement tools rather than simply fall on compliant tests. Chen (1997) introduces a new idea of measurement power or scaling effectiveness to indicate the relative degree of success in attaining the full measure of the relationship under inquiry. This directs research effort to the maximum exposure of specific relationships rather than aiming at some isolated, "absolute," but elusive individual constructs. Aiming at the power of unconfounded measurement or the effectiveness of scaling methods, the use of criteria will be part of an aggressive scaling process in order to achieve the fullest theoretical results.

The above shows that confounding is unavoidable by conventional understanding. On the other hand, clear boundaries are possible by tracing the roots of the problem and stressing the role of purpose in understanding the specific meaning of a theoretical formulation. In terms of a particular design of a research investigation, the question is how to form a meaningful relational research as

assistants, or postdoctorates coordinating a study. Alternatively you may be a health or social services worker who needs to learn more about research to inform your profession, or you could even be an experienced researcher bringing in grants and managing a research team. This book is aimed at all of you. If you are just starting out, it will give you skills and confidence to get going; it will help more experienced researchers manage their own work and help with the development of any staff they are supervising. Most importantly it will help you carry out research in a way that protects your well-being, and that of any participants you encounter.

On that note, the aims and objectives of this book are to:

- Cover issues not typically addressed in research methodologies texts or courses
- Make use of "expert researcher opinions" to highlight common problem areas
- Assist researchers to complete more accurate, ethical, and product-ive research
- Ensure good treatment of participants
- Improve the skills of researchers in terms of writing and presenting information
- Save researchers time and money, and help them work more efficiently
- Encourage debate and discussion about the practicalities of research.

How is this book different?

The official explanation goes something like this. Social science research has traditionally focused on methods in order to teach ways of completing studies. Much of what we learn in research tends to be acquired in practice, and most information around research assumes rather than checks that people know how to conduct work, resulting in poor science, wasted time, and a negative effect on the morale of the researcher. If many of these practical issues were taught to researchers, higher quality research could be completed, yet there seems to be a resistance among academics to sharing information they have learned.

The alternative story is as follows. As an undergraduate studying social psychology I got a grounding in methods that is probably similar to most people's experience if they've been taught research in an academic setting. Once a week we'd spend three hours in a lab being taught about experiments, variables, and validity, and debating qualitative versus quantitative methods—with the latter usually faring better (see also Howitt, 1991). We practised running studies on each other, and we helped our tutors with their research by participating in their studies. We didn't really think about these ideas learned in "the lab", or get a chance to apply them in the real world with real people, but we were given plenty of confidence that by knowing our methods off pat, we'd be able to carry out studies and collect data. I also spent three years studying statistics, where I learned, panicked about, and then promptly forgot the different types of statistical tests you could use on numerical data. Nobody taught us data management, how to cope with large datasets—and data cleaning wasn't mentioned at all. Neither was the analysis of qualitative "data".

As a postgraduate, I continued to live in this research bubble. I was now designing my own studies using qualitative and quantitative approaches, and I had no problem with recruiting participants. Why would I? They were undergraduates, and many of them were my students, meaning it was easy for me to ask them to take part, and probably quite hard for them to refuse. The ethics of this didn't really occur to me until a lot later (Banyard & Hunt, 2002). Due to my 100 per cent response rates I didn't have to think about how to deal with people refusing to participate, or even about including exclusion criteria for people who might not fit my study design. Everyone was welcome to the party, and it seemed they all turned up.

I probably continued believing research was this easy until I completed a study that entirely changed my outlook. I was hired to look at the issue of prostitution in a West Midlands town (Boynton, Bucknor, & Morton, 1998), and suddenly saw a different side to life, and to research. For a start, people said "no". A lot. They said "no" to being asked to participate, gatekeepers wouldn't give access to participants, steering group members didn't like suggestions for the study design, and often when people did say "yes" to be in the study it was a nightmare trying to get an appointment to see them (Boynton, 2002). It was all wrong! I'd been taught that if you produced a good design and controlled your variables, your study would work—nobody had told me that a steering group, or the participants themselves, might have their own ideas on what would happen. Nobody had said "no" to me before: people loved being in my studies; in fact I often had to turn participants away! I had not been taught that research took up so much time, so many letters and phone calls, so much cajoling and persuading, and so many late evenings. I knew a lot about methods, but, I realised, I knew very little about applying those methods in "real-life" situations (Robson, 1993).

The prostitution research also had another angle that taught me a great deal. Two local women had heard about the study and had volunteered to be researchers. They were of a similar age to myself and the prostitute women we'd be interviewing, and had grown up in the same neighbourhood, sharing the same regional dialect. They were enthusiastic, bright, and feisty. Both women have now become dear friends, and I am indebted to them for the questions they asked me. When I was being taught about research I listened and took notes, as did the undergraduate students I was now teaching. Nobody really asked questions. The two women we hired for the prostitution research asked them endlessly—"Why do you do it that way?," "Why can't we ask this instead?," "That won't work, nobody'll understand you," "What's the point of that?," and so on. Through trying to answer their questions I realised that much of what we take for granted about methods is changeable, and can be quite flexible—it's just that we're frequently taught it in a very rigid way. I came to realise that my (and the steering group's) well-meaning suggestion of using qualitative interviews to find out why women worked as prostitutes wasn't all that helpful given their association of "taped interview" with something that unscrupulous journalists or the police inflicted on them. We eventually compromised and used a questionnaire for the more personal issues we wanted to cover (Boynton, 2002). True, it went against everything I'd been taught about methods—where qualitative studies were always presented as being more "sensitive"—but it was what the participants wanted, and we needed to hear what they had to say.

My training in research methods wasn't bad, and in fact much of the teaching was quite liberal. Even so, I could picture several of my tutors having a problem with the above statement that participants might select or direct the methods used. Again, one of the underlying themes of my teaching was the researcher decides on the problem, how it is to be measured, and what will be said about the issue. The participant's job is to turn up and do their task (without saying "no" or asking difficult questions), and then to leave and let the researcher get on with the end product—a paper or similar. Nowadays we're fortunately embracing a more equitable view of research, thanks to efforts of groups like Involve (formerly Consumers in NHS Research), and charities like MIND. It is still unsettling for many researchers to have to consider participants in this way, but my steep learning curve with the prostitution study showed me that if you don't ask it right, you don't get anything back.

Since working on that study I've continued to work in community-based settings, and with each project realised there's more to learn. With the work I completed on intermediate care for older people (Boston, Boynton, & Hood, 2001a) I learned how to introduce a study and adapt letters, consent forms and other literature for those with visual or hearing problems. I learned how to close an interview, often when the participant was lonely or depressed and wanted me to stay longer. I also experienced dealing with ethics committees, and managing large datasets—including noting participants who didn't fit the study criteria, or who refused to take part. I've worked with participants who do not speak English as a first language, or who speak no English at all, requiring me to use interpreters and alternative methods. Other studies within primary care have taught me a great deal about fitting in with staff who are overburdened with work and demands from researchers (Boston, Boynton, & Hood, 2001b). In short, I've learned to sell my research to others, to network, to think about the needs of my research team and our participants, and to be aware of when things are falling behind or going successfully. Pretty much everything I wish someone had told me before I started research.

I'm not saying that working in the community is harder than working within a university setting. It would also be wrong of me to imply that involving students as participants is less valid than including other members of society. It can be tricky to do research full stop, whatever the setting or the participants. Things can, and do, go wrong. Much of this book is a testimony to mistakes I've made along the way, or things I had to learn through trial and error. However, none of the issues covered in this book are particularly difficult or mystical—they just don't tend to get recorded or talked about. Reasons for this include younger researchers blaming themselves for perceived "mistakes" and not admitting to them, and more senior researchers not being aware that their staff need training (Boynton, Catt, & Wood, 2001). When work is published we hear only the final "cleaned up" result (Woolgar, 1996), and don't tend to hear what goes on "behind the scenes" (Slife & Williams, 1995). Frequently problems can be avoided if anticipated (which this book should help you achieve). We need to start thinking about research as a changeable entity that requires a flexible approach, not a set bank of methods to be learned and stuck to come what may.

How to use this book

You can use this book in several ways. You may want to read it through as an accompaniment to your other studies. You may want to focus on the exercises within the book, or pick out key issues to discuss with your manager, students, or colleagues. Alternatively, you may want to use it as a resource, to dip into at different times during a project. Table 1.1 provides an outline of each chapter and what it covers, in case you need to find a particular topic straight away. It's advised that even if you don't read the whole book in one sitting or in the order it's set out, you do read it through at some point. Even if you are an experienced researcher it may remind you of topics that you ought to be discussing with your staff—and for junior researchers it may flag up areas where you know you need to focus.

Covering all your bases

As mentioned above, many excellent books on research, analysis, and writing skills are available. No one text can teach you everything about completing research in the social or health sciences. To that end, this book is aimed at filling the gaps between some of these texts. Table 1.2 outlines what this book will teach you, and other resources available to increase your research skills.

If you feel you need to brush up on your research skills, you may want to start with them first before reading this book—or a better idea would be to use this book and work on your other research needs as you go along.

TABLE 1.1

Where to find information in this book

I need to know how to . . .	I can find out more in . . .
Deal with ethics committees	*Chapter 3* covers ethical issues and approaching ethics committees. *Chapters 5 and 6* deal with the ethical treatment of participants and project staff.
Work with participants	*Chapter 3* discusses consumer involvement. *Chapter 5* covers everything from voluntary informed consent to dealing with difference.
Look after my own/my staff's well-being	*Chapter 6* discusses safety when working within the community or in university settings.
Plan a study	*Chapter 2* runs through literature searching, planning, and networking.
Get started	*Chapter 3* covers objectives and timescales.
Avoid making mistakes	*Chapter 4* outlines piloting, selecting methods and running research. *Chapter 7* discusses data cleaning and maintenance.
Stay motivated	*Chapter 4* offers tips on coping with boredom, workload, etc.
Work out what my role is	*Chapter 3* covers research hierarchies and accountability.
Manage my staff	*Chapter 3* (see above) and *Chapter 4* (motivation) may help. *Chapter 6* may be of use if your staff are challenging.
Know who owns the research	*Chapter 3* addresses intellectual property and research ownership.
Cope with all my data!	*Chapter 7* will help you cope with data management, cleaning, and entry.
Stop my project wasting time and resources	*Chapter 3* covers timescales; running an efficient research office is addressed in *Chapter 7*.
Write my work up	*Chapter 8* outlines possible publication/ presentation sources, writing for different audiences, etc.
Stop my manager/ participants/colleagues bullying/harassing me	*Chapter 6* covers all aspects of bullying, harassment, and coping with problem research situations.

TABLE 1.2

Other resources to help with research

Skills gap	Where this book fits in	You can also use . . .
I want to learn how to get a degree in the social or health sciences.	This book gives you skills that may help when studying for a degree, but doesn't cover topics like study skills, completing a course, or preparing for an exam or viva.	*How to get a PhD: A handbook for students and their supervisors* (3rd ed.), Estelle M. Phillips & Derek S. Pugh (2000), Open University Press, Buckingham, UK. *The research student's guide to success* (2nd ed.), Pat Cryer (2000), Open University Press, Buckingham, UK. *The doctoral experience*, Paul Atkinson, Sara Delamont, & Odette Parry (2000), Falmer, London. *How to get a good degree: Making the most of your time at university*, Philip Race (1999), Open University Press, Buckingham, UK.
I want to learn what different methods are out there, and which one's the best.	This book will give you a brief outline on different methodologies (see Chapter 2), in the context of choosing the right method to suit your research question and your participants. You should read this book in conjunction with other texts on methods, as it will teach you how to plan, design, organise and coordinate research using different methodological approaches.	*Ground rules for good research: A 10 point guide for social researchers*, Martyn Denscombe (2002), Open University Press, Buckingham, UK. *Qualitative researching*, Jennifer Mason (1996), Sage, Thousand Oaks, CA. *Qualitative health psychology: Theories and methods*, Michael Murray & Ken Chamberlain (Eds.) (1999), Sage, Thousand Oaks, CA. *Research methods in social relations* (6th ed.), C. M. Judd, E. R. Smith, & L. H. Kidder (1991), Harcourt Brace Jovanovich College Publishers, Fort Worth, TX. *Research methods in psychology* (3rd ed.), Gary A. Heiman (2002), Houghton Mifflin, Boston. *Handbook of qualitative research methods for psychology and the social sciences*, John T. E. Richardson (Ed.) (1996), BPS Books, Leicester, UK.
I need to become a better manager and/or to supervise students/staff.	This book covers many issues that will help you manage your research and any staff in a better way (see Chapters 3, 5 and 6), from time management through to staff and participant well-being.	*Communicating with your staff: Skills for increasing cohesion and teamwork*, Karla Powell (2001), American Medical Association, Washington, DC. *Managing for dummies* (2nd ed.), Bob Nelson & Peter Economy, Wiley, New York.

		Supervising the PhD, Sara Delamont, Paul Atkinson, & Odette Parry (1998), Open University Press, Buckingham, UK. Managing scientists: Leadership strategies in research and development, Alice M. Sapienza (1995), Wiley, New York.
I can't do qualitative or quantitative analysis.	This book isn't a guide to statistics (or analysis of qualitative "data"). However, if you don't design a good study, manage it well, and clean, organise, and enter your data appropriately, you won't even get to the scary stats part. Use this book as an accompaniment to analysis guides so you can be sure your work is robust.	*First steps in research and statistics: A practical workbook for psychology students*, Dennis Howitt & Duncan Cramer (2000), Routledge, London. *Critical textwork: an introduction to varieties of discourse and analysis*, Ian Parker & the Bolton Discourse Network (1999), Open University Press, Buckingham. *Discourse analytic research: Repertoires and readings of texts in action*, Erica Burman and Ian Parker (Eds.) (1993), Routledge, London. StatSoft Online Advice—http://www.statsoftinc.com/textbook/stathome.html
What about computer packages for research?	This book touches on computer support. However, you may also want to talk to your manager, supervisor, and colleagues if you need further training. Many colleges, community organisations, and charities offer training in Access, Excel, Word, or statistical packages like SPSS. See what is available in your area. If you are a community researcher you may be able to get a discount—talk to your local university for more details.	*Microsoft® Office 2000 for Windows® for dummies®* Wallace Wang & Roger C. Parker (1999), Wiley, New York. *The SPSS book: A student guide to the Statistical Package for the Social Sciences*, Matthew J. Zagummy (2001), Writers Club Press, Lincoln, NE. Tips on using SPSS—http://www.ats.ucla.edu/stat/spss
How do I learn to write reports or papers?	This book will teach you the skills to ensure that what is written about in your report is of a high standard, and how to create and disseminate research (see Chapter 8).	*How to write health science papers, dissertations, and theses*, Shane A. Thomas (2000), Churchill Livingstone, Edinburgh, UK. *How to write a great research paper: A step-by-step guide*, Leland Graham & Darriel Ledbetter (1995), Incentive Publications, Nashville, TN.

Who are you?

I've told you a bit about me and how I came to write this book. We are rarely asked to consider our role or skills as researchers (Cherry, 1995b), or what our training needs are. Before continuing with this book, you may find the following exercise helpful. It requires you to think about your abilities and needs. You may want to revisit these questions as you progress through this book, or studies you are working on—or you may want to use your answers to help appraise your staff, or discuss with your manager/supervisor what training you may benefit from.

Exercise: Researcher Skills and Abilities Checklist
(adapted from Health Services Management Centre [HSMC], University of Birmingham, 1996)

There are lots of different aspects of research. This questionnaire contains a number of statements that describe important aspects of research work. You are asked to indicate your current skills and abilities for each aspect. If you feel capable of completing an item, score 1. If you feel you need further experience or practice, score 2. If you are completely unable to do a task, score 3. If there is any item you believe you require additional training/experience in, write T alongside your numerical answer. Some of the questions do not necessarily fit this format, but wherever possible try to complete them. Remember this questionnaire is for you to assess your own strengths, weaknesses, and attitudes towards research. There are no right or wrong answers, and you don't have to share your answers with anyone if you don't want to. It is important that you think about how each statement relates to your undertaking research before making your choices. Try to complete all the items on this questionnaire. Interpret each question alongside the statements provided.

Being an effective researcher would give me the opportunity to . . .

1a.	Examine organisational change issues and implications with contacts and colleagues.	
1b.	Organise arrangements for maintaining performance standards.	
1c.	Identify current deficiencies in theoretical understanding.	
2a.	Critically assimilate and evaluate relevant literature.	

2b.	Ensure research approach is politically acceptable to key stakeholders.	
2c.	Guide others in performing specific tasks and activities.	
3a.	Identify alternative research hypotheses that can be tested.	
3b.	Ensure relevant information is properly organised and up to date.	
3c.	Integrate data and information from a variety of sources.	
4a.	Obtain all the necessary information before making decisions.	
4b.	Analyse how concepts relate to one another.	
4c.	Undertake formal review of relevant (scientific) literature.	
5a.	Examine transferability of results to other contexts.	
5b.	Develop efficient audit procedures.	
5c.	Pose problems as answerable research questions.	
6a.	Assess costs and benefits of undertaking alternative research approaches.	
6b.	Design research studies with appropriate controls (if necessary).	
6c.	Develop efficient information retrieval systems.	
7a.	Identify representative sampling frames.	
7b.	Consider organisational priorities and their potential future impact.	
7c.	Advise on work methods and performance standards.	
8a.	Obtain or devise standardised measuring instruments (qualitative and quantitative).	
8b.	Avoid the distractions of organisational politics.	
8c.	Interpret research information in the context of the organisational setting.	
9a.	Design strategies for reliable and valid data collection.	
9b.	Develop a wide variety of working relationships.	
9c.	Use research results to assist others in making decisions.	
10a.	Ensure the continuity of programmes and policies.	
10b.	Improve understanding of organisational processes.	
10c.	Plan research and schedule research activities.	
11a.	Design new management structures and systems.	
11b.	Know when it is appropriate to use standardised instruments.	
11c.	Make necessary value judgements about collected information.	
12a.	Be aware of the different meanings of "objectivity" in research.	

(Continued overleaf)

dissertation will have to do with some of the areas chosen.

(2) Make a course schedule, or a timetable, for the courses you expect to take. If you do not yet have a particular topic for your thesis/dissertation, the selected courses will help you expand your scope and search for candidates for the most interesting topic. The selected course readings could also be the first material you would like to include in your literature review as part of your thesis or dissertation. It seems that nobody can really jump into her thesis or dissertation. The search for an appropriate research topic takes time and the understanding of the issues involved is an accumulative process. If you wait until you finish everything but your thesis/dissertation, you are leaving yourself in a vacuum that would delay your advancement to your degree candidacy for weeks, months, or even another year.

(3) Decide on the kind of research skills you want to pursue. Although all kinds of research methods appear to be useful, you are limited in time and energy and thus must choose a few that seem to be the most useful to the conduct of your intended research. It is apparent that you should apply the methods that you know well, or at least relatively better, to your study. Therefore, your decision in this respect will have significant implications to your thesis and dissertation research.

It is safe to say that undergraduate education follows a more generalist model while graduate training is more specialized. Generalization and specialization, however, can only be talked in relative terms and an oversight or denial of either need will hurt the students at both levels. There is a difficult trade-off in anybody's educational preparation: you will prolong your course of study if you overemphasizes its extensiveness, or you will limit your career choices if you end up with premature specialization. In thinking about your study plan you should anticipate the educational consequences and make it suit your needs to the maximum degree.

The theory and research papers

In the course of your study you will be writing a lot of papers to satisfy various academic requirements. If you are a doctoral student, you are likely to be required to write some papers, in a very formal manner, as part of your qualifying examination. Such papers, beyond the term papers you write for particular courses, are commonly called the "comprehensive papers." Typically, there are

opposed to the comprehensive measurement of an individual construct. Methodological study has not well articulated the difference between these two kinds of research. Probably this is because behavioral and social measurement ideas such as reliability and validity are established mainly as an effort of psychometrics. The primary concern of psychological testing, however, is not the relationship between variables but such individual constructs as IQ or ability. The focal interest is how to achieve the most complete and valid measure of the construct itself. Such testing, of course, is very important in education and screening. The requirement of validity would therefore demand a comprehensive coverage of the content area, possibly including anything relevant. However, if this requirement for validity is applied to a relational research which is most frequently seen in social science studies, it might bring about some serious consequences. Recently there have been scholars pointing out the confounding issue in social research, and some good points have been raised to deal with the situation. However, the issue is far from settled and many social researchers are still perplexed by this problem. The measurement effectiveness principle discussed above in contrast to the traditional validity principle provides a guide to relational research in social science studies. To recapitulate, this principle underscores the importance of research purpose, which requires attention to the issue of overlapping of different constructs in the same study, not just the content or construct validity of the individual constructs.

Strictly speaking, researchers should adopt the mutual exclusiveness criterion. That is, the content included in one construct cannot be included in any other construct in the same study. Otherwise it will cause a confounding problem. However, many theoretical constructs in social and behavioral sciences are made overlapping with one another. If the mutual exclusiveness criterion is rigidly applied everywhere, it will change the definition of some important constructs and seriously conflict with the traditional validity principle. Chen's measurement effectiveness principle allows the researcher to use a more flexible treatment. In other words, it allows a certain degree of overlapping in certain research situations. However, the researcher must clarify the research purpose, and give the reasons for the specific choice. Especially, when presenting research results and their implications, the researcher must point out the degree of overlapping in measuring constructs, and clarify how much of the correlation, discovered or validated, is simply due to the overlapping in measurement. The understanding of social research results, therefore, is a complicated and dialectic thing. Simply applying existing measures, even if they are perfect, or attempting to develop a

12b.	Build a (demanding) future role.	
12c.	Examine the feasibility of proposed changes emanating from research.	
13a.	Use exploratory "ideas frameworks" and "mental maps".	
13b.	Gain insight into work processes.	
13c.	Ensure information is collected in a methodical and systematic manner.	
14a.	Ensure all evidence is presented accurately, accounting for stakeholders, consumers/participants, colleagues, additional studies/publications, etc.	
14b.	Locate organisational areas with scope for improvement.	
14c.	Develop career prospects.	
15a.	Ensure that all research evidence is as "reliable" and "valid" as possible.	
15b.	Ensure the research techniques/methods are appropriate to the question(s) being investigated and participants to be used.	
15c.	Carry out long-term planning.	
16a.	Construct logical/mathematical models of problem areas.	
16b.	Adopt a sympathetic and understanding approach to others.	
16c.	Generate innovative ideas for exploration.	
17a.	Consider the theoretical significance of research ideas.	
17b.	Adapt research plans as circumstances demand.	
17c.	Produce and modify work schedules.	
18a.	Understand what makes colleagues "tick".	
18b.	Interpret research findings in the context of organisational "realities".	
18c.	Use research ideas to construct abstract theories.	
19a.	Assess information from a number of different sources.	
19b.	Pursue my own academic interests.	
19c.	Understand debates around "neutrality", "objectivity", and "value-freedom", and apply them to my work.	
20a.	Deal with health/research issues rather than business pressures.	
20b.	Integrate current findings with established knowledge.	
20c.	Assess costs and benefits of implementing research findings.	
21a.	Work in an interesting workplace.	
21b.	Explore the practical value of applying research-based options.	
21c.	Publish research findings in refereed academic journals.	

22a.	Present papers at (scientific) conferences.	
22b.	Earn a good reputation for my work.	
22c.	Convert research results into feasible organisational action plans.	
23a.	Evaluate the theoretical outcomes of research programmes.	
23b.	Identify available data sources and methods of information collection.	
23c.	Feel confident that my skills are appreciated.	
24a.	Report research findings in a way that facilitates action and future replication(s).	
24b.	Collate information that is relevant to my research area/question.	
25a.	Write and disseminate research reports for a variety of audiences.	
25b.	Improve the job-satisfaction of those I work with.	
25c.	Clarify problems by critically appraising all relevant issues.	

Once you have answered the questions on what being a researcher would allow you to do, take time to consider where you feel competent, and where you require further training. Don't worry if you feel there are many areas where you require support—the aim of this book is to give you information on how to acquire the research skills you need.

After thinking about what research allows you to do, think about your skills and abilities in more detail by answering the following questions in the same way as before. (If you feel capable of completing an item, score 1. If you feel you need further experience or practice, score 2. If you are completely unable to do a task, score 3. If there is any item you believe you require additional training/experience in, write T alongside your numerical answer.)

I feel I have a particular ability to . . .

1a.	Collect (appropriate) data in a systematic way.	
1b.	Keep up-to-date databases (and clean data regularly).	
1c.	Link pure and applied aspects of research.	
2a.	Know where best to target organisational change.	
2b.	Structure problems into various conceptual "models".	
2c.	Involve myself in a range of important tasks.	

(Continued overleaf)

3a.	Evaluate ideas on their merits.	
3b.	Design balanced and/or controlled research projects (if appropriate).	
3c.	Link research findings to specific innovations/outcomes.	
4a.	Pinpoint strengths and weaknesses in current theories.	
4b.	Gain a clear picture of complex issues.	
4c.	Solve day-to-day work difficulties.	
5a.	Produce novel ideas that are worthy of further examination.	
5b.	Deliver research presentations at conferences.	
5c.	Improve my professional skills.	
6a.	Understand the objectives and priorities of the organisation.	
6b.	Identify evidence and "factual" information.	
6c.	Make future projections about the impact of organisational plans/outcomes.	
7a.	Use research to clarify the structure and functions of an organisation/issue.	
7b.	Appreciate the contribution of other staff (whatever their grade).	
7c.	Translate theory into focused research questions.	
8a.	Debate the causes and consequences of research issues.	
8b.	Intervene in personal problems of staff.	
8c.	Define representative sampling frames.	
9a.	Maintain personal enthusiasm and commitment to change.	
9b.	Use social interactions as a rich source of additional information.	
9c.	Distinguish between evidence and opinion (but know how to utilise both).	
10a.	Compare and contrast relevant (scientific) methodologies.	
10b.	Inform decision-making on the basis of pertinent research results.	
10c.	Influence the behaviour of others.	
11a.	Assimilate new results into established knowledge.	
11b.	Acquire relevant knowledge about work activities.	
11c.	Assess the wider value of research results to other contexts.	
12a.	Construct or adopt reliable and valid research instruments.	
12b.	Identify and apply practical outcomes of research activities.	
12c.	Delegate appropriate tasks to others.	
13a.	Work well in a team.	

13b.	Present findings in accordance with academic convention.	
13c.	Take account of organisational/social "realities" in assessing research implications.	
14a.	Persuade others to make effective decisions.	
14b.	Maintain (strong) objectivity when integrating research evidence.	
14c.	Explore links between concepts and constructs.	
15a.	Ensure quality is monitored and maintained.	
15b.	Appraise relative costs of following up research recommendations.	
15c.	Adopt a structured approach to data collection.	
16a.	Communicate research work to all levels.	
16b.	Modify research strategies as situations evolve.	
16c.	Evaluate the theoretical contribution of a research programme.	
17a.	Design detailed work schedules.	
17b.	Gain the support of influential others.	
17c.	Think analytically about research ideas.	
18a.	Maintain the quality of all information used as research evidence.	
18b.	Question policies I do not agree with.	
18c.	Select a research strategy using cost and benefit assessments.	
19a.	Understand the feelings of those working in my area/discipline.	
19b.	Extract useful "data" from available sources.	
19c.	Specify research questions so that they can be tested.	
20a.	Match research approach to social issues.	
20b.	Undertake organisational planning.	
20c.	Manage the stages and phases in research projects.	
21a.	Target different audiences with different styles of report-writing.	
21b.	Teach others about research design(s).	
21c.	Sift relevant "informal" or "grapevine" information.	
22a.	Recognise values and drawbacks of using standardised instruments.	
22b.	Reason using mental maps and/or images.	
22c.	Maintain my own sense of purpose and motivation.	

(Continued overleaf)

23a.	Assess the value of research "data" from a practical perspective.	
23b.	Assess the theoretical value of research reports and articles.	
23c.	Cooperate with others in the organisation.	
24a.	Write academic research papers.	
24b.	Appraise the technical feasibility of implementing research recommendations.	
24c.	Keep up to date with new developments.	
25a.	Develop higher-level theoretical abstractions from basic research "data".	
25b.	Initiate staff development projects.	
25c.	Evaluate the relative value of disparate types of information.	

What is research?

This book uses the term "research" frequently. However, what this term actually means has come under close scrutiny over recent years. People within different disciplines, or favouring different method-ological or philosophical approaches, have diverse views about what "research" might be. Further confusion arises when people are uncertain whether what they're doing constitutes research, or whether it's an audit, an evaluation, or something else. I've taken an open view on "research" here, using it to mean a variety of things. You can use this book and the questions it raises to discuss whether you're completing research; and whether you end up thinking you're doing research, evaluation, audit or other, you can use the techniques outlined here to improve your practice and the process of completing your work.

Let's get started

I hope you enjoy the rest of this book. One of the striking character-istics of methods books is that they aren't always all that interesting to read. It's not their authors' fault, it's just that methods aren't really considered a sexy subject (see also Benson & Blackman, 2003; Terre Blanche & Durrheim, 1999). I hope that even while this book inevit-ably covers issues that may seem mundane or dull, the stories from researchers and tips within it may make it less arduous. What methods books often miss out is the excitement, humour, and anticipation that underlies research. The stories within this text are a testament to the many sides of studies.

Remember, although this book can cover issues for you, it is not designed as a replacement for actual experience: *"All the reading in the world won't make you into a skilled enquirer. There is the danger of the centipede problem (it never moved again after trying to work out which leg moved first) and much to be said for jumping in, carrying out enquiries and developing skills through experience"* (Robson, 1993, p. xvi). As well as jumping in and trying things out, the main aim of this book is to get you thinking about research—and to get you talking about it. Much of the work we do seems to be done without discussion or reflection, so talk to other researchers and share with them ideas raised here—that way research may become a lot more interesting, and you'll certainly get more out of it.

Planning research 2

Research is generally presented to us in a "backwards" format: that is, we see the end result first. This means that research tends to be in reports or journals that may not always tell the whole research story. While they give us a "finished product", we're discouraged from thinking about how the research was created or conducted (Slife & Williams, 1995; Woolgar, 1996). Planning is probably the most important aspect of any study, but is frequently hurried or overlooked. Yet if we miss these key skills, we may never get to see our work as a report or paper.

This chapter will cover the issues and questions that will form the focus of a project or study, including:

- Research questions
- Possible methods to be used
- Analysis (qualitative/quantitative)
- Purpose, scale, and proposed end result of research
- Making research plans and stakeholder analysis
- The needs of participants/researchers
- What support is available to complete a study
- Making links
- Budgets and funding sources
- Literature searches.

These issues all need consideration, but different studies at different levels will also have different requirements. Sometimes you have to deal with all of the above factors, while for smaller projects you may share the tasks, and in certain cases you may not need to complete all of them (for example, if you are carrying out a student project you may not need to think about budgets).

Thinking about your research questions

In the previous chapter, we looked at the idea of thinking about your role in research in terms of your skills, and what research could do for you. Before considering research questions themselves, it's also worth thinking about why you need to complete a study (see Denscombe, 1998, p. 5).

Exercise: Why are you doing this?

Take a moment to think about yourself in relation to research. You might find it difficult at first since it's not something we tend to do, given that much of research is tied up with getting a study started, not thinking about our place in it. The aim of this exercise is to get you thinking about why you do research—and how you feel about it. Set aside 15 minutes and think about why you're doing research. *Is it because you:*

- *Have to do it?* For example you have to complete a study for your dissertation, or as part of your job.
- *Want to do it?* This may include because you find people or a subject area interesting, or perhaps you want to increase your existing skills, or want to do a study because it might be fun or enjoyable.
- *Need to do it?* Maybe there's a social issue that's important to you, or you feel needs to be addressed urgently; perhaps there's a problem that needs explaining or sorting out that research could help with.

You may find that you identify with one of the categories above, or perhaps a mixture of them. Think about this list and see what reasons resonate with you—either that you agree with, or that you feel don't match your idea of research. Then on a blank sheet of paper write "I am a researcher because . . ." and note down as many reasons or explanations as spring to mind. You may want to keep this record, because as your research career progresses your reasons may alter. The point of this exercise isn't to create a fixed researcher identity—it's to start you thinking "why am I doing this?" During research we should consider our motives all the time, and sometimes question why we're doing the work at all. Rather than seeing it as an unrelated idea, or an anguished cry when things go badly, you should continue to question who you are, and what is going on.

Once you've focused on why you need to do your study, the next step is to think about a clear rationale for your work. Thinking about why an issue requires assessment can keep you focused on your study question. You may need to think of a study idea because it's expected of you (for example, you need to complete a project for your course), or because there's some funding available you want to bid for, or even because you're aware of an issue or problem that you think you may be able to find an answer to. Whatever the reason, work will be difficult if you don't have a clear focus on what you want to ask. However, you need to be flexible. If you are completing action research or ethnography, you won't be beginning a study with a fixed hypothesis or idea—instead you'll be thinking around a broad area you wish to investigate. If you are completing an experiment or evaluation you may have a highly specific question you wish to answer. This means that while you're thinking about the question/area/issue you'd like to investigate, you should also begin thinking about what kind of method would best suit your needs.

> Some studies I've supervised haven't worked out simply because the person doing the research wasn't clear about what they wanted to do. Having a vague idea, or often far too many, means that the research may get done, but it also may not tell us very much. (Clive, tutor)

Before you get started, think long and hard about exactly what it is you want to find out. Keep your question as simple as possible—avoid having lots of different things you want to ask. Instead, condense your thoughts down to a clear aim or idea. If you have a clear question it will help you consider how best to go about answering it. Frequently problems arise in research because the question was too broad, confused, or perhaps not very original (a good idea, but something someone else had already answered). Don't feel that your question has to be carved in stone, or even sound very formal, in the early stages of a study. As you move through your literature searching and designing your study, you may find that your original question alters slightly. That's fine—problems will arise only if you start with one idea but research something else, or lose track of your original question part of the way through a study.

universal measurement scale, even though you can, will unlikely achieve the best results. The researcher must be guided by a specific research purpose to understand and deal with the content relations of the constructs. However, if the most stringent mutual exclusiveness criterion is adopted, then all kinds of scales can be used in order to attain the maximum degree of exposure of the relationship under study. This is a multiple and systematic measurement approach to social and behavioral research. For each construct, different results obtained with different scale instruments can be compared, and those proven more powerful or effective in detecting the relationships among the theoretical constructs should be recommended.

Exercise: Scoping your question

If you have an idea about what you want to do, but it's not entirely clear to you, or perhaps you have lots of issues you want to investigate, this exercise can help you condense your thoughts. On a sheet of paper write down what you want to investigate. This may take the form of a number of questions, or a set of reasons why your work needs to be conducted. You may also have key ideas or phrases that fit with your study idea, and perhaps even some general thoughts that may fit in with the work. Once you've noted everything you can think of about your possible question, leave it for a couple of days. Then return to it and read through what you've written. Can you see a general theme or idea—a specific question? You might see several. In this case, focus on the one that interests you most, or is the most pressing. Don't discard the other ideas though—they may be something you can return to later.

Background and backup information

Once you've worked out your question the next step is to find out two things—"Has anyone already done this?" (in which case you may need to alter your question or even abandon your original idea); and "What literature exists to support what I'm planning to do?" If someone seems to have already carried out a study that seems to match your idea, don't despair—it can be very beneficial. For instance, you may be interested in looking at the use of a community centre for older people and their carers. You may discover a paper that has done exactly that, but in another country. You can take the ideas and findings from that work (ensuring you fully reference/credit it), and apply them to your study setting. There's no point in reinventing the wheel. Alternatively you may find a study that's similar to your idea but hasn't covered what you want to look into, which can be used as further justification for your research.

We frequently use literature to show what's already been done, and why our work is still needed. However, don't limit yourself to this. By reading papers and reports smartly, you can also find out other issues—for example, in the studies you've found that match your research idea do they talk about any methodological difficulties (around recruitment, any questions asked, etc.)? By using papers as more than a justification for your work you can gain a useful insight into how to run a project. While you are searching for literature around your question, consider also how you think you may want to go about answering that question (for example, through a survey, observation, or interview). You can also complete literature searches around using these methods in the population you want to look at, as it may be that your question is right, but the initial way you plan to approach it is not suitable for your participants (more on this later). At this stage of a study you are working through literature to see what helps support and inform your study. Keep a record of papers, and make notes around what aspects of them are useful. You also need to consider what you're collecting literature for at this time—are you looking to write a project or report, or are you going to create a bid for funding? If it's the former, your literature review should be detailed and systematic; for the latter you need to cite key papers and justify your question, but it is acknowledged that you'll continue literature searching during the course of the study (once it's funded).

> *I begin writing about my study pretty much as soon as I think of my research question. I create an "introduction" and label differ-ent sections which I then add to as new papers come to my atten-tion. I move it around a fair bit and some references get dropped out at the end, but it keeps me focused on my work and saves me loads of time at the end of the project when we're really busy with other tasks.* (Kim, lecturer)

Where can I get information?

It's often assumed that we all know how to carry out literature searches, but this isn't the case (Table 2.1). It isn't the purpose of this section to teach how to carry out a literature search; there are several guides that cover this issue should you feel you need more informa-tion (see Cooper, 1989; Galvan, 1999; Hart, 1998). In searching for papers you should begin with peer-reviewed literature published in journals. If you are based within a university or research organisation you should have access to search facilities such as Web of Science, PubMed, Medline, Ovid, and Silverplatter. Many are free online, while some require a licence and permission. Alternatively your local library may be able to help you search for books or papers. Many journals and book publishers have online information—you may have to pay to view full papers, but a general search is permitted (see Table 2.2). Literature searching is complicated, so if your library offers training in how to use any search facilities, make use of it (if you are a junior researcher or haven't ever been trained in this area, you may wish to ask for this as part of your career development). The reason

TABLE 2.1

Some common worries about literature

Problem	Solution
I don't know where to start!	Focus your searching on one key area or database; from this you can build outwards.
I don't know how to read papers/reports.	A guide on how to read a paper can provide hints on what to focus on (see Greenhalgh, 2001).
I can't follow some of the sections.	Again, using a guide may help. If there are particular sections you struggle with (e.g. "results") then ask a colleague or friend who can follow such sections to help you. You can also find out what's going on by reading the other sections in the paper/report. Don't avoid the sections just because they are hard, though; it may mean you miss some crucial information. Some people find they improve their skills by reading the method and results first, and then try to guess what the discussion should say.
There's too much literature—do I have to read all of it?	Nobody can be expected to read everything. However, you should show that you've covered the key areas surrounding your research question. If you are generating too much literature you can limit your searches (e.g. to a period of time or source of information)—although you'll need to justify why you made such a choice. Alternatively you can hone down your question in order to make it more specific and reduce the literature you need to search.
I can't find any literature in my area of enquiry.	Often if we're over-specific or too literal, it seems there's no literature on our question. You may have to think laterally to begin with (e.g. if you can't find something on stress in nurses (which is unlikely), look for stress-related research on other health professionals). If you really can't find any literature then you may want to flag this up in your writing, but do so with caution—don't claim there is no literature out there because chances are there is, but you haven't found it. Instead say you've not been able to find any.
I can read the literature, but how do I write it up?	If you are writing an essay, you can describe studies in more detail. If you are writing a report, you tend to list studies to support points you're making (this book follows the latter method). A good tip on learning how to write up papers/reports is to search for existing literature in your area and copy that format.
I keep getting muddled with what I've read and what I haven't.	You may find a database helpful (e.g. Reference Manager), or you may want to use a card index system. Keeping a list of what you've read and its usefulness can cut down on repetition.

TABLE 2.2
Examples of search engines and research archives

- Web of Knowledge: http://wos.mimas.ac.uk
- Evidence-based medical information: http://www.tripdatabase.com
- Social Science Search Engine: http://www.sosig.ac.uk/harvester.html
- PsycINFO (psychological research): http://www.apa.org/psycinfo
- Cochrane Database of Systematic Reviews: http://www.nelh.nhs.uk/cochrane.asp
- PubMed (medical research): http://www4.ncbi.nlm.nih.gov/PubMed/clinical.html
- General Practice Research Database: http://www.gprd.com
- National Statistics Online: http://www.statistics.gov.uk

for getting training is that many search facilities include ways of combining searches, making it easier for you to find exactly what you want, and narrow down your work.

As well as searching through the published literature, you may want to see whether there is ongoing, unpublished research in a similar area. Examples of facilities that allow this include the National Research Register (NRR) (http://www.update-software.com/National/default.htm), the Economic & Social Research Council's list of funded research (Regard) (http://www.regard.ac.uk), the National Foundation for Educational Research's database of Current Educational Research in the UK (http://www.ceruk.ac.uk/ceruk), and the NHS Centre for Reviews and Dissemination (http://www.york.ac.uk/inst/crd/crddatabases.htm).

Books are another useful source of information, as is "grey literature" (papers, reports and internal documents created for use within organisations, which may not have been published). Articles in magazines or newspapers can also be helpful, and should not be excluded because they are not "peer reviewed" (although if you are preparing a rigorous study you will need to show you've considered information from a variety of sources).

Literature searching—some dos and don'ts
(adapted from Hart, 1998, p. 219)

Do:

- Identify and discuss the relevant key landmark studies on the topic
- Include as much up-to-date material as possible
- Check the details, such as how names are spelled
- Try to be reflexive; examine your own bias and make it clear

- Critically evaluate the material and show your analyses
- Use extracts, illustrations, and examples to justify your analyses and argument
- Be analytical, evaluative and critical and show this in your review
- Manage the information that your review produces; have a system for records management
- Make your review worth reading by making yourself clear, systematic, and coherent; explain why the topic is interesting.

Don't:

- Omit classic works and landmarks or discuss core ideas without proper references
- Discuss outdated or only old materials
- Misspell names or get date of publications wrong
- Use concepts to impress or without definition
- Use jargon and discriminatory language to justify a parochial standpoint
- Produce a list of items, even if annotated; a list is not a review
- Accept any position at face value or believe everything that is written
- Only produce a description of the content of what you have read
- Drown in information by not keeping control and an accurate record of materials
- Make silly mistakes, e.g. orgasm in place of organism
- Be boring by using hackneyed jargon, pretentious language, and only description.

Once you've started searching through literature you also need to consider what method(s) you want to use to answer your question. Don't forget that your literature searching should continue throughout the time you are completing your research, in case any new information becomes publicly available.

Possible methods to be used

When thinking about methods, it's important to think not of whether one method is better than another (for example, that tired old debate around qualitative versus quantitative), but rather of what method is best suited to your research question, your timescale, the budget (if appropriate), your skills, and the needs and abilities of participants. This book is not a methodologies text, but you may find reading around this area useful (see Blaxter, Hughes, & Tight, 2001; Bowling, 1997; Cresswell, 2002; Denscombe, 1998; Robson, 1993), particularly if you need to know how to apply a method, and also any problems or drawbacks associated with it. Table 2.3 summarises some of the more popular methods used in social and health research (although it is by no means exhaustive).

The methods listed in Table 2.3 can be used individually or in combination (sometimes known as "triangulation"—where different methods are used to explain or shed light on a complex problem) (Blaxter *et al.*, 2001, pp. 84–85). These are traditional methods to collect information, but there's no reason why other approaches may not be applied—including photography, film, painting, participant diaries, or poetry (NHS, 2001; Norris, 1997—see also Chapter 8 of this book). You need to think of the method in the way that you'll collect information—as well as being aware of how that information will be used. A complex statistical survey may not, for example, be the most appropriate approach for a project looking at how it feels to live with a terminal illness. Chapter 4 (piloting) explains more on how methods may be selected and rejected. Drawing on existing literature can also help shape your future research, as it can tell you what research has been successful in the past.

Thinking about analysis

It's never too soon to start thinking about analysis. As soon as you've decided on the method(s) to use in your research you also need to think about how you're going to analyse them. Firstly, be clear in your own mind about whether your question requires a qualitative or a quantitative method, and then think about what analysis will match your method. The reason for this is twofold. If you aren't sure of how to analyse quantitative or qualitative data, it gives you time to learn (or time to find someone who can help you do it!). It also means you can design your study questions so that analysis suits your needs. For example, if you're going to use a questionnaire but know you're not very good at statistics, you have two choices—either design questions that have simple yes/no/don't know responses rather than rating scales, or, if you have to use an existing measure that will result in complicated statistical analysis, build payment of a statistician into your budget (or ask a friend who's good at stats to help you). Alternatively, if you plan to use qualitative analysis you can organise your questions to fit your study time limit so you can cope with the information generated.

TABLE 2.3

Methods you may want to consider

Method	What it does	Data generated
Case study	This is the small-scale evaluation of a particular person or organisation (for example, a local religious group; a patient's medical experience; a sports team).	Qualitative (reports/write-ups), quantitative (coding of events). Additional data may include photographs/film, etc.
Observation	In this method the researcher(s) watch and record activity in a systematic way (for example, hand washing by staff in a restaurant could be one area that is observed during a study of the experience of restaurant working).	As above.
Action research	Is a tool commonly used to improve practice, and utilises community involvement. Problems or issues are identified by key informants/communities, and options are explored to find a workable solution.	As above, plus this method usually produces tangible results. For example, a community realises there's a problem with vandalism in a certain area. By working together it is discovered that the culprits are teenagers who have little to do after school. An after-school club and drop-in centre is introduced and the problem is reduced.
Nominal groups	This method sets out a number of key issues, and small groups of participants discuss them, eventually prioritising the issues. The method works well where a decision about an issue needs to be made and informed participants can help prioritise.	Nominal data around the group's beliefs. For example, using the example above, another way of solving the problem of teenage vandalism might have been to produce a list of solutions and get local community representatives to agree on the main issues requiring change.
Focus groups	These are discussions among small groups of participants (usually face to face, but can also be conducted via email or in chat rooms). The researcher may ask questions for the group to discuss, or the group may generate their own topics of conversation.	Qualitative (taped interviewed), and quantitative if questionnaires are used within the groups.

Method	Description	Data type
One-to-one interviews	These are usually face to face (but can be conducted via phone, email, etc.), with a participant and researcher. As with focus groups, the researcher may set the agenda, or the participant may suggest what is discussed.	Qualitative (taped interviews).
Questionnaires	This tool allows you to ask questions of a sample of participants. The researcher sets the topics for research and participants' replies are coded and analysed. Researchers may design their own questionnaire, or make use of one previously used in research in a related area. Questionnaires can be administered by post, by a researcher direct to participant, or using a computer or website.	Quantitative (yes/no or scale-based data); some qualitative if open-ended questions are used.
Experiments	These are based on natural science studies and aim to show a causal link between independent and dependent variables.	Usually quantitative (results on a task, for example), but can include some qualitative components.
Randomised controlled trial (RCT)	A quantitative evaluation to assess how one factor performs against others (commonly used in medical research to investigate the performance of drugs).	Predominantly quantitative data.
Ethnography	Research is completed with people in their natural surroundings, where the researcher observes and talks to participants about their lives.	Mainly qualitative, but some quantitative work may be involved (e.g. noting of occurrences of activity). Examination of case notes and other information can be used (e.g. documents relating to the community under study).

When I first began research I didn't realise I had any control over it. If I were doing a questionnaire I'd set it up using rating scales and multiple answers. Then I'd have a nightmare trying to analyse it and often had to drop questions out of my analysis. With qualitative questions I assumed it was easier so asked loads of items, only to find it took me hours to transcribe and, worse still, I found it difficult to wade through all the text produced. Luckily I went to a conference where one of the speakers told us WE were the ones who determined how we asked questions and ultimately could set how we analysed our data. It was a revelation to me, and I now design my work to fit in with my abilities as a researcher, along with limitations of time and money. (Nisha, senior research manager)

On my first research job I was surprised about what they asked me to do. I've got a masters in health psychology and I was worried they'd ask me to complete analysis, do statistics, etc. Stats have never been my strong point! But I didn't do anything like that at all. Even though I knew in theory about research, my job involved interviewing patients and entering data. I didn't do data analysis at all. They had a statistician for that. I felt a bit deskilled on the one hand, but relieved there was an expert there to do the stats I knew I'd struggle with. (Geoff, researcher)

While you're choosing your method and working out what you want to ask, you can concurrently decide on how you think you may analyse the data. This may change as the study progresses, but considering what you think may be required can be another means of focusing you on your research question and may set you off on the right route.

Purpose, scale, and proposed end result

Chapter 3 covers timescales and research objectives in more detail. However, in the planning stages of a study it's important to make feasible research designs. This means that if your research is for a dissertation or small project, you don't need to think up complicated designs with large numbers of participants and huge amounts of data to process.

Whatever research you are planning, it's better to keep your original question as straightforward as possible, and make sure whatever methods you use are simple too. (Lucy, lecturer)

Two issues—time and money—will affect the scale of your research. But you do need to consider what the work is for and what you want to get from it. If you are planning on making wide-ranging conclusions, you need to have utilised a representative and appropriately sized sample. This doesn't mean lots of people, but it does mean recruiting the right number of the right sort of participants (people who reflect what your research is about). For a small-scale project, a smaller sample is appropriate. If, however, you want to run a study to show how a new teaching method works, or how an alternative form of healthcare could benefit people, you will need to design a bigger project with more support (assistants, secretaries, and so on).

Finally, think about the end result of your work. Is it for an undergraduate or postgraduate degree? Is it to make a difference within your community or place of work, or are you intending to make recommendations on a local, national, or global level? Chapter 8 covers the writing-up and dissemination of research in more detail, but again, as you are planning a study you need to reflect on where it is going to end up, and how you will present it. This may affect the way certain results are reported, what is made public, and what claims you are making. As you begin a study, think about the ultimate aim you have for it—and keep asking "why am I doing this work? What is it for and where will it end up?"

Making research plans and stakeholder analysis

There are many parts of a research project, and different people are involved in the different stages of a study. It is worth being aware of the following factors that will affect your work: the project sponsor; the customer (person or organisation that will use the results); the objectives and scope of your work; constraints (e.g. time, access to participants); costs and resources; deliverables (what the final study will look like); project phases and timetables; your methodology; risks (what could foreseeably go wrong and contingency plans); and responsibilities (who does what by when).

This chapter takes you through how to address these issues, but it is also worth creating your own stakeholder analysis, so you can establish what you need to do to complete your research, the tasks others will be required to complete, and what the eventual aims are for everyone in the research. For example, the project sponsor will want a report and outcomes for discussion, you may want career

CHAPTER THIRTEEN

Presenting Your Findings

The teaching of behavioral and social science research has produced a linear model that is most familiar to students and professors. It starts with defining and refining the research problem associated with a specific population by reviewing the literature as well as other sources of information. Then the researcher may articulate some research hypotheses based on previous studies, existing theories, and personal beliefs. She also needs to explain her ideas by clarifying the terminology and giving a research rationale. After establishing the specific research objectives, the researcher works out a research design by selecting an appropriate type of study and choosing one or more research methods. The data collection and analysis plan will include sampling and instrumentation with careful measurement of the key variables based on their appropriate operationalization. In a formal or institutional procedure, the above steps will form a research proposal submitted for approval, usually with application for funding. The implementation of the research plan includes activities in staffing, organizing, evaluating, and adjusting the data collection, management and analysis process. The results will then be sorted, examined, interpreted, and chosen to draw the conclusion. All these will be documented in a final research report, which summarizes the findings and discusses their implications or significance to theory, practice, and future research.

This chapter, therefore, is supposed to be dealing with the kind of after-implementation activities, that is, the examination, interpretation, and selection of the results, the derivation of the conclusions, and the writing of the report. The real research process, however, tends to be much more complex and complicated than the linear model. The kind of practice may not follow the development, and the local community may need a resource evaluated. A stakeholder analysis allows you to identify key people who need to be brought or kept onside within your research. The reasoning behind identifying key stakeholders is that it can speed up your research (for example, a lead union representative could get you access to other union groups for a project on trade union membership). For more on how to complete a stakeholder analysis, visit http://www.mindtools.com/pages/article/newPPM_07.htm.

Exercise: Who are your stakeholders?

On a sheet of paper write down everyone who could be involved in your research (from your boss, to a funding body, to potential participants). You may wish to do this with your project team. On a second sheet prioritise these stakeholders—whom do you need to make links with/win over first? This will help you direct your networking to the correct people. Finally, go back to your first sheet and look at each person you have listed (even if you don't know them, you know what they represent). Ask yourself what would motivate them to be part of your study, what information you would require from them, what they may think of you and what you think about them, who else may influence their opinions that you may approach, and what you'll do if you can't get them to support you. By doing this you can anticipate all the different needs of people involved in your research, as well as planning a strategy for those who may be opposed to it.

Participant/researcher needs

As well as thinking about your question, method, and timescales, it's also worth considering whom the research is going to be carried out with. You may have identified a problem clearly, and know who your participants are, but frequently studies run into difficulties when the needs of the participants, the study question and the proposed methods don't match up.

> We wanted to look into the problem of bullying for children from refugee populations. We felt it was a really important and worthwhile issue, but our first idea of using a questionnaire went really wrong. Not all of our participants could read English proficiently. We eventually opted to use the kids to interview

each other about their experiences, worries, and concerns about bullying. (Nancy, research coordinator)

Work out whether your method will suit the needs of your participants. Your two priority issues are what question you want answered and who you want to recruit to help you answer it (participants). The method should be suited to those two requirements, rather than trying to force a method onto a study question or group of people (more on this in Chapter 5). If your study will require additional costs of translators, developing new methodologies or trialling different approaches, this is not a problem, but you will need to reflect these extra costs in both your time plans (see Chapter 3) and your budget (if appropriate).

If you are designing a study where you plan to employ researchers, you may also need to think about their needs in the planning stages of research. If you intend to use a standardised measure or interview, will they need extra training in how to use this? If particular equipment will be a feature of your study (say a computerised interview, or a blood-testing kit), will you need to teach staff how to use it? Finally, will your staff be placed in risky situations requiring training in assertiveness, breakaway techniques, or negotiation skills (see Chapter 6)? If so, support for this will need to be factored into your study plan—as will the need for any counselling or emotional support your staff might require (for example if your research focuses on a particularly distressing or emotive issue).

Making links and getting support

The planning stage of any study is the time when you focus on getting the research off the ground. What can be missed is making links with other researchers, services and support groups that can greatly improve your study—and save you lots of time. As you are reading through papers or reports, note who has written them and, if appropriate, make contact. You may want to call or email them if you feel they can help suggest other projects you may be unaware of, recommend any existing papers or measures, or give you an insight into the practicalities of a study (tell you the whole story about what went on in the research you've just read in their paper). This can prevent you encountering similar problems to them (around recruitment, analysis, etc). A note of caution, though—network with other researchers appropriately (Boynton, 2003c).

I get several requests about my research per month, usually asking me questions about measures used, or advice on following a particular study path. I'm happy to answer these emails since it's always good to share information, and some of these contacts have now become collaborators on research grants with me. What I object to are the letters I get, usually from students, saying things like "I'm doing a project on such-and-such. I would like all the papers you have on this topic. You can write to me/phone me here." Like I don't have anything better to do! It's not my job to write somebody's essay and tutors ought to advise their students against this approach. It annoys me and I never write back. If you are making contact with others, do so respectfully and ask them a short question they can answer. After that you may find you can communicate with them about your project, but don't let your initial approach be a demand for them to work for you.
(SL, professor)

Keep your networking varied. You may want to use professional groups or research organisations (see list in Table 2.4). Alternatively you may want to set up your own group, or ask around—many departments or organisations have their own, informal study groups or journal clubs you could join. Reading the letters pages in journals relevant to your study can flag up like-minded people, as can writing to introduce yourself if you read a paper that fits your area. Making links with charities or other support groups can add a practical focus to your research, and they are a great place to involve

TABLE 2.4

Potential networking sources

- Social Science Information Gateway (network for social scientists): http://www.sosig.ac.uk
- British Psychological Society: http://www.bps.org.uk
- American Psychological Association: http://www.apa.org
- British Sociological Society: http://www.britsoc.co.uk
- British Medical Association: http://www.bma.org.uk
- British Dental Association: http://www.bda-dentistry.org.uk
- R&D Direct (research advisory service): www.rddirect.org.uk
- Charity Choice Directory Online: http://www.charitychoice.co.uk.ccdonline.htm

You can use these sites to gain access to other organisations in the rest of the world.

consumers as researchers or grant proposers. It is fair to say that not everyone values the importance of networking, and some people may want to guard their research. Don't be put off if you approach someone who doesn't seem interested, simply keep increasing your networks and find others who want to collaborate or communicate. Remember, you can publicise your work as well (see Chapter 5) since this can put both participants and other researchers in touch with you.

Some people are busy or don't really network; others may just be in touch with you for a short time. Whatever happens, it is worth making a wide range of contacts since they can help guide you away from problems, support you as your work continues, and possibly help you find outlets for publication once the work is over.

> *I keep a database with the names, contact details and people's specialities. I can refer to them whenever I need to—and I can also pass on to others who are working in this area. It's all about making and then sharing networks.* (Archie, GP)

Budgets and sources of funding

This chapter covers general issues about planning a study. Many organisations or universities offer training or in-house courses on how to create budgets or obtain funding. Your finance department may offer invaluable advice about what to include in your budget (you may be surprised that you need to include for items such as stationery, refreshments for participants or travel costs, as well as bigger costs, like computers or salaries). Alternatively you may want to talk to colleagues who have obtained funding and ask to see their proposals and budget sheets.

> *Making links with your finance department can be invaluable. I liaise with the finance staff in the research office at my college, and I find talking to them when I'm thinking of applying for research funding, and involving them with the proposal can mean I get the financial parts right, and they remind me of the correct way to get research signed off too.* (Bina, research manager)

There are some fairly easy ways to lose out on getting a research proposal accepted or funded, as outlined by Robson (1993, p. 468) under the heading *"Ten ways to get your proposal turned down"*:

1. Don't follow the directions or guidelines given for your kind of proposal. Omit information that is asked for. Ignore word limits
2. Ensure that the title has little relationship to the stated objectives; and that neither title nor objectives link to the proposed methods or techniques
3. Produce woolly, ill-defined objectives
4. Have the statement of the central problem or research focus vague, or obscure it by other discussion
5. Leave the design and methodology implicit; let them guess
6. Have some mundane task, routine consultancy or poorly conceptualised data trawl masquerade as a research project
7. Be unrealistic in what can be achieved within the time and resources you have available
8. Be either very brief, or, preferably, long-winded and repetitive in your proposal. Rely on weight rather than quality
9. Make it clear what the findings of your research are going to be, and demonstrate how your ideological stance makes this inevitable
10. Don't worry about a theoretical or conceptual framework for your research. You want to do a down-to-earth study so you can forget all that fancy stuff.

If you are carrying out a project for an undergraduate or postgraduate degree, you don't need to worry about funding for a study—if extra money is required, your supervisor should be able to help and advise you with this. For other research you will need to think about who is going to pay for it (Carter, 1997). Some studies are completed on a shoestring, with everyone volunteering their time to help out. However, this is not ideal, so try to get funding wherever possible. It's acknowledged that getting research funded is very difficult (Hopkin, 1998; Schepers, Sadler, & Raun, 2000), although guides are available (Table 2.5) (Carter, 1997; Reif-Lehrer, 1995).

TABLE 2.5

Resources for funding

- How to write grant proposals—list of websites/guides:
  http://www.pitt.edu/~offres/proposal/propwriting/websites/html
- Resource list for grant writers:
  http://www.people.memphis.edu/~ressvc/resource.htm
- Research funding (list of sources): http://www.rdinfo.org.uk
- Sources of funding: http://www.usc.edu/dept/source/grantsweb.htm

Table 2.6 gives a checklist for obtaining funding.

In my experience studies don't get funded for the following reasons. They are vague, badly described, or talk about research that seems unethical or unfeasible in the timescale suggested. If you've continually gone over time or budget on previous studies this can count against you, as can applying to the wrong funding body. Most often research goes wrong, though, because although you get the money to do it, it's not been well designed or thought out, and the staff working on the project aren't supported. This means work doesn't get done, or it turns out the original idea just doesn't work in practice. My advice is to sort out the study and pilot it first before trying to get money, because there's no point in having a fantastic grant if you just can't deliver what you promised. (Mike, Professor)

TABLE 2.6

Checklist for obtaining funding

❑ Do I have a clear, well-argued, and well-supported study idea?
❑ Have I chosen the most appropriate method to answer my research question?
❑ Does the research team contain people who have already obtained funding for research and seen studies through to a successful completion?
❑ Is the research budget reasonable (not underselling or overselling itself)?
❑ Is it realistic that the research will be delivered on time and to budget?
❑ Will I offer relevant training and support to staff so their tasks are completed?
❑ Will the research have relevant and deliverable outcomes?
❑ Am I applying to the appropriate charity or funding body, at the right time?

This chapter has summarised the main issues to consider when thinking about a study. The next chapter builds on this, and focuses on how to get your idea into action.

Starting out 3

Building on the issues outlined in Chapter 2, this chapter asks you to think in detail about structuring your work. This includes:

- Workspace essentials
- Timescales (from a two-week investigation to a long-term study)
- Research objectives
- Staffing/support for a study (including advertising research posts, applying for research jobs, working with volunteers, and utilising (community) support)
- Training and supporting research staff/volunteers
- Roles of project staff
- Setting up and dealing with a steering group
- Your/staff's career development, training, and appraisal needs
- Publication, accountability, and intellectual property rights
- Research governance and ethics committees.

This chapter will discuss the needs of researchers at all levels, from those who are junior researchers or working alone to those who are responsible for a large research team. This is particularly important given that most researchers have little or no knowledge about their rights and responsibilities as research workers or managers, and may not have received formal training in this area. Some of you will not have been trained in making applications to ethics committees, and may find such applications very difficult. Delays in obtaining ethical approval (if necessary) can seriously affect research, so this chapter closes with an explanation of how to apply to ethics committees. However, before we look at these serious issues, we need to consider what you need to get a study started, as outlined in Table 3.1.

TABLE 3.1

What you need to get going: workspace essentials

A desk or table—or some form of space dedicated to your work	*Writing materials:* Stationery (letter-headed paper, notelets, envelopes, plain paper), pens, pencils, ruler, eraser, highlighters, etc. *Guides:* local maps or an A–Z, train or bus timetables—whatever you require to help you find your way around your research environment. *Research diary:* This should be kept in part of your desk that is lockable, and should be used to record what you are doing and where you will be. If you intend to record more personal details this should be done on your computer and kept password-protected. Some people prefer to use the diary feature on their computer or buy an electronic organiser. However, keeping a desk diary is useful for safety purposes (see Chapter 6). *"Personal effects":* These are up to an individual, but canvassing my colleagues, the top items for keeping at work include tissues, deodorant, antibacterial hand wipes, sanitary towels/tampons, lip balm, painkillers, an emergency sewing kit, and throat sweets.
A computer and printer	Preferably with Office (particularly with Word for Windows, since many journals or reports are requested in this format; and Excel and Access for data storage, analysis and management) (see http://www.show.scot.nhs.uk/bitsandbobs/microsoft_faq.doc for information on buying packages). It is also worth having an additional presentation package, such as PowerPoint, that will allow you to make slides, along with a reference support pack (e.g. Reference Manager), and Acrobat Reader (as many papers are in PDF format). Many organisations or universities have these packages, but it is worth checking that you have an up-to-date version before you start on a project. Access to email or the internet is pretty much essential, but ensure your participants' data is secured and protected if your machine is networked.
A lockable storage cabinet	You can get large-scale lockable cabinets, or smaller storage boxes (depending on the size of your project and your budget). Remember, if you have a lockable cabinet, keep it locked, and keep keys in a safe place. Don't forget issues of data protection (see Chapter 7). Within your cabinet you need to have files that apply to everything you need to run your study: ethics forms, study publicity information, consent forms, contact and follow-up letters, questionnaires or interview schedules (blank questionnaires do not have to be locked away; those that have been completed should be stored separately from participants' consent forms—see Chapter 5). You may also find having a shredder helpful for destroying personal records.
A poster board	Or space to pin up research information (e.g. progress records, reminders). Remember to consider confidentiality—patient details or personal aspects of research should not be visible if others not relating to the study will see the board or space. If you are interviewing participants in your office, think carefully about what messages any visible material will give: this also applies for any pictures or photographs you have up (see text).

Other materials you may wish to consider include

- An audio and/or video tape recorder (if appropriate to your study)
- A telephone and answering machine (see Chapter 5)
- A mobile telephone if you will be working outside the office for any length of time (see Chapter 6)
- A notebook for recording calls and contact numbers—particularly if you share an office (see Chapter 5).

Depending on where you're doing the research, you may want to think about making your office as comfortable as possible, with pictures, flowers, rugs or comfy chairs. This is important if you will be interviewing people for any length of time.

> *I think if you need to keep research information in your office, things like recruitment details or study design information, it's a good idea to keep a larger picture or poster to use to cover any notice boards if you are having visitors to your office and want to keep anything private. It saves you having to change your notice board each time someone comes to visit or do research.* (TP, research manager)

Some researchers keep photographs or other personal pictures in their office—this is entirely up to you, but consider whether this will compromise your safety, or perhaps upset a participant (for example, if you are doing research on cot death, having your baby's photos everywhere may not be appropriate). Keep your work area as clean or tidy as possible—particularly if it is within your home or if you are sharing office space. Don't forget safety issues. If you work within your home, it is better to complete interviews or other work involving participants outside it, although you must not forget that you need to apply safety considerations wherever you are working (see also Chapter 6).

Timescales

Once you have identified your research idea and how you want to implement it, the next stage of your study is to create a detailed plan to show how you are going to go about completing the research (many grant applications have to include this, so you may have to write a time plan in order to get funding). It is worth creating a time plan whether your study will take place over a few weeks or months, or

standard phases, nor may they conform to any single and particular research model. The researcher will be faced with challenges as well as given choices as he moves each step forward. Not only must he follow an order of getting things done but he is also responsible to a large degree for determining that work order. Somewhat similar to the "garbage can model" of policy analysis initiated by Cohen, March and Olsen and explicated by Kington (1990), research projects may also look like the "organized anarchies" influenced by problematic preferences, unclear technology, and fluid participation. Although this may be more debatable with regard to scientific research, it is not uncommon that answers would search for questions and hypotheses would go after results. Even in the most ideal case, you may not have to follow a "standard" flowchart waiting for the completion of the prior steps to launch a supposedly later task. The writing of the research report is a good example to illuminate this idea.

Compiling your research report

Practically, the researcher starts the preparation of the final research report at the very beginning of a research project. In the smoothest case, the researcher carries out her original research idea without a hitch based on a well thought out plan. It is therefore important to refer to the original research documentation when compiling the final research report. Even if the original ideas and designs have been revised from time to time, it is still helpful to review the process and see the reasons. In any case, you should try to document all the major aspects and steps of your project. Specifically, your written research proposal will serve as the best starting point to generate your research report. You should also keep a good record of what has happened in the research process in terms of the implementation and revision of your research plan. The readers will fully understand the meaning of your results only if you let them know the background, process, and purpose of your research.

Your research report does not have to repeat your research proposal and other process documentation. However, if you know how to write or have actually written a good proposal, probably you also know how to write a good research report. The final report is usually a more comprehensive one, with an executive summary and/or an abstract attached. It should clarify the background of the research interest, state the research problems and objectives, provide a review of previous research and current theoretical understanding, articulate the

will run over several years. Your time plan should block out the weeks/months covered by your study, identify the tasks that require completion by particular deadlines, and show who is responsible for what task (see below).

> *The way I do things is like this: rather than working from your start date through to the end, I work out the deadline for my study (when funding runs out, or a specific date I have to complete it by), and work back from there.* (Nic, research coordinator)

One way in which you can manage what needs doing is to create a Gantt chart (Table 3.2) that sets out tasks by week/month of your research programme. Alternatively you may wish to use a critical path analysis (CPA) to identify and break down all tasks necessary for completing a study, and prioritise them (see http://www.mind tools.com/pages/article/newPPM_04.htm for instructions on CPA). Remember that in creating these time plans you are predicting what you want to happen in your research. You should be realistic in your goals, build in spaces for problems, and have clear targets. These plans tell you where you should be going. For day-to-day recording of a study's progress (or lack of), you also need to keep a research diary (which is covered in Chapter 7).

TABLE 3.2

Example of Gantt chart

Task/Month	Jan	Feb	March	April	May	June
Renew ethics approval	░					
Participant interviews	░	░				
Enter data	░	░				
Analyse data		░	░			
Write and edit report			░	░		
Disseminate findings					░	░

You can find a more detailed guide to creating a Gantt chart at
http://www.mindtools.com/pages/article/newPPM_03.htm

> *I create an overall study diagram using a wall planner. I highlight what tasks should be done by when, and I note what my jobs are and what my assistants are doing. If there are key dates, such*

as deadlines for progress reports or meetings with ethics commit-
tees, I factor them in too. (David, research coordinator)

What if things go wrong?

Hopefully, if you plan your research in a realistic manner, you should
bring the research in roughly on time. However, sometimes events
occur that weren't predicted in the study design or time planning (for
example, participants refusing to take part, or research staff having to
take long-term sick leave). In such cases, research can be put behind
schedule. Piloting can help avoid some of these problems (see Chapter
4), but if it's not possible to overcome problems and the study looks
like it could be in trouble, it is better to share this as soon as possible.
This may mean telling your tutor or supervisor if your study has
run into difficulty, or writing to your funding body asking for an
extension on the project or possibly more money.

> *Usually problems can be sorted if they are caught early enough—*
> *even if it seems like you may look bad to admit things aren't*
> *going to plan. It is better to acknowledge any difficulties and ask*
> *for assistance than to try and keep going and end up with no*
> *results and wasted time/money. I know if I'm managing a study*
> *and I hear it's getting into trouble, I can do more to help if I hear*
> *early than if someone hides it from me until there's nothing I can*
> *do to fix it.* (DK, professor)

Objectives

Chapter 2 outlined the need for clear aims and objectives for research.
As well as having a set study focus, it is also beneficial to set out well-
defined tasks for all those involved in working on a study. Evaluate
research and workload to identify who completes sharing what tasks.
Those collecting data or carrying out interviews/projects need to
know how much work is required of them, and over what time
period. Project coordinators should be told what is expected of them
in terms of their own performance and that of the staff they are supervising. Finally, those in charge of the study overall (the grant holder,
or possibly just you if you're a lone worker) need to keep a check that
the work is running correctly, and is within time and budget (see later
in this chapter for more on roles/tasks).

> *Getting good at research is a lot like running a hotel. If you were*
> *to become a manager of a really successful hotel you'd need to*

know what it was like to do everything from cleaning the rooms to managing the catering and finance. A good hotel manager knows everything about their hotel, and what everyone working in it should be doing. A good research manager knows what needs doing on their project, and preferably will have had experience of doing all the tasks required to run a study. (Charlotte, senior lecturer)

Advertising and selecting staff

If you are going to include staff within a study (for example to help you collect, manage, or analyse data), their tasks need to be included in your timescales and objectives—as does time for advertising, recruiting and interviewing staff. Often studies run into trouble because this aspect of research is overlooked. Even if you have a human resources department that can help you with advertising and interviewing, it can still take several days (even weeks). The costs for advertising for staff also needs to be included in your budget, as this can be a hidden expense.

If you plan to advertise for and interview staff you need to ensure you are following correct procedures. Take advice from your human resources department while you're still planning your study, since they can advise you on the legal requirements of creating job adverts, descriptions, shortlists and running interviews. I found that I also needed extra training in this area, since there are many issues about recruitment and interviewing I wasn't aware of. (Nobu, statistician)

It sounds obvious, but place your adverts for staff in places where potential staff will look (newspapers, websites, etc.). Spend time thinking about appropriate places to advertise for staff. It may be worth tailoring adverts to fit different projects—for example, if your research is on the emotional health of lesbian and gay teenagers, you may want to advertise for researchers in the gay press, as well as job sections of other sources. Your human resources department can help advise you on the content of adverts, or you could look at existing advertisements and follow their format.

Create a list of essential and desirable characteristics for the staff you wish to appoint. The essential skills should be summarised within the job advert (for example, if you want someone with a PhD, or who is a service user, then this must be made clear). You should also send out these characteristics to applicants enquiring about the post. It is worth liaising with your human resources department about this, as they may have a template you can use, and will advise you on the law relating to equal opportunities and employment. An example of selection criteria for an academic research post is shown in Table 3.3. If you require community researchers, or those with personal rather than academic experience (e.g. a user of mental health services), this should be specified.

> *Interviewing isn't easy. I prefer to be interviewed than be the interviewer. If you've not had this experience before, talk to more experienced colleagues and/or your human resources department; alternatively some colleges/organisations offer training days in interviewing. And don't forget that if you ask someone to be proficient at a given task, you need to get proof they can do this. If I need someone to be competent at using statistics databases I ask to see them perform some analysis for me in interview. I've been caught out in the past by people saying they can use different analysis packages, and it turns out they have only a basic knowledge.* (Bill, lecturer)

TABLE 3.3

Example selection criteria

	Essential	Desirable
Qualifications	BSc	MSc
Experience	• Experience of research involving person-to-person contact. • Experience of data handling, data input, databases, statistical packages, and wordprocessing.	• Familiarity with quantitative data. • Familiarity with computer interviewing.
Personal skills	• Able to work on own initiative as well as in a team. • Able to work to deadlines. • Good interpersonal skills.	• Willingness to participate in the university department's research and education programme.
Physical requirements	• Able to travel. • Good command of written and spoken English.	

Applying for research posts

If you're on the other side of the fence and are interested in a research position, there are a number of ways of finding posts. The main ones are through adverts in the health/social science pages in newspapers, or through websites specialising in academic jobs (for example http://www.jobs.ac.uk or http://www.appmemo.co.uk). Some charities also advertise for researchers, so it is worth searching for jobs in this category too. Many universities advertise positions on their own websites (start from http://www.scit.wlv.ac.uk/ukinfo/uk.map.html), so it is a good idea to look at work available in your area.

> *It's always worth asking around and telling other people you'll be free for work soon. I've got two research positions in this way, simply by telling people in my department my project was soon due to end. I wouldn't do it instead of applying for other posts, but if you're known within a department and have key skills, particularly about the local area, then you may find your talents will be in demand.* (Sharon, research assistant)

It is worth remembering that many research projects are short-term, and that junior staff contracts are particularly precarious (see Dickson, 1998; Shelton, Laoire, Fielding, Harvey, Pelling, & Duke-Williams, 2001). You may find there are research posts available, but these tend to be for a short time (a few months to a year). However, once you have a research job it places you in a better position to find other positions. It is also important to consider that many research vacancies are oversubscribed. For one research assistant position I advertised, I received 275 enquiries and just over 100 applications. Of course many were not suitable, but even so, getting a research job can be competitive.

A few years ago, a colleague, Sue Catt, and myself were involved in interviewing for research assistants. We were overwhelmed with applicants, and astonished by the standard of many of them. Application letters were badly spelt or wrongly addressed; people hadn't read the essential and desirable characteristics, and didn't fit the job spec; and many accompanying CVs were scruffy or incorrect. We decided to write a guide on how to apply for an academic post (Boynton & Catt, 2002). A summary table from this paper is shown in

Table 3.4, as a checklist for your applications. You may also want to have a practice interview with a colleague or friend familiar with the area where you'll be working, and do as much homework as you can about the post you are applying for: for example, finding out what research goes on at the department you are applying to, and reading up on the area that covers the post you want (Boynton & Catt, 2002; Parkinson, 1994; Yate, 1992).

Remember, more senior posts may require longer CVs, more detailed application letters, and additional information such as a list of publications. If in doubt ask for details from the human resources department or contact person named on the job advert.

Consumer involvement—what is it, and why is it important?

Over the past few years, we have heard more about consumer involvement in research (Carr, 2001; White, 2003). The reasoning behind getting others involved in studies is that although researchers can set out research ideas, they may not have the best insight into the study issue, or be the most appropriate people to carry out research (Boote, Telford, & Cooper, 2002; Tallon, Chard, & Dieppe, 2000). Consumers, or lay members, could be patients who are service users, charity workers, employees, or other forms of stakeholders; and can be involved in studies as researchers, advisers on a steering group, or co-applicants on grants (for details of places to contact potential consumers, try this charities/organisations directory: http://www.charitychoice.co.uk). Within many large-scale studies now, the involvement of consumers is requested as part of the criteria for funding, particularly since consumer involvement has been proved to strengthen research and empower participants, researchers, and wider communities (Dickerson, 1998).

It is necessary to state here that "consumer involvement" does not mean including more participants in research, or even a cynical attempt to get free labour. Involving consumers means inviting key individuals with particular expertise to inform, direct, and reflect on research. To that end, lay or consumer members of a research team are more than just an information resource or a means to access extra participants. They are key project staff and need to be treated as such.

Luckily, Involve has produced guidelines to enable lay involvement in research (2003). These guidelines inform researchers what types of consumer involvement may suit projects, how consumers can

TABLE 3.4

Tips for applications for academic/research posts

✓	✗
• Use good-quality paper.	• Avoid notelets, lined paper (particularly if torn from a workbook), very heavy or very flimsy paper, coloured paper.
• Unless specified, use a wordprocessor to produce your CV and application letter.	• Avoid handwriting an application if your writing is untidy or illegible (unless specifically asked to write).
• Write neatly on application forms (and if possible make photocopies and work out how to print into the spaces provided using a wordprocessor or electric typewriter).	• Don't hand in work that is crossed-out, typed-over, stained or scruffy—it will look like you can't be bothered (and may reflect badly if the post requires high standards of written and verbal communication).
• Use a standard-sized font (12 is appropriate).	• Avoid fonts that are too small (this tests the reader's eyesight) or too big (may seem like you are trying to waste space, or draw attention to yourself).
• Use a standard font (e.g. Times New Roman or Arial).	
• Consider what line spacing looks best.	• Avoid different-coloured fonts, or unusual lettering (these may seem ostentatious, and can be hard to read).
• Use a consistent format throughout (you might want to use different-size fonts for headings, etc., but keep these consistent too).	• Only enclose a photograph of yourself if it is requested. Omit pictures or sketches that you think might brighten your application. They detract from the important information the employer is having to work through.
	• Don't bunch up all the lines, or leave large gaps.

- Provide what is asked for in the advert—no more, no less (e.g. if they ask for the names and addresses of referees, or five copies of a CV and application letter, provide these)
- Use the spelling and grammar check on your computer and get someone to read through your application. Make sure it reflects everything you want to say (and your prospective employers want to hear).
- Be prepared to write a number of drafts, and always read a rough copy thoroughly first.
- Submit something that looks like you've made an effort.
- Keep a copy of the letter, application form, and accompanying CV on file, along with the information sent to you by your prospective employers. Make a note of when you sent it.

- Don't leave spaces on application forms: if something doesn't apply, write N/A, or refer the reader to your CV or covering letter.
- Don't ignore instructions, or hand in work that looks like it's been thrown together.

- Avoid keeping all your CVs, applications, etc. in one folder—organise in relation to each post. You can then discard any unsuccessful applications, keep pending ones in case you need to make further enquiries, and you'll be ready when you are called to interview.

Source: Boynton & Catt, 2002, p.12

be identified, and when they ought to advise on a study. The guide outlines where consumers can be involved, including:

- Identifying a topic area
- When research topics need to be prioritised
- When research is to be commissioned
- When research is being designed
- Managing research
- Undertaking a study
- Analysing and interpreting research results
- Disseminating research findings
- Evaluating the research process.

In addition, the guide contains a draft job description that can be used when one is employing consumers (p. 38). For more information visit Involve (formerly Consumers in NHS Research): http://www.invo.org.uk.

Training and support

Once staff have been appointed, you may find the format shown in Figure 3.1 helpful to ascertain what their training needs are, or you can utilise the researcher-skills questionnaire in Chapter 1 (if your project has no scope to offer such training, it may be worth stating that these skills are required when advertising for a researcher—see above).

Figure 3.1. Checklist for staff training

Please tick which of the following areas you would like to receive additional training in:

Packages

Word ☐   SPSS ☐   Access ☐   Excel ☐   PowerPoint ☐

Research skills

Using the internet   ☐   Presentation skills   ☐   Statistics   ☐
Evaluating measures ☐   Qualitative methods ☐

Writing and presentation skills

Writing conference papers ☐   Writing for publication ☐
Writing research bids   ☐   Disseminating research ☐
Other (please explain below)

_____
_____
_____

Within research, many of the skills we're taught are around learning methodologies and analysis. We are usually not instructed how to work with others, or manage staff. This means that many staff end up being managed by people who have no formal training in how to motivate or look out for others. If you are placed in a managerial or research coordinator position, or are required to supervise projects in some way, you may wish to request additional support or training in this area to help you (many universities or research organisations have started to offer these courses). You need to know how to manage people's time (and your own), motivate staff, offer constructive feedback/criticism, and possibly give appraisals. It is necessary to learn how to manage effectively, since projects can be stressful, and you don't want to end up making staff feel bullied because you find management difficult (see Chapter 6). Ask your employer to arrange training for you (this can be part of your career development) (Have a Job, Give a Damn Project, 2003). If you are a member of staff being managed, and you feel it isn't going well, you may wish to ask for formal management sessions, and request that your career be supported by your manager (it may be they don't know to offer this to you). For many contract staff members with universities, charities, or other organisations, your human resources office should offer you options for career development; if these are not offered then ask for them.

> *You should always get something out of any job you do. They pay you to do research, but you should leave with more new skills too. The first time I asked for extra training it felt scary, and my employers haven't always said "yes" to everything, but I've got most things I needed. I make a list of what I need to learn to get onto the next stage in my research career, and then I ask for it.*
> (Luca, researcher)

Steering groups

The purpose of such a group is given away in its title—it guides the research. That's the theory anyway. Some people find steering groups extremely helpful, while others find them an interfering and limiting menace. Steering groups are usually made up of people with an interest in the research, and knowledge about the issue under study (Rhodes *et al.*, 2002). For example, in the prostitution research I conducted, the steering group consisted of representatives from the police and youth justice, an outreach worker, and someone from the

research assumptions and hypotheses, and define the terms used. It should also show the research design and justify the choice of specific research methods and techniques. Information regarding the sample, instrumentation/measurement, and the implementation of the data collection and analysis plan should also be included. As you can see, these are also the major components for the research proposal. Indeed, making reference to your research proposal is not only necessary but also expedient to the writing of your final report. The difference is that the proposal is only a plan of your project, whereas the report must be written according to the research as implemented. If the implementation process involves significant alteration of your research plan, you may need to describe the original design and the changing process. In terms of both content and format, the final report should be much more mature than the proposal. The part of literature review, for example, should be more extensive as well as more intensive for the final report since the researcher usually keeps reading and using the information until the project is completely finished.

Generally speaking, you may elaborate on some parts of the report while only briefly mention others. The content and the format of the final report, therefore, may vary considerably from project to project. You need to keep in mind, however, the primary audience and the main purpose of the report. As a researcher you need to follow available agency guidelines. Or if you are a student you need to pay careful attention to the comments of your advisor(s). Generally, you should consult your "boss(es)" and find sample copies of research reports written for a relevant purpose. For example, to satisfy the requirements for a degree, you can get copies of well-written theses or dissertations recently filed with the library in your field. To fulfill the requirements of a funding source, you can make reference to research reports previously submitted to that agency.

What eventually distinguishes the research report from the research proposal are the results of a project. Although the proposal is also aimed at intended research results, only the report actually has them in it and your conclusion will be drawn from the selected findings. The interpretation and communication of the results, therefore, constitute the key task for report writing. Some authors would wait until most of exploratory data analyses are done. Some others may initiate writing even before data analysis gets started. Generally, data analysis and report writing constitute an interactive process. The rough ideas, questions, results, and answers will gradually form an organized and coherent body of information and knowledge in such a dynamic process.

probation service or drug care. Steering group members do not usually carry out the research, nor design the study. Instead they offer support, help with networking, and check that the research is running on time and to budget, and is representative. Groups work when they are supportive to researchers and participants, and offer solutions rather than just "checking up" (for more on effective group work see Elwyn, Greenhalgh, & Macfarlane, 2001). Groups tend to be less effective if they do not meet regularly, don't have a clear focus, and have a number of revolving members:

> On one study I worked on the steering group was pretty useless because several of the people in the group rarely turned up. Instead they sent along deputies and junior staff on their team, who of course knew nothing about the study, and wasted loads of time at the start of every meeting having to have the whole study explained to them. And often they'd make suggestions for change which just dragged the whole study down. (Rebecca, GP)

It is the role of the grant holder to set up a steering group (and many group members may also be grant holders—see next section). If one isn't in place, other researchers may suggest that a steering group could be established if it's deemed helpful. It is advisable to invite consumer or lay members to be involved on the steering group, since they can provide an insight from a "user perspective". Create a list of guidelines for group membership: an example of possible contents for a contract is shown in Table 3.5.

TABLE 3.5

Factors on which membership of the steering group is dependent

- Attending _____ meetings per year.
- Giving adequate notice if a meeting is likely to be missed.
- Offering support and advice to researchers and other group members.
- Giving notice and suggesting a replacement if I am unable to attend sessions.
- Providing assistance and contacts to researchers.

See also Greenhalgh & Donald (2000), pp. 3–4

While having a steering group can sometimes feel restrictive, involving different members from various disciplines or types of work can enhance the progress and quality of your research, and the usefulness of its outcomes. This may not be necessary for undergraduate and many postgraduate projects, but in many other studies it can be very useful. Even if you don't use a formal steering group, you can use informal networks to support you.

Accountability, hierarchies, and who exactly does what

Frequently roles within research aren't clear, which can make it difficult to know who is supposed to be doing what. Where roles aren't defined, this may lead to people feeling annoyed or undervalued if they perceive others working alongside them to be doing less. Furthermore, if roles are not outlined early on, this may lead to tasks being missed out. When it comes to work being written up, if who shares what role isn't defined, people can feel upset if their name doesn't end up on a paper when they expected it to (Wilcox, 1998) (see Table 3.6).

TABLE 3.6

Authorship guidelines

Significant contributions	Minor contributions
<ul><li>Origination and formulation of the research idea and hypotheses.</li><li>Design of the research.</li><li>Designing and conducting major analysis.</li><li>Interpreting findings.</li><li>Writing a major section of the report/paper.</li></ul>	<ul><li>Collection of data (including interviewing) and data entry, if these do not include a significant intellectual/scientific input.</li><li>Supervising data analysis.</li><li>Designing or building research apparatus.</li><li>Recruiting research participants and other administrative duties.</li><li>Advising on statistical issues.</li></ul>

Adapted from Game & West (2002); see also http://bmj.com/advice/article-submission.shtml#author

In order to counter some of these problems, the job title and corresponding tasks are outlined in Table 3.7. This is a rough guide, however. The fact that someone holds a senior position shouldn't mean they automatically qualify for first authorship if they've done little or no work on the research.

TABLE 3.7

Roles of different people working on a research project

Job title	Role
Grant holder(s)	Comes up with the idea for the research, writes the research bid and obtains funding. Oversees the study progress (usually through the research coordinator/manager). There can be more than one grant holder on a study. Has the final say on what gets published and has their name on any papers/reports arising from the research. They are the spokesperson for the research if it receives any publicity. In some studies grant holders do not collect data or have direct contact with participants; in other cases they take a more "hands-on" approach.
Research coordinator/manager	Manages the project overall. They don't design the study but can suggest improvements. There is usually one manager on a study, who oversees the progress of the project and the research assistant(s). The manager usually analyses the data and writes the research report. They may also write papers arising from the research.
Research assistant	Collects data, interviews participants, etc. They don't tend to have input into the study design. They may have responsibilities for data entry and cleaning, but possibly not for analysis. They are usually acknowledged on any publications arising from the research, but not named as authors on the research paper.
Steering group member	May also be a grant holder, or could be a representative of a charity group, organisation, or local service. The steering group members direct the study and ask questions about its purpose, progress and outcomes. Steering group members get their names on papers only if they contribute significantly to the writing-up of the research.

Statistician/ Qualitative analyst	If the analyst is employed purely to analyse/organise qualitative/quantitative "data" they will be paid for this task, and be acknowledged within any subsequent publications. If, however, they were involved in the design and management of the research and contributed to end reports/papers they may be cited as an author.
Secretary	Some projects require secretarial support, and many departmental secretaries assist with projects as well as carrying out their regular work. In such cases they won't have input into the research but should be acknowledged if without their help the study wouldn't have progressed.
Research manager	Some large-scale projects employ managers who check that data is being collected, entered, cleaned, etc. They may not have input into the design or writing of the research, in which case they will be acknowledged in final publications. If they have contributed to the writing and analysis of research, they may be a co-author. On smaller scale projects the research coordinator heads the organisation and running of the research.
Consumer	Consumers can fill many of the above roles, from being a grant holder or steering group member through to a researcher. It is important that when consumers are included in research their role is documented and rewarded—a name on a research paper may not be as meaningful as a training certificate or a good reference, or an opportunity for work in other projects.

Don't be afraid to bring up discussions of roles—if you've earned authorship, believe your job isn't clearly defined, or think you're being overloaded or experiencing a shift in workload then talk about it as soon as you can. It's better to say this at the start when everyone is calm and the research is moving along, than at the end when everyone is overworked, stressed and may feel resentful about the work they've been doing. I always get everyone to state what their role will be and agree this at the start of a study. We can review as the research progresses, but at least there are no nasty surprises for anyone when we come to write up the work. (Julianne, senior lecturer)

Setting out roles in the planning stages of a study isn't a guarantee of preventing queries about tasks, but can reduce confusion. You may find the checklist of tasks in Table 3.5 helpful in deciding who has earned what authorship.

If you are working with consumer groups, or as good practice with participants, it may be worth letting them know who the lead researcher is on a study so that they can get further research information from that person. Frequently the person participants have the most contact with is the research assistant, the most junior member of a team. The assistant may leave before a study is written up, and will therefore be unable to share results with participants. It is up to the lead researcher to ensure that this information gets shared at the end of the study (see Chapter 8 for more on this).

As well as the people listed in Table 3.6 there will be numerous others with whom you'll have to work, ranging from IT support staff to the finance department. It is worth working out who is involved (even marginally) in your research and ensuring you establish good links with everyone. You never know when your computer will need fixing, or a package will need to be delivered urgently. If you are working by yourself or outside an academic institution, again, work on building your networks to support you.

Intellectual property and research ownership

As well as setting out work tasks and job descriptions, it is also worth understanding and agreeing who owns what in relation to a study. Again, this should be set out at the beginning of research, when a study is being planned. Knowledge of these issues is frequently assumed, which may mean that new researchers, consumers, or others not used to research procedures may expect different outcomes from studies. The research is owned by the grant holder and funding body—the person who got the money to conduct the study (see Table 3.6). They are named as authors, speak about the research and have to be consulted if it is to be discussed elsewhere. If you are not a grant holder you do not have rights to the data, and cannot discuss the research without permission—nor can you publish the research under your name.

> I've found staff who collect data frequently feel aggrieved that they seem to do all the work, but don't get any credit. If you want to be involved in writing the paper or presenting the research, you should ask your manager to see what you can do to become more involved. I think managers also have to think about giving staff other bonuses. If they aren't going to get their name on a paper, then you should offer them other skills training so they can develop as researchers. (Roger, head of department)

But even if you've sorted who has done what, whose name goes first on a paper and who takes the lead? Who gets the prime spot of first author and research representative can cause disagreements if not sorted early on (the reason for this is that the first author is recognised as the person who had the biggest input into the research) (see Drenth, 1998; Guide to Intellectual and Financial Ownership: http://www.corec.org.uk, select the category that best decides you from the home page; Hoen, Walvort, & Overbeke, 1998).

Research governance and ethics

Those completing studies within the field of health and social research in the UK (and in other countries too) need to be aware of the Research Governance Framework. This covers five key areas: ethics; science; information; health and safety; and finance and intellectual property (see http://www.rcgp.org.uk/research/governance/key.asp for an outline of each category). The Framework covers everything from guidelines for those running clinical trials through to the roles and responsibilities of participants and researchers, and issues of indemnity and insurance. At the time of writing, much confusion exists over what research governance means, and what issues apply to different forms of research studies. I suggest erring on the side of caution, and for all research you are involved in consult with the guidelines for Research Governance. You can find an outline of the Framework here: http://www.dh.gov.uk/PolicyAndGuidance/ResearchAnd Development/ResearchAndDevelopmentAZ/ResearchGovernance/fs/en.

If you are uncertain about issues of research governance in health studies, you can also ask for, or offer, help and advice at the R&D Forum: http://www.rdforum.nhs.uk. We will also update people about any changes to the Framework, and offer explanations of research governance, on this book's website (see Chapter 9 for links).

Research cannot proceed without ethical approval. This may be from your university ethics committee (if your research is at undergraduate or postgraduate level; or you work within a university and your participants are members of the public who aren't patients). If you are completing research with patients or through a health care setting you will require ethical approval from your local research ethics committee (LREC), or an MREC (MultiCentre Research Ethics Committee), which deals with studies that cross geographical boundaries and span four or more health authority areas (see Chapter 5 for more on ethical guidelines, and http://www.corec.org.uk). For psychologists or those in other social sciences, the British Psychological Society offers an ethics advice surgery (email conduct@bps.org.uk with your question).

It is the role of the ethics committee to check over your research in terms of its design, method and predicted outcome (Kendall & Carter, 1997). You will need to provide full details to the committee about your proposed research, which includes the following: letters to be sent to participants; publicity or information sheets relating to your study; consent forms; any questions, measures, or schedules for your study; and a protocol for your proposed research (most committees require either copies of these sent electronically or multiple paper copies, so be prepared to build time into your project for this, and check what form of submission they require).

Exercise: Is this ethical?

Consider your research/study question. What are you going to study, and how are you going to do it? Who will be in the research (participants and researchers)? Write your study aim and method at the top of a large sheet of paper. Draw three columns on the paper. Write "participants" in column 1, "researchers" in column 2, and "others" in column 3. Keeping your research question in mind, write what you think the study will involve for people in your three groups. Consider this from the inception of the study idea through to the production of a research report. See how the different groups have different needs, and consider how you would go about ensuring that these ethical requirements were met.

Ethics committees are made up of a chairperson who leads the group, a secretary, and a number of volunteers including those with expert knowledge in the area of health/social research and some who are lay members. The committees meet regularly—busy committees within hospitals or local authorities tend to meet monthly, while university committees usually meet on a twice-termly basis. It is therefore important to find out how often committees meet and place your application with them on time. Your application will be reviewed alongside other proposals, and the committee will then contact you with its verdict. Usually this is provisional approval, but you'll need to answer some questions or make some amendments for the committee. Occasionally it may refuse a study, in which case you can appeal or question this with the chairperson.

> *I always attend ethics meetings, and when I have new staff I take them with me so they can see what they are like. Committees always seem to ask you loads of questions, but I think that if you are on hand to answer them, it reduces the chances of any confusion. Also, they can see who you are and know that you know what you're doing.* (Angus, lecturer)

The best way to view ethics committees is as a resource to help develop your research and safeguard the public. If you have any questions or uncertainties, rather than avoiding getting ethical approval, or delaying your application, read the guidelines for ethics committee applications (available from your university or local research ethics committee). If you are still uncertain about part of your research, then email or call the chair of your committee and ask them for their advice—this can help you shape your application, or even help you decide whether one is required.

> *The best advice I ever got was about keeping a dialogue with an ethics committee. I didn't know it was possible to communicate with the chair of the committee, but once I found out this was possible, it was a positive strategy in the planning of all my research.* (Grayson, lecturer)

Remember, if your study is running over a period of time you'll need to renew your ethics application each year for its duration.

Ethics committees get a bad press from researchers, who frequently see them as gatekeepers or busybodies who don't know much about the realities of research. My experience with committees has ranged from their being very helpful, through to being downright obstructive (one ethics committee chairperson, who will remain nameless, once told me he wanted to get my study on sex stopped because he didn't see the point in a study on sex and the topic was "trivial"). If you feel that a committee has shown ignorance with regard to your method, study question, or design—or that they are biased against your topic, or make inappropriate remarks to you—you can complain to the chairperson. Committees are there to protect the well-being of participants, and so their role is to be respected. However, if you feel they are obstructing research or being disrespectful to you or your research, you have a right to question it.

Finally, remember that you need ethical approval for research to take place (and many savvy participants and collaborators will ask to see ethical approval). Furthermore, journals should not accept papers for publication if they do not have approval from an ethics committee, so as well as considering ethical issues when planning a study, you also need to keep ethics a priority throughout your study (see Chapter 5 for more information). Many journals list what they expect from ethical research, so it may be worth consulting the websites of the leading journals in your area of research to see what they expect from you.

This chapter has set out general issues that need consideration as you begin a study. The next chapter covers how to prepare research and check it to ensure that your final study really will work.

Completing research 4
Or the importance of piloting, and how to stay focused

The previous two chapters outlined issues to consider when planning and setting up research. The early stages of any study are crucial in terms of spotting factors that could get overlooked and lead to work building up beyond your control. This chapter takes things up a level by focusing on the stage between planning and running a study, including:

- Maintaining literature searching
- Reviewing methodologies
- Piloting
- Staying motivated.

The most important part of this chapter focuses on piloting. Many research books outline methods and how to do them, but do not explain how to get your study into shape, which can be achieved only by good design and piloting. If you pilot your work, you can save time, check whether an idea will work, and make improvements to a study before it gets out of control. Unfortunately, piloting is frequently rushed or missed out completely, so this chapter will stress its importance and show how to do it.

Reading never ends

As mentioned in Chapter 2, literature searching isn't a one-off exercise at the start of a study. Although you need to conduct a thorough literature review at the outset, it is worth continuing with searches throughout the duration of research, as this can help you to keep on top of new developments, and also to be sure you've covered

Interpreting and communicating the results

The issue of causation

One of the most important issues in the interpretation of research results is the problem of causation. Statistical causal modeling tells us what variables are truly correlated by controlling for spurious correlations. It does not determine whether or not the relationship is really causal by itself. You must use logical judgment and take into consideration additional information such as the time sequence of different variables.

The notion of causation, however, has been expanded as a recent trend in behavioral and social science research. Pedhazur and Schmelkin (1991) point out that the scientist *qua* scientist seems to find a causal framework indispensable for central concepts and principles of design, analysis, and interpretation of scientific research. Even in the modest claims of "descriptive" findings we see various causal allusions in euphemisms such as: independent and dependent variables; mediating or moderating variables; proportion of variance accounted by; effect; influence; risk factors (ibid.). Additionally, any single regression may be referred to as an analysis of "multiple causation" (Li, 1988). Nevertheless, as "a notorious philosophical tar pit" (Davis, 1985, p.8), causation is one of the most controversial topics in philosophy and science (Pedhazur & Schmelkin, 1991). Generally, "the design type has important implications for the validity of conclusions, inferences, and generalizations from research" (ibid., p.697), and various authors have asserted that it is only through variable manipulation that one may hope to study causation. Indicating problems of internal validity in experimental and quasi-experimental designs, however, Pedhazur and Schmelkin point to the fact that inability or unwillingness to manipulate variables has led many to make causal inferences from nonexperimental research. "This in turn has led to conferring the status of cause on variables that are not manipulable in principle (e.g., race, sex) or in practice (e.g., religious affiliation, marital status)" (ibid., p.698).

Indeed, one can hardly imagine the popularity of modern structural equation modeling techniques without the idea of causation applied in nonexperimental settings. Saris and Stronkhorst (1984, p.2) contend that "Although this non-experimental research may seem to be less convincing or conclusive, it can still be used in tests of causal hypotheses." Historically, Simon (1954) and Blalock's (1962, 1964, 1970) work laid the foundation of such causal analysis. The Simon-

literature thoroughly. This includes checking over the topic area you're studying, so that methods you intend to use can be checked against existing literature.

> *If it seems someone has carried out a similar study to you, and has, for example, used a set of questions or study design it is worth replicating their work since you can utilise it. There's no point in repeating work if somebody's already started it for you.* (Aaron, research nurse)

If you incorporate existing designs into your research at the earliest opportunity, you can pilot the measures to see whether or not they suit your study. If they work, you can use them; if not, you'll be able to explain and discuss this in your research write-up.

Reviewing and selecting measures

It's not always clear how to select a measure, and some people I've met seem to be under the impression they shouldn't use existing study design since they believe research is given more value if it's original. This is a simple confusion, but one that can waste time and money. What should be original in research is the question or idea— what you want to study. How you go about investigating that idea doesn't have to be original. So if there's something you can incorporate that's been proven in existing research, then use it! This is also very helpful when you want to compare your results with those of other studies.

> *Don't forget, if you are using a standardised questionnaire/ measure or interview schedule, you cannot alter the wording; otherwise it ceases to be a validated measure. I made this mistake a few years ago when I got hold of a standardised measure and I changed it to fit my study. When it came to being published the reviewers rejected the paper since they said I'd altered a validated measure and therefore lost the purpose of the research.* (Martin, lecturer)

However, there's no reason why you cannot think of additional issues you want to measure that you can ask before or after the validated, pre-existing one.

A further confusion arises around how to find existing measures. A quick way is to incorporate this into your literature review.

You've probably noticed that many papers include the question-naire, interview, or experimental design used in their research; and where they are not included the author's details are cited so you can contact them for copies. If I can't find what I'm looking for in the publication I email the author. Not only do I usually get to see the measure or interview questions they used, but I also make contact with another professional working in my area. (Annette, senior lecturer)

It's important to remember that when you use existing measures, you need to reference them fully, and some are licensed, which means you have to pay to use them—make sure you check this when considering what questions/schedules/designs you want to use in your research. Many publishers print collections of assessment tools and measures, so as well as literature searching through journals, examining publishers' web pages and catalogues can help—as can calling stockists who'll be able to let you know if they know of existing study materials that may save you time and effort.

Don't fly without a pilot

Did you hear the one about the researcher who sent out a question-naire but didn't think to enclose return stamped addressed envelopes? Or the one who sent out letters with key terms spelled incorrectly? Or the survey that had pages missing? Or perhaps you heard about the interview that included questions nobody understood? Perhaps not, but I expect most researchers have heard some tale of a research "disaster"—possibly one they were involved in.

Although research can be changeable and unpredictable, most errors occur for two clear reasons. Either you didn't plan your study thoroughly (see previous two chapters), or you made plans but you didn't test the research to see if it was feasible. The second problem occurs if piloting was missed out. In my opinion piloting is the most important and least valued aspect of all research. We rush into research and make mistakes, whereas if we took a breath, tested our ideas and took things slightly more slowly, chances are we'd spot mistakes that could save our blushes and wasted time later on.

So what is piloting? It is more than just proofreading. Piloting involves checking all aspects of your research—from your correspondence, to your recruiting approach, through to your work with participants and subsequent creation of databases/means of coding (Blaxter, Hughes, & Tight, 2001, pp. 135–137; Robson, 1993).

When we think of piloting, we often focus on the method itself, and whether participants will understand the task we wish them to complete. However, that may not be where the problem lies. If the introductory letter/approach isn't appropriate, or the end outcome is poorly written, then the good study that was sandwiched between them will go unnoticed. Therefore think of research as a collection of different parts (see Table 4.1), all of which require testing—not just the method itself. In one of my studies we had the idea of using a computerised interview for our sex survey, since it was believed that such an approach leads to participants feeling safe, less embarrassed, and more likely to give "honest" answers. In reality, this only happened with participants who were well educated and accustomed to using computers. Participants with literacy problems, or for whom computers were a novelty, were deeply suspicious or scared of revealing their ignorance about IT in front of a researcher, and so refused to use them. We had to amend our design to a patient preference study, where we offered the questionnaire on paper as well as on computer—two-thirds of the participants opted for the former. Piloting of the method itself rather than just the questions might have shown us that on approach with less emphasis on the computerised interview was more appropriate in a diverse group of participants (and saved us a lot of money).

Table 4.2 gives a checklist for piloting.

Exercise: Checking comprehension

Pick a series of papers and see what they're asking: this may mean their research question, or any measures used in the research. Ask friends or colleagues what they think the questions or points mean. Look at where there are consistencies and differences in the topics they do and don't understand. Make a note of where confusions arise, and see whether these are factors you can avoid when designing research of your own.

TABLE 4.1

Aspects of research where piloting is required

Study item	What to pilot/test
Participant letters/consent forms/information sheets (see Chapter 5 for more on this)	Spelling and grammar (using spelling/grammar checker and proofreading by colleagues). Readability by participants—you need to test this on people who are representative of your participants, not your colleagues, who may not spot problems.
Means of approaching participants (see also Chapter 5)	Work out a rough script about what you want to say to introduce yourself and your study. Practise on colleagues and people representative of your participant group. Check for accuracy as well as whether your approach seems interesting and inviting. Test study logistics, such as how long it takes to call or write to participants, how long travelling to reach them takes, or how much time is spent on stuffing envelopes with questionnaires and letters.
Questionnaire/Interview schedule	Again, check spelling and grammar. For questionnaires test for readability using colleagues and people representative of participants. Do the questionnaires look easy to complete, as well as attractive? Can participants follow them? Are any pages/questions missed out? For interviews, are there any questions participants don't understand or that need repeating?
Instructions for researchers	Check that researchers understand what they have to do, and, if they are reading out questionnaires/interview questions, that they can do so correctly. If they are coding participant replies or filling in observation schedules, check they are doing it in accordance with the study aims. If more than one person is completing this task, check that they are doing it in the same way.
Setting up a database (see also Chapter 7)	There may be more than one way of setting out your database. Consider the best way of laying it out—take advice from a statistician where possible. Once data is being entered, double-check that everyone who is using it knows how to enter the data and is doing so in the same manner.
Final reports and papers (see also Chapter 8)	Check for spelling, and have others read through drafts. If reports are being made for different audiences, ensure that each report is suitable for the group question. Ensure that your publications are as easy to read and accessible as possible.

TABLE 4.2

Checklist for piloting

- ❏ Was there any aspect of your study that had to be repeated or explained before the participant understood it?
- ❏ What comments did the individuals who completed the pilot study make? Did they give feedback that suggested the study was flawed, or explain how their answers/actions were affected by your research?
- ❏ Note any persistent errors or misunderstandings by either participants or researchers.
- ❏ Ask the participants to tell you exactly what they thought the study meant and how this affected their responses/reactions.
- ❏ Record any problems participants had with the design, layout, phrasing, or format of your research.
- ❏ Assess how long your study will take to complete (this includes recruitment time).

Keep on keeping on

Research can be very rewarding and positive. But some of it is mundane, repetitive, and downright dull. We are often taught about the hands-on aspects of research, and are not aware of the scope of the behind-the-scenes aspects—the envelope stuffing, database maintaining, transcript reviewing side of our work. Chapter 7 outlines strategies to make some of these factors less arduous, but it is important to acknowledge that while research can be trying and difficult, what can be just as draining is the daily grind of a study. So how do you cope?

The main way to deal with the problem is to acknowledge it. Some studies run over time, and even the shortest study can include peaks and troughs, where you feel that you're either running the best study ever, or have the worst job in the world. Accept and understand there will be times when you feel tired, bored, or frustrated. If you can't access participants, or if you seem to have hit a brick wall in your analysis, it's understandable that you'll feel stressed. You can share your feelings with your research team, or, if it is getting too much, ask for a break or to talk to a counsellor or adviser. Research can be very boring: after all, you repeat the same task on a regular basis, or look at the same sort of words and numbers when the data is being analysed. When you are working with participants, it's important that they don't feel you're doing the work off pat, so, if possible, alternate tasks (for example, interviews can be alternated with transcribing or contacting participants and literature reviewing).

There are other ways to stay focused on research: I asked a few colleagues how they coped, and their answers are given in Table 4.3.

When you are designing research, the temptation is to plan for the maximum number of participants in the minimum amount of time. The problem with this is that researchers can easily feel overloaded and burnt-out (see Haivas, 2003). On one of my studies the only way to fulfil the number of interviews specified in the original research proposal was to see two participants per day. Fine in theory, but not so good in practice where each interview took up to two hours and participants lived in different parts of the city, meaning lengthy journeys between them. Also, there was no space for data entry, meaning we often had to work into our evenings to keep on top of the research. Because the study hadn't been adequately piloted, we were given no leeway, and we were exhausted. A rate of two interviews per day doesn't seem much, but requires emotional involvement and

TABLE 4.3

Researchers' motivational strategies

You know those books *Little book of calm* or *Don't sweat the small stuff*? I've found sometimes those self-help books can contain some useful ideas that help me feel better and less bothered about my work. (Robert, GP and MD student)

I go to somewhere like Lush, I buy up loads of bath stuff, go home, open a bottle of wine, put on my favourite music, run a bath, light some candles, turn off the phone—and forget about everything. (Kathy, research nurse)

We have a gym attached to my work and I take out all my frustrations there. (Nicky, research coordinator)

I've got a big group of friends and they don't do research, so I talk over my work when I'm at work, and when I'm with my friends we talk about everything else. (Lili, PhD student)

My work's mostly in the community, so even when I get bored or fed up, I know that there's a reason for my research, so it's more than being about me—it's about everyone in the community and they need help and support. You'd have thought it would put me under pressure, but actually it makes me want to do more to help. (Brian, outreach worker)

I do short-term projects and I leave gaps between them. I couldn't do research permanently, but I miss it when I'm not doing it. By alternating between teaching and research I can keep my outlook fresh. (Mahesh, lecturer)

Each time I write a paper or give a conference presentation I get a real buzz. Even though I've a list of publications I still get a thrill from papers or grants being accepted. It may sound strange but the more acknowledgement my work gets, the more I want to do it. (Suzy, professor)

concentration—and is tiring. Therefore, studies should build in time out for researchers—and where that isn't given, ensure you take all holidays you are entitled to, and don't work over your allotted hours. If you feel under pressure to do more than you are paid for, see the coping strategies outlined in Chapter 6.

Even if you are working with a research team, and studying members of the public, research is still a very lonely job (Blaxter *et al.*, 2001, pp. 185–186). You may spend a lot of time travelling, waiting, and talking to people you don't know and probably will never meet again.

> *I would travel on my own, spend time being cheery and doing my interviews, then sit and eat lunch on my own, before doing more interviews and going home on my own at the end of the day. I saw my supervisor once a month, for about an hour. I've never felt more lonely in a job in my life.* (Christina, project assistant)

It is therefore important to keep in touch with others, and to share issues. If you feel lonely or isolated, or that you are becoming demotivated, then tell your research manager or supervisor as soon as possible; don't hope it'll just "go away". If you're a lone worker, take a break or share your feelings with colleagues. Frequently if you are feeling bored or demotivated, you may find that your emotions are noticeable to participants and can be off-putting. On one study I managed, a researcher who said she "couldn't be bothered" with the project had the highest number of people refusing with the reason "can't be bothered"; her team-mate who felt embarrassed having to approach participants had more people refusing due to the sensitive topic of the study. If you feel you are putting people off, it's time to take a break!

> *Because research can seem repetitive and boring, it's tempting to only do the tasks you like, or the ones that seem more exciting or interesting. The problem is that at some point you'll have to get on with the rest of the work, and there's nothing worse than having to face a backlog of interviews, data to enter, or papers to search for.* (Matt, research coordinator)

Although it may seem tedious, keeping on top of even the most repetitive tasks can make for the smooth running of a study. If you are working as a team, it is worth discussing what tasks need doing. I like recruiting participants into a study, but am not keen on data entry.

Ideally working with someone who liked data entry might suit me, since I can recruit while they sort the data. Of course you need to ensure that tasks are shared fairly, and it is important that everyone on a study take their turn at different tasks (particularly if they are learning how to research), but sharing and balancing work can keep a study running on time.

Other useful strategies include keeping a separate work and home life. Often research has to be fitted in around participant availability, which can mean some weekend or evening work. However, this doesn't mean you should be available 24/7—something you should reinforce with your employers and your participants. Build in set days off, so you get clear time to yourself. The following sites could be useful (Meretrix, 2001; p.140): Doc Potter's advice site (http://www.docpotter.com); or a guide to recognising and coping with stress from the Mental Health Foundation (http://www.mentalhealth.org.uk/page.cfm?pagecode=PMNZST).

Ordinarily, methods texts would now talk you through how to do an interview, survey, or similar; and lecture you about validity, reliability, and bias. But since there are many books out there to guide you, this book doesn't go down that route (see Chapter 1 for more information on methods and analysis, if required). Instead, the remaining chapters cover how to manage your study—from approaching and recruiting participants, and monitoring researcher well-being, through to data management and maintenance, and presenting research findings.

Participants 5

The previous chapters addressed preparing for research. This chapter deals with arguably the most important feature of any social or health study: the people who will participate in it (although it is acknowledged that health and social research doesn't have to involve people). If you studied a social or health science topic at A Level, undergraduate, or even sometimes at postgraduate level you may be used to using fellow students in your studies. You may not have experienced recruiting non-student samples to research, and may be unfamiliar with issues around participant recruitment (Boynton, Catt, & Wood, 2001). This chapter will get you thinking about participants in a planned/actual study, including:

- Who are the participants going to be?
- How will they be accessed?
- Participants' needs (e.g. translators)
- Sampling/selecting participants
- Making contact with participants
- Issues of publicising research and participant recruitment (including using the internet)
- How to provide clear information to participants.

As research done "badly" can cause distress to participants and researchers, this chapter encourages you to think about treating participants with care and respect, and suggests ways of maintaining their well-being.

What's in a name?

Before moving on to address the issues listed above, it's worth clarifying terminology. I use the term "participants" here deliberately. In the past we used the term "subjects" to refer to those who completed research, and many people and publications continue to employ this descriptor. However, I believe the term "subject" implies someone who

Blalock approach is based on statistical control, which is considered more efficient than experimental design (Saris & Stronkhorst, 1984). Path analysis is a somewhat different procedure suggested by Boudon (1965) and Duncan (1966) based on the work of Wright (1934). "In this approach causal theories are specified including all important variables. Furthermore, procedures have been developed to establish the relationship between the causal effects specified in the theory and the measures for covariation between the variables" (Saris & Stronkhorst, 1984, p.4). Most importantly, since 1973 the program LISREL has been available which not only provides an efficient estimation procedure for the causal effects but also a test of causal theories (ibid.). This test is based on the relationship between the measures of covariation between variables and the causal effects. As Saris and Stronkhorst write, "If the theory is correct, the measures for the covariation derived from the estimated effects should be the same as the measures of covariation obtained from the data, apart from sampling fluctuations. If they are not the same, the causal theory on which the computations are based has to be rejected" (ibid., pp.4-5).

In terms of a structural equation model, conditions for causal inference should be borne in mind. James, Mulaik and Brett (1982) stated the logical foundation, including the following principle: "A structural model is confirmed if the predictions regarding correlations ... among manifest variables are consistent with the observed (i.e., empirically derived) correlations ... among manifest variables. A structural model is disconfirmed if predictions and observed correlations ... are inconsistent" (ibid., p.59).

All these illustrate that it is possible to test causal hypotheses on nonexperimental data, including those obtained from cross-sectional surveys. In fact, many explanatory studies are cross-sectional (Babbie, 1992). However, explanatory cross-sectional studies have an inherent problem. "Typically, their aim is to understand causal processes that occur over time, yet their conclusions are based on observations made at only one time" (ibid., p.99). Nevertheless, there are ways in which the problem can be dealt with. Especially, due to the difference between experimental and nonexperimental designs, one has to pay more attention to theory formation in nonexperimental research than in experimental research. "If important variables have been omitted in a nonexperimental study the conclusions from the analyses of the data are questionable, while this is not necessarily true in experimental studies" (ibid., p.5).

A causal model may involve some conceptual difference in the interpretation

is "subjected to" research, and who is relatively powerless within a study—a hierarchy is implied, where the "subject" is there to do what the researcher wants. It is for this reason I challenged the *British Medical Journal* in 1998, requesting they use the term "participants" (Boynton, 1998). You may find terms such as "volunteers", "consumers", "patients", or "people" can be used instead—just not "subjects"! I'm not alone in suggesting this—organisations such as the British Psychological Society and the Standing Advisory Group on Consumer Involvement in NHS Research have also led the way in advocating this terminology. Using alternative terms can make your research seem more accessible—as well as being more participant-friendly.

What are your participants' needs and wants?

It stands to reason that if people have a good experience of research they are more likely to continue with a study, participate in the future, or recommend taking part to others. This means ensuring that your study is well thought-out, and participants can clearly see the point of your work, and know exactly what is required of them. All researchers involved in working with participants ought to be aware of their interpersonal skills so they appear friendly, approachable, but not patronising. Role-playing the research prior to completion may help researchers feel more confident about this.

Exercise: Getting to know you

In pairs or more, practise introducing yourself in different ways. One part of the pair makes an introduction of themselves, and who they are (appearing friendly, busy, embarrassed or shy, abrupt- etc.). The other party (on the receiving end of the introduction) feeds back on how the approach makes them feel—and whether they want to carry on the conversation. Note what factors draw you into a conversation, and what ones make you want to get away!

You can identify the needs of your participants by looking at your selection criteria (who you want to be in your study). Do your potential participants have any particular requirements? It is worth being aware of them since they may need implementing right from the start of the research. Items you may wish to consider include:

- Translation services (for individual interviews, or any written materials you'll be using) (these are often organised through social services, so contact your local office for more information)
- Wheelchair and/or pushchair access to wherever the research is taking place
- Signing, or items in Braille (see also http://www.signpostbsl.com)
- Access to advice or counselling (see also http://www.bacp.co.uk)
- Refreshments, and transport to and from research venue
- To allow parents or carers to participate, crèche services for young children, or support and care for ill or older people
- Flexible time limits for research (to allow for translation; people with learning, visual or hearing difficulties; young children's concentration spans; or to permit conversation between you and participants)
- Advice, information, and consent forms aimed at those with different needs (e.g. children, those with learning difficulties, or who speak different languages—see also http://www.dh.gov. uk/PolicyAndGuidance/HealthAndSocialCareTopics/Consent/ fs.en).

If you have no plans to exclude people on the basis of their health, abilities, languages spoken, etc., then you need to have procedures in place to assist anyone whose needs are not met by your study. This can increase the cost of the research, but should not be a barrier to a study unless there are other good reasons for excluding such groups (which you'll need to justify when reporting findings). Once you have thought about who your participants are, and what they need, you are in the right position to invite them to be in your research.

Approaching participants

Making contact with people about research is one of the most crucial aspects of a study, and yet frequently this area is left to chance, or hardly reflected upon. A letter or call that is well thought-out and presented in an interesting way is far more likely to gain a person's approval than something that seems to show a lack of forethought.

By letter

If you are going to write to participants, save yourself time by setting out a letter in a clear format and saving it to disk and/or making paper copies (see Table 5.1). Do this for every type of letter you'll need for your study (so you don't have to keep rewriting the same letters).

TABLE 5.1

Composing your letter

Think about who it is for	What will participants' reading skills be like, and what font size do they require? (For example, older participants, young participants, or those with visual problems may require a bigger font than usual; see NHS (2002), p. 9.)
Write clearly	This means short sentences and an accurate account of what is required. Avoid using complicated phrases or terms, and if using abbreviations or acronyms, explain these within your letter (Plain English Campaign, 2001).
Consider the impact of letter-headed paper	Letter-heads make correspondence appear more official, and (depending on the nature of the letter-head) more impressive. For example, some letter-heads include logos that show your department is award-winning or approved/supported by a related organisation or charity. These factors can be very helpful in getting people to feel happier about supporting a study. However, they may also carry other connotations. For example, a letter-head from a doctor's surgery, hospital, psychiatric service, or other health-related organisation could cause people anxiety, fear, or embarrassment. The same applies for correspondence that appears to be from official (government) organisations, the police, or other legal groups. Therefore decide whether your existing letter-head looks inviting or off-putting, and if it's the latter design a new letter-head that is appropriate to the needs of participants within your study. Finally, don't forget that you need permission from your organisation to use its letter-headed paper. If you are in doubt, check with your tutor or manager to find out whether you can use a letter-head.

It may sound obvious, but by setting out different letter formats you'll save time (just remember to make sure you change the date each time you print new copies). You may want to create letters to those who may help with the research introducing the study, letters to participants inviting them to join the research, apology letters to those who are upset about the research, or "thank you" letters to those who have assisted with your study. It may be worth using an electronic signature to save you signing every letter, but consider the impact of this—sometimes people will prefer to see your actual written signature.

Ethics committees frequently want to see copies of all correspondence to be sent to participants, and those completing a research degree may be required to include letters in an appendix of their report. Those who are experienced researchers may get correspondence from other academics/researchers about their work—in such a case a set letter explaining the work may be a time-saving device.

Similar issues arise when the name of your workplace is included as a frank or stamp on an envelope, as the following example shows.

> *I was sent a letter asking me to take part in a study on insomnia. My GP had told me about it and I was looking forward to taking part. But when the letter came it was franked with the words "Department of Psychiatry" as the study was being run from that department at our local hospital. I live in flats and all our mail is put out in the hallway, so my neighbours saw what looked like a letter from a psychiatrist. I felt really self-conscious and upset about it and didn't want to do the study after that.* (Maggie, patient, Liverpool)

If you are writing to participants inviting them to be in a study, be sure to outline clearly the study, the role of participants, and their right to refuse, and to explain what will happen next. Many ethics committees and research organisations have existing templates for letters. An example for a participant information letter/sheet is shown in Figure 5.1; tips on setting out correspondence are given in Table 5.2.

Things participants worry about

People can be concerned or maybe just curious when they get a letter about a research project, so your contact should include an explanation of how and why they were selected, and the contact should only be made if you have ethical approval for such an approach. Many ethics committees will ask to see a copy of this letter before giving you approval for your research.

> *On my first project I was keen to get started and impress my boss, and I sent out letters asking people to take part in my research, which was looking at the impact of caring for a relative with Alzheimer's. Unfortunately I didn't know I needed ethics committee approval, and one of the doctors who heard about my research was also on our local ethics committee. He contacted my*

Figure 5.1 Patient information letter

YOUR ADDRESS GOES HERE
YOUR LOGO GOES HERE

PARTICIPANT INFORMATION SHEET

We are working in —— for a study on ——. You have been selected [explain how—randomly, purposively, etc.], and we hope you will assist us in our research.

Why is this study important?
Outline for the participant a brief background about your research, what you are doing (brief title of study), why you are doing it and what the results will be used for. [This section should be two or three lines.]

What will the study involve?
Tell the participant what the research involves (for example, answering a questionnaire, taking part in a focus group). Remind them that what they say will be treated in the strictest confidence, and explain in a sentence how you will protect their anonymity. If possible inform participants that a researcher will be available to answer any questions. Give them time to think about opting into the study, and let them know how they can take part (for example, if there's a choice, where they can complete the research). If you want to do anything else (for example, look at a person's work or medical records, or take blood or other measurements), you should mention it here—along with telling participants who will be doing this task. If you are going to reimburse participants, you should mention it here. [This section should be between three and five lines.]

What if I change my mind about being involved?
You can decide not to be part of the research at any time. This will not affect any services or treatment you are currently receiving or will receive in the future.

What do I do now?
Let the researcher know whether you would like to take part, and when you would like to complete the study. If you have any further questions, please ask the researcher. You can telephone [give researcher's name and job title] on ——.

boss and complained about me. The result was our study was delayed and I ended up looking bad—even though it wasn't really my fault. Nobody told me to wait! (Phuong, research nurse)

Practicalities of sending letters
Sending out research letters can quickly become laborious. Apart from

TABLE 5.2

Tips on setting out correspondence

Font and size	The best fonts are Arial or Times New Roman, and you should use a minimum of 11pt Arial or 12pt Times New Roman. Bigger is acceptable, although you should make sure it is not so big it looks patronising or off-putting. Small text is hard to read, and if it's hard to read people won't bother finding out about your research (see NHS, 2002, p. 9).
Paper colour	Pastel colours (cream or light yellow) or plain white are the easiest to read. Other colours may be eye-catching, but be sure they are still readable.
Address	Ensure you include your correct address, with a contact telephone number and your email address if you have one (and if your participants are likely to correspond with you in this way). And check you have their correct address too!
Date	Ensure you include the correct date on each batch of letters you send out.
Spelling	Run your letter through a spell and grammar check, and get it proof-read by a colleague. You should pay particular attention to the spelling of participants' names, since incorrect spelling here doesn't bode well for the rest of your research relationship with a person.

See section on piloting in Chapter 4 for more on this

setting up templates for your letters, other ways in which you can save time are as follows:

- Use a mail merge for both your letters and envelopes/address labels
- Invest in self-sealing envelopes (licking hundreds of envelopes is nobody's idea of fun)
- If participants have to return anything to you, enclose a stamped addressed envelope
- If you need to send follow-up letters, have these prepared (as a template) at the same time as you write your initial research letter.

Mail-outs

If you are sending lots of letters, particularly if they will enclose more than one item (e.g. a letter and information sheet, questionnaire, etc.), then you'll need to plan a mail-out strategy. This means working out how long you need to put together your letters, and checking with your mail room that they'll be able to process your post. You may wish to send out all the letters in one go, or over time, but whatever way you do it you'll need to record what letters have gone out to whom, and ensure the letters are correct (including checking that the person named in the letter matches the name on the envelope). If you are assuring someone anonymity and confidentiality in your research, they may not feel reassured if you send them a letter with someone else's name on it.

Names and addresses

Check that names are correctly spelled, and if you know the person's gender use the prefix "Mr" or "Ms" unless another title is specified. Make sure you get the first or family name and surname the correct way round.

Problems with letters

Even if you've done your best to create letters that are comprehensive and interesting, problems can emerge if you're given the wrong address to write to, and letters are returned to you. If this happens, check or request the correct address. Alternatively, you send the right letter to the right person, only to find that there's a problem:

> I completed a study on home care for older people. My job was to write to them to ask if they would like to be in the study. Many of the participants didn't understand I was a researcher, so called me asking about benefits or other issues I couldn't help them with. This wasn't so hard to deal with, since I found out whom to refer them to. But it did add to the time of the study, which my boss didn't really appreciate. What was worse was I wrote to two people who had, unbeknown to me, recently died. In both cases their relatives called me and were very distressed. In one of the cases the relative was angry since I'd been given the person's details from the GP, and they felt the GP hadn't paid attention to the fact their parent had died. (Rav, research manager)

Make sure you check everything over before you send out letters. I've heard reports from colleagues who forgot to sign or give their name on letters, or who forgot to provide a return address for patients to contact them (see Chapter 4). Ask a colleague or member of your research team to check letters for you. A checklist is supplied in Table 5.3.

TABLE 5.3

Checklist for sending out research letters

❑ Does my letter look interesting and inviting?
❑ Is it clear and concise?
❑ Is it spelled correctly?
❑ Do I have the correct details and address for the person I'm contacting?
❑ Am I giving accurate information about my work in the letter?
❑ Am I promising more or less than I can deliver, or the study involves?
❑ Have I signed the letter?
❑ Is it in the correct envelope?
❑ Is it sealed and stamped appropriately?

Approaching participants by telephone

In most projects, whatever their size, you'll probably have to use the telephone for some of the work—to get information, to talk to participants, or to talk to other researchers you may be working with. Many people find it difficult to use the telephone in research, as it's not face-to-face contact and is often hard to know how you're being received. Again, if you are recruiting by telephone or plan on using telephone conversations as a major part of your research, this needs to be explained in your application for ethical approval. Remember, "cold calling" (approaching participants by telephone or personal visit) without an initial letter or email introducing the study is unlikely to get ethical approval unless you can prove it is integral to your research.

Tips for telephone talk

If you have to make a number of calls, prepare a script or checklist of key points you need to raise. Practise going through them and have them available as an *aide-mémoire* (although you don't need to read them through verbatim each time). Think about whom you'll be talking to. Make your verbal communication as clear as possible—in the tone of your voice and the words that you use. If you are speaking to older people, those with hearing difficulties, or those who don't share the same language as yourself, you'll need to remember to slow your speech and speak slightly louder than normal. However, don't shout, and rehearse this with a colleague to ensure you sound clear, rather than patronising. Pilot what you'll be saying—it might sound trivial, but you need to consider what you think your key message is and test it out on someone to check if you're right (it's best to try this on someone who you know will give honest feedback, but who doesn't know what your study is about). Keep this in mind as you go through your study, as you may find that you introduce your work in different ways that may give out different messages.

When to call

Pick a time when you know your participants will be most likely to be in. Then consider whether this will be convenient. If it's appropriate you may call people at work, but only do so if your research relates to their work—if it does not, and particularly if your study is of a personal nature, you should not call them at work. You may find calling people at home in the early evening is best for participants who are at work in the day, but be aware that for many with busy lives or who have children, this might still be a busy time. Calling people very early in the morning or very late at night is off-putting, or may seem threatening, and should be avoided.

Leaving messages

If you get an answering machine, it's better to call back later, since you do not know who else checks the messages and you don't want to inadvertently breach confidentiality. If, however, you are calling a group or organisation that is expecting to hear from you, and you know you are through to the correct person's voicemail, then you may wish to leave a brief message stating your name, that you're calling about research, and when you will call back.

Cold calling

As mentioned above, calling people to introduce your research is regarded as unethical, as it may seem to participants to be an invasion of privacy, and may be coercive. Therefore before you call anyone you should have sent an introductory letter outlining and introducing your research. Within that letter you should specify if you will telephone a person, and tell them when this is likely to happen. You may also need to offer them an opt-out option (for example "if you do not want to be contacted by me in relation to this research, please return the enclosed form indicating you do not wish to be part of the study"). When you call the participant you can say you sent a letter already and remind them about your work. This rule of cold calling applies particularly to participants, but also relates to those who may give you access to participants (for example, an office, a GP surgery, or a school). You should never call someone you don't know to talk about a study they have no prior knowledge of.

Making calls

If your project will involve a lot of telephoning, you may find the following helpful.

- Invest in a hands-free earpiece or headset—it avoids neck ache and you can move around when talking. You may also use a speaker-phone, although you should be aware of confidentiality issues with having your conversation with participants heard by others
- Take regular breaks between calls, stretch, and move around
- Keep a glass of water on your desk, and take a drink between calls
- Know the name of the person you want to speak to (and get advice on pronunciation if you're unsure of how to say a particular name)
- Be polite at all times, even if the person doesn't want to do your study, or is difficult. (That doesn't mean you have to listen to abuse. If a person is difficult then apologise for troubling them and put the phone down—see Chapter 6 for more on this)
- Be patient, and be prepared to explain your study in a number of ways
- Smile
- If it doesn't make you too self-conscious, keep a mirror by your desk to check you aren't looking tense or sitting awkwardly. This can be reflected in your voice
- If you have one, get your health and safety adviser to give you support and check your office is set up to make calls.

How to start a telephone call

It may seem obvious, but people struggle when starting a telephone conversation, particularly if calling someone they don't know, but whom they want to be part of research. A guide on how to get started is shown in Table 5.4.

Be prepared

Create a participant database with the name and number of people you call (ensure this is password-protected). Record the outcome of the call (an agreement to participate, a date to call out, an incorrect number or a refusal) (see Chapter 7 for how to create a database for this information). If possible, make a note of why they are refusing (too busy, topic of research, etc). You may also wish to keep a note of the calls, particularly recording problem areas, discuss with your manager or colleagues if there are persistent misunderstandings or

of results derived by the same procedure. For example, the causal explanation of a suitable analysis may consider a variable as an antecedent variable. It may also be taken as an intervening variable in a causal link interpretation. In addition, it can be treated as a conditional variable if the different groups are regarded as different conditions in a conditional analysis. Even in the most straightforward bivariate analysis, sometimes you may need to control for the dependent variable rather than the independent variable. In such a case, row percentages will be used instead of column percentages if you put the values of the independent variable in the first row of the contingency table as usual. This technique is especially useful when the sample is drawn disproportionately on the values of the dependent variable. The logic of reasoning may be reversed accordingly based on the contingency table.

Longitudinal data analysis greatly facilitates the interpretation of the causal relationship but demands special formats for presentation and communication. Frequency tables of the key variables for different time periods are usually combined into one table, which constitutes a basis for so-called time-series analysis. This is especially useful to show the secular trends of the key variables. The key variables can be put in the first row; the time periods (years, months, days, etc.) can be put in the first column on the left-hand side. A trend line can be drawn by linking the data points in a coordinate system. The line can be simplified by using the method of moving averages (i.e., means of different groups instead of individual data points) or semi-averages (i.e., means of two general groups instead of individual data points). Least squares linear regression analysis may also be performed for this purpose by using time as the independent variable. Sometimes nonlinear regression techniques are necessary to obtain more accurate description and prediction of the secular trends. Generally speaking, the presentation of longitudinal data may only show irregular movements, or may reveal some regular patterns including cyclical movements.

Longitudinal data analysis can deal with the relationship among different variables in terms of their correlation with one another. This is important because researchers often need to know reasons of change other than simply the "aging" factor. In statistical terms, the method of "serial correlation" is exactly the same as what we have learned about correlation. However, a variable here is formed by the change of the individual values or group parameters (e.g., means or percentages) of a measure when repeatedly applied to the same subjects or groups along the time dimension. This is different from the cross-

TABLE 5.4

Example of phone conversation

"Hello, my name is _____. Can I speak to _____ please? Is this a convenient time to call?" (If it's not, arrange a suitable time to call back.)

- If the person you want to speak to answers, remind them you've already written to them, restate the study, and explain what you would like them to do (e.g. participate in your study, help you gain access to participants, give you advice).

- If someone else answers your call, ask if you can speak to the potential participant, and if they aren't available, check a convenient time to call back. Arrange a time and give your contact number (if you feel it's appropriate). Do not ask the participant to call you back—you want them to help you, so you have to do the work. If they want to know more about why you are calling, tell them it's about research but give no more details unless you feel it's absolutely necessary. You are protecting your (potential) participant's right to confidentiality. They may not want others to know they are taking part in your research, and you have no idea who you may be talking to (or what their relationship is with your potential participant), so be polite, brief, and call back later. As you have given your name at the start of the study, if the participant has told their friends/relatives/colleagues about the study they may recognise your name and know why you are calling. In such cases you still don't give details about the person you want to speak to. If a friend or relative says the person won't be doing the study, patiently remind them the participant needs to refuse themselves. However, be flexible: a relative or carer may be able to tell you a person is too ill to take part, which you need to respect. You don't want to cause offence or lose participants, so use your discretion about getting someone on board.

- If you get the wrong number, ask the person you are talking to to confirm the number. If you dialled incorrectly, redial. If you dialled the number you believed to be correct then check whether the person whom you were trying to call has ever lived there. Apologise for interrupting the person whose number you called.

problems, and find solutions for them where possible. I've encountered participants whose reactions have mostly been positive, but some have reacted differently—one woman accused me of having an affair with her husband, while another man believed I was from a radio show, trying to "stitch him up". It's worth remembering that although the research seems sensible and meaningful to you, it may not feel the same to participants (again, piloting can help iron out possible misunderstandings).

Other problems you need to be prepared for are participants who are:

- Unable to speak your language
- Upset and angry about you contacting them, or about an issue related to your research
- Lonely (or whom you can't stop talking)
- Unsuitable for the study, but want information or advice from you anyway
- Sceptical about you, or don't believe you/your study is genuine.

Ending your call

If people do want to take part then explain the next stage of the research, thank them and remind them of your contact details.

Ansaphones/Voicemail

Some people hate speaking to ansaphones. Some believe it's better talking to a person rather than a machine. However, it's not good if someone calls back about a project and ends up talking to someone who is not related to that work, or who is unable to help them. In these cases an answering machine may be better. Consider what best suits your needs.

Making a message

Consider the essential details for your message and write a script (an example is given in Table 5.5). Keep it clear and concise. Rehearse it, keeping your speech slow and clear. Record your message when you won't be interrupted and when it's quiet. Check the message by playing it back and dialling from outside, and be prepared to change it as and when necessary (for example, if you'll be out of the office for a while, then callers need to know for how long and when you'll be getting back to them).

TABLE 5.5

Hello, you have reached the answering machine/service/voicemail for [person/project name]. I'm sorry I'm [we're] unable to take your call at the moment, but please leave your name and number, and I'll [we'll] call you back as soon as I [we] can.

> *Dial your message and check it works. And remember to keep it up to date! I forgot once and it was only when someone pointed out to me in May that I had a message saying when I'd be back after the Christmas holidays that I realised I'd let it slip.* (Marni, research assistant)

Extras

You may want to give other numbers for people to call (for example, your mobile). If you are giving your mobile as a contact number, then make this clear as these calls may be expensive and some people may prefer to leave a message on the answering machine. Let people choose to call your mobile rather than putting your phone on divert to a mobile, as this can also lead to unnecessary expense for participants.

Decide whether you want to give details other than your name on the message. Your department/organisation/project name may be encouraging, but it may also be off-putting (particularly if the person calling doesn't know much about your study). People can often trace the telephone number of calls they have missed. Getting through to an answering machine could be the first someone hears about a study, so ensure your message is appropriate to anyone in this category.

It is important to think about safety issues here. Giving your name and other contact numbers can make you more vulnerable. If you receive any upsetting calls, make a note of them and report them to your boss and to the police if necessary (see Chapter 6 for how to deal with this). Unless absolutely unavoidable, do not use a home number for research. Use a mobile or keep an office address. Don't overload your message. It's costing someone money, and people may get frustrated if they have to hang on for a long time. If you are going to give people different contact numbers, be sure to say them slowly and clearly (repeat if necessary, and you may also wish to include alternative numbers on your letter). Check your machine regularly. Return calls promptly, and delete old messages once they are dealt with. If you note down the caller's details, ensure these are kept privately—do not leave numbers and names in open view.

Introducing research/publicity

You can publicise your research in a number of ways: in the press, or on other media (television, radio, website), or by using posters where potential participants might see them. It's important to keep the publicity ethical, and proportional to your research. You don't always need advance publicity. If you are planning a national evaluation of cancer care, utilising the mainstream media could help. If you are investigating a local service, the local paper or radio station would be more appropriate, and if you are doing a small-scale or student project, you probably won't need to use the media to publicise your work. Always check with the study leader (and/or your workplace) whether publicity is permissible.

> *One of my students decided to go off and advertise her final year project. She didn't check with staff first, but made posters for local pubs inviting single mums to be part of a research project. She gave the department's number as contact and we were suddenly swamped with calls from women thinking the poster was advertising a crèche or child care, was about benefits, or was someone checking up on them. The secretaries were overloaded and it took us a while to work out what was going on. She didn't have a clue about why it was a problem, or why participants were misled. I always use this as an example of how a person's wish to do well can actually cause problems—to them and others. (Steve, lecturer)*

You may want to use posters, leaflets, websites, adverts or articles in magazines or papers, or slots on television or radio (see NHS, 2001, 2002). Remember, if you are doing any of these as your main means of recruiting participants, those in your sample may not be particularly representative, and this will need to be declared in the methods section of subsequent reports or papers. You will need to explain that they were viewers of TV, readers of magazines or papers, radio listeners, or those able to read posters or access the internet and find the site about your study. Those who respond may have a particular reason for participating, so you may wish to incorporate questions to assess this into your research design. You may need to pilot methods of publicity/recruitment if you are uncertain about participant responses. Some pros and cons of publicity are listed in Table 5.6.

TABLE 5.6

Publicity—who needs it?

Positive aspects	Negative aspects
• You can raise the profile of your research. • You can reach a wider audience. • You can get more participants. • You can make contact with others working in a similar field.	• You may get lots of contacts from people who aren't suitable for your study (but who still take time to deal with). • If publicity is in the media, it is less under your control—you could get lots of interest, but your research (or yourself) could be misinterpreted.

When to publicise

When you tell others about your research depends on the type of study you are completing. If participants in your research are all volunteers you may need to publicise research early on. You will need to think about where to get publicity—where those on whom your research is based are most likely to be (see Table 5.7).

You may also want to try other ways of selecting people, and introduce a publicity campaign at a later stage. However, if you have a set means of selection (for example, recruiting participants through a play-scheme or hospital), then any additional publicity campaigns may interfere with this. You could also use publicity at the end of the study to draw attention to findings and give out information, and could circulate a short press release to media sources you think might be interested (see Chapter 8).

Exercise: Sell that study!

Choose a selection of diverse journal articles. Write a short press release for each (explain how the study was done, and summarise the key points from it). Consider how you would tailor these releases for local radio, tabloid or broadsheet papers, a television science show, or a women's or men's magazine.

TABLE 5.7

Publicity sources

Magazines or newspapers	Those who can read, and who read those publications when you are advertising in them.
Radio	Listeners to that station who hear the programme where your research is mentioned.
Television	Those who own a television, and who watch the programme/station where your research is mentioned.
Posters	Those who can read, who are in the area where your poster is placed, and who notice your poster.
Internet	Those who have access to the net, who can use a computer, and who can find your site.
Professional publications	You can describe your research in advert pages of some journals or members' magazines (e.g. *The Psychologist*, *Pulse*, or *Nursing Times*). However, don't forget that most participants do not read these publications, and so you're better served making research contacts via this medium.
Postcards, leaflets, or flyers	Those who can read, who notice your publicity, and who feel it applies to them. Some people may not realise a postcard is advertising research.

On top of this, you'll only hear from people who are prepared to take the time to contact you, or who are able to do so (have a phone, have money to call, can write in or email, etc.).

Website

You can create a study website (or include a link on your department site). This can be used to describe the study, invite participation, keep people aware of the study's progress, and publicise results. You may also want to give links to copies of papers or support groups related to your study (the Plain English Campaign has a guide for designing clear websites: see http://www.plainenglish.co.uk/webdesign.html).

Other ideas

Some researchers have combined other incentives to get participants to be part of their study—for example giving out gifts or money in return for taking part. However, many ethics committees take a dim view of this, since it constitutes coercion. You can provide a gift (monetary or otherwise) to participants, but it is unethical to use this approach as initial recruitment, and therefore it needs careful consideration. You must inform the ethics committee if such an approach is planned.

When to think twice

If publicity will put people off, cause offence, or draw attention to a study at the "wrong" time, then it is better to avoid or downplay participation. A researcher being well known, in the media, the local community or the organisation being researched, could have positive or negative effects on recruitment that also need consideration.

Looking after participants

Ethics

When completing any social research, it is important to plan for and overcome any potential ethical problems (see Howitt & Cramer, 2000, pp. 26–28). Universities, social science organisations and medical organisations usually have their own ethical guidelines for the treatment of humans (and animals) in research, so be sure to consult these when planning a study (see also Chapter 3) (e.g. British Psychological Society, 2000). Utilise, but do not rely on, ethical codes set out by your professional body. These are helpful but are not a replacement for applying to an ethics committee.

> *I was given a questionnaire to overview from a student who wanted to complete a study with some of the young lads who use our drop-in centre. She was interested in looking at their experiences of visiting the doctor, and part of the questionnaire was a long and detailed health assessment form—which included questions about their mental and physical health. I wasn't sure if it was appropriate for our lads to complete, nor whether the student was qualified to administer such questions. I asked her if she had ethical approval for the research—from her university or from the local research ethics committee. She breezily replied "Oh you don't need to worry, I'm a member of the psychological society,*

and I've followed their ethics". I declined support for the research and suggested she talk to her tutor about what ethical approval she needed. (Wale, youth worker)

Many people tend to focus on the most obvious aspects of ethics when planning research, but frequently ethical problems emerge that could have been anticipated, but perhaps weren't, and sometimes ethical problems occur even though steps have been taken to ensure participants' emotional and physical well-being.

Remember also that each new study requires ethical approval. I recently heard of a chiropodist inviting GPs to take part in what she was calling "enhanced service delivery" for patients, where patients were asked to fill in a questionnaire on foot care, and the chiropodist was later available to offer advice to those who wanted it. This was approved by the local Primary Care Trust (PCT), but one of the GPs pointed out that this wasn't a service, but was in fact a research project. When asked, the chiropodist stated she had no ethical approval since the questionnaire she was using had been given ethical approval on a previous study completed in Manchester. The fact that a measure or method has been used before doesn't automatically make it ethical, and care needs to be taken to ensure that your participants are protected. It's also good practice to check, since in the case of the chiropodist the GP surgery refused to help out until she'd gained ethical approval for what they deemed "research". The chiropodist, and arguably the patients, lost out on this occasion.

The trick is to identify whether you're doing research or whether you're delivering a new service or similar. If your work in any way involves working with people, asking questions, taking measures, then it may well require ethical approval and thorough piloting (see Chapter 4). If in doubt check with colleagues or contacts at your local ethics committee or university. There's nothing wrong with doing work with people that isn't research, but there is something wrong with researching people without the proper regulations being followed. Those who supervise work, and sit on charitable, social, or health committees (particularly PCTs), need to be aware of work completed within their area, and advise those who are bordering on completing research on how to proceed in an appropriate manner (see Tables 5.8 and 5.9).

TABLE 5.8

Ways to complete ethical research

❑ Familiarise yourself with research governance and ethical codes and guidelines.

❑ Plan your research using said guidelines.

❑ Show your research plan to others—ask for their feedback about the research design, paying close attention to the well-being of participants.

❑ Consult your ethics committee if you have any questions, and be sure to gain ethical approval for your work before you begin.

❑ If appropriate, involve a steering group and consumer representatives on your study team.

❑ If in doubt, discuss any design or study issues with members of a professional organisation linked to your work (the British Psychological Society, the British Medical Association, etc.).

TABLE 5.9

Items that your checklist for ethics should include

❑ Who will be in your study?

❑ What will it involve?

❑ Does the methodology you have selected represent the choice that is most ethically suited to the needs and abilities of your participants?

❑ How will participants be approached and selected?

❑ How will participants be made aware of their role and rights, and how will you ensure they understand these?

❑ How will you ensure confidentiality and anonymity before, during and after the research?

❑ How will you obtain voluntary informed consent?

❑ How will you protect your participants (and reflect them fairly) in any reporting of your research?

❑ Have you considered issues of data protection?

Voluntary informed consent

We often hear the term (voluntary informed) consent used about a project, but are not always clear why consent is important, or how to go about obtaining it. Voluntary informed consent (VIC) refers to participants being fully aware of the research they are about to become involved in. This includes a knowledge of the research itself and any adverse effects it may have on them, their families or their communities, both during and after the research period, and an understanding of what the research will be used for (Bulmer, 2001). VIC means that participants have chosen to be in the study, know what it entails, and have agreed to be part of it. It is of particular importance given past research (particularly the atrocities committed by Nazis during the Second World War—you can find out more at the Imperial War Museum's Holocaust Exhibition http://www.iwm.org.uk/lambeth/holoc-ex1.htm), where people were subjected to "research" that was abusive and distressing, and caused health problems, pain, infertility, and in many cases death. It had little basis in science. The Declaration of Helsinki, outlined in 1964, is now used to ensure humanitarian treatment of participants (you can read the full version at http://www.wma.net/e/policy/63.htm). Remember, you need to know about humanitarian guidelines, but again, these are not a replacement for gaining full and formal ethical approval for your research.

Why is it important to get VIC?

The need for VIC is to show that those who take part in your research do so willingly, and are fully aware of what the research involves—the implications of participating (including any negative aspects) and the benefits of taking part (Howitt & Cramer, 2000, pp. 29–30) (see Chapter 3 for more on research ethics).

How do I get VIC?

It is customary to get participants to sign a form or letter to show they agree to take part. The researcher usually countersigns this. Many ethics committees provide a pro forma consent form with their application packs, which you may want to use or adapt. Make sure you use the form specified by the ethics committee you are using. Don't forget that many forms may be designed for medical or experimental research, so you may need to amend them slightly if yours is a social science study.

In all research people have to volunteer to take part, no matter how they are recruited/selected. This means the researcher must ensure that participants completely understand their role in the research. Your

sectional variation of a measure applied to different subjects or groups at the same time. The explanations are therefore different. In the former case, special attention should be paid to the time difference in determining a causal mechanism. If an independent variable does not take effect immediately, various kinds of "lagging correlation" can be calculated. The type of causal effect can be determined by comparing serial correlation with various lagging correlations.

A time period can be regarded as a "case" or an "observation" in a longitudinal data matrix. It may involve many variables, which have values either as individual measures or group parameters (oftentimes percentages of group members) to represent different things that represent a social trend. If the number of independent variables is larger than one, then methods of multiple correlation and regression may be performed to analyze the relationships among different variables that represent different components of the social trend.

Longitudinal data analysis helps to clarify the secular trend of change, which is the first step toward a better understanding of the issue under study. This kind of trend study, nevertheless, may obscure the reality since it does not require study subjects to remain the same except for internal secular changes. The danger in the interpretation of the results, therefore, is to mistake the differences among various groups of subjects as part of the pure secular changes that the researcher is looking for. The panel design discussed in chapter eight aims to get rid of this danger by using the same group of subjects for the entire duration of a research project. Yet the strategy of aggregated trend analysis within the panel may still involve the risk of misinterpretation, if we draw a conclusion about individual subjects based on the trend of the whole group. This is somewhat like the "ecological fallacy" in dealing with the analytic units of a study as mentioned in chapter eight. To avoid this potential problem, a more detailed "turnover analysis" based on the change of the situation of individual subjects can be performed, which may reveal a deeper seated tendency different from what is shown by the trend analysis. Various methods of statistical control such as the use of subtables in elaboration may also be applied for the purpose of more accurate multivariate analysis. And this kind of analysis is supposedly to best satisfy the criteria for causality, that is, appropriate time order, correlation, and control for spurious associations.

Epistemological considerations

There are a number of ways that the researchers could get into trouble with the

forms need to be clear, easy to follow, and appropriate for your participants, and to reflect fully the purpose of the research. You do not want them to be ambiguous in any way, otherwise you can't be said to be collecting VIC. The researcher keeps the consent form, but it is helpful to give participants an information sheet (including researcher's name and contact details). Some researchers have relied on explaining the research fully to participants and then asking them to complete the study—assuming this will cover VIC. This exercise is imperative, but you should still collect a consent form. An example of a consent form is shown in Figure 5.2; Table 5.10 offers a guide to obtaining consent.

Figure 5.2 Example of consent form

YOUR ADDRESS GOES HERE
YOUR LOGO GOES HERE

CONSENT FORM

Title of Project:
Names of Researchers:

Please initial box

I have read and understood the information letter for participants and a researcher has explained the study to me. ☐

I have received enough information about what my role involves. ☐

I understand that my decision to consent is entirely voluntary and that I am free to withdraw from the study at any time without having to give a reason; and I know this will not affect me in the future. ☐

I consent to participate in the study on _____ ☐

Signed: . . . . Date: . . . .

PARTICIPANT'S NAME IN BLOCK
LETTERS: . . . .

Researcher's Signature: . . . .

TABLE 5.10

A stepwise guide to obtaining consent

(1) Explain to participants what the study involves, either verbally or using an information sheet (it may be worth using the latter method if your study involves participants reading questionnaires or a similar task, since those who struggle with reading an information sheet may not be suitable for your study overall).

(2) Let them know they can have time to think about participation (most ethics committees will ask about this, and often specify you need to give people a minimum of 24 hours to consider your research). Even if you are recruiting people where this 24-hour notice isn't possible (for example, customers in a pharmacy), you need to give them clear instructions and a some time to reflect on participation.

(3) Provide participants with a consent form (in one of the following formats: checklist, letter, cover sheet on a questionnaire, a page in an internet or computerised interview). You may want to include the contact details of an independent person the participant can call to discuss the research—for example in a hospital study the advocate could be a doctor who is not involved in the design or completion of the research.

(4) Check and double-check with participants that they fully understand the research, their role in the study, and any implications it has for them. Ask if they have any questions or concerns. (You will need to continue to check their well-being even after getting consent, during the study itself, and after the study has finished.)

Consider your participants and the circumstances under which you are obtaining VIC. Is there anything about them/the situation that might mean they feel pressured to consent (or not reveal that they don't understand something)? People may also consent because of peer pressure, fear of being left out of something they perceive to be important, fear of being the odd one out, or a concern about their status.

> We were completing an evaluation in an office. I noticed several of the people in the study consented but I didn't feel they really wanted to answer the research questions. I overheard one guy saying he didn't want to miss out, and I think he thought our work was more around evaluating staff than the organisation. He seemed to be under the impression that being in the study might help him get a promotion—which of course it wouldn't. (Raj, research manager)

It is important you make it clear to participants that being involved in your study won't affect their future care or status, while avoiding implying they'll get benefits from the work that can't be delivered.

Exercise: The confidentiality test

The aim of this exercise is to get people used to being aware of keeping confidences. Work in small groups. One person acts as an observer, and tells one other person a "secret" that they mustn't reveal. The "secret" shouldn't be too personal or likely to cause upset. It could be a made-up case, such as "Mr Smith is an awkward patient—he's got so bad his GP is considering having him removed from the practice register". The person who knows the secret is aware that others in the group know they have information. The task of the other group members is to find out what the secret is by using as many different strategies that they can think of to discover it (without upsetting the secret holder). The secret holder must find as many tactful ways as they can to hold onto their information— they can ask for time out when they need to. After the exercise the group shares with each other the strategies they used. If the secret holder accidentally gave their story away, that is fine. The aim is to show how people may give away information even though they are trying hard not to, and as a group to think of strategies to pre-empt this in future.

Giving consent

Some people require lots of information before consenting; others need time to think the study over—you may have to come back to them later. Still more may agree to your study without needing or appearing to want much information about it. As a researcher, you'll need to practise explaining research and getting consent without pressurising a person. You also need to become adept at negotiating what your research may mean to someone who may be anxious about it, or perhaps may not fully understand your purpose.

I had a colleague who was completing a study in a nursing home. Part of the study involved talking to residents about their care. She carefully explained who she was, what she was doing, what she'd be asking, and the role of the residents in the study. She then invited them to answer some questions about their experiences of care. Those who agreed completed a consent form, and were given an information sheet about the research that she also explained verbally and let them keep. She then asked them her questions, checking the whole time that they were okay. After she'd completed the questions with one resident, she thanked them, and as she was leaving she overheard the person chatting to a member of staff. The resident was saying how much they'd enjoyed talking to my colleague. "Why was the lady here?" she overheard the staff member say. "I have absolutely no idea," the resident replied. Sometimes even if you try hard to explain things, not every participant will understand. However, this should not prevent you from doing your utmost to explain your research. If in doubt, even if you feel under pressure to recruit participants to your study, it is better not to include someone who may not seem to understand your research than to go ahead and include them.

Those who can't consent

There are legal and ethical issues for those who are unable to consent (e.g. children, the elderly, those who are physically or psychologically ill). In such cases you need to consult with both your professional guidelines and ethics committee (British Psychological Society, 2000). For those aged under 16, permission can be given by the child and parent (parents or caregivers will need to be notified of any research). Those who have mental health problems or physical illnesses that mean they are too ill to participate in research or are unable to understand what's involved in the research (and give informed consent), should be excluded. Those who are in looked-after or prison settings may be included in research so long as they are not compromised or coerced into the research by virtue of their situation.

Those who don't/won't consent

In order for consent to be voluntary, people have the right to refuse to participate—and they can refuse to take part at any time. Many people will say "no" before knowing much about research, others may refuse while the study is being explained to them, and still others may withdraw during the study. It is useful to keep records of those who refuse or are unsuitable for your research—although you'll need to obtain ethical approval to collect such information (see Chapter 7 for more on collecting this sort of routine data).

What should a consent form include?

Many ethics committees or organisations have standard forms/sheets for obtaining consent and giving information about a study (see Howitt & Cramer, 2000, pp. 29–31; http://www.corec.org.uk). Remember the consent form is a written explanation of the study that a participant and researcher sign. The researcher keeps it. An information sheet explaining the research and giving contact numbers of the research team should also be given to the participant to keep. A checklist for consent forms is given in Table 5.11.

A consent form should be written in the first language spoken/read by the prospective participant (which may mean you need consent forms translated into different languages). It should be presented in lay terms—and this should be piloted to ensure participant understanding. If appropriate, illustrations may be used, for example for participants with language difficulties or learning disabilities. Accompanying illustrations should be informative, appropriate, and

TABLE 5.11

Checklist for consent forms

❏ The researcher(s)' names, position and affiliation (supervisors/project managers ought to be named on the form, as well as junior staff who may be collecting data).

❏ The sponsors of the research.

❏ That the participant is being involved in a research study.

❏ How and why the person has been chosen (at random, purposively sampled, etc.).

❏ The method to be used (interview, questionnaire, observation, procedure, drug trial, etc.).

❏ The aim/purpose of the study (explaining why the research is being done).

❏ What the research involves (what's going to happen to the participant, what they'll be required to do, whether they'll be randomised into any conditions).

❏ How long the study will take (this could range from a half-hour questionnaire to a number of visits over time).

❏ Any harms, adverse effects or likely inconveniences the study may cause (you should endeavour to keep these to a minimum).

❏ What benefits the study can offer the participant and/or others.

❏ The option to refuse to take part, and the participant's acknowledgement that they know what the study involves and are taking part anyway.

❏ What level of confidentiality and anonymity will be provided, and how it will be maintained (including telling participants who will have access to the data, how it will be stored, and whether participants will be identified when the research is written up).

❏ That the participant has the right to refuse at any time, without it compromising them in any way.

❏ Any details of remuneration.

❏ That any participation is voluntary.

not patronising. It's advisable to design and develop them with the support of consumer representatives.

Any terms that may be ambiguous should be explained (for a guide on good writing practice see Paasche-Orlow, Taylor, & Brancati, 2003, p. 723). You should **never** include statements that release the researcher, their sponsor or organisation from liability of negligence, and, as mentioned above, you are required to include a copy of your consent form when applying for ethical approval.

By using a consent form, along with verbally explaining your study, you are checking that participants understand your study, what their role in it is, and what the study will be used for. They should be aware of any negative aspects (questions that may be upsetting, or drugs that may have adverse effects, for example). You should also feel confident that your participants understand they have the right to withdraw from the research at any time, without having to give you a reason, and without being pressured or compromised.

Exercise: Getting someone to say "yes"

Working in groups of three, decide together on a study idea, how it'll be completed, and who potential participants might be. Think about any ethical issues the study presents, and consider how voluntary informed consent will be collected. Draft a consent form. Elect one person from the group to be the researcher and another as the participant; the third member and participant decide (out of earshot of the researcher) on how the participant will behave— overly agreeable, sceptical, afraid or nervous, etc. The researcher then discusses the study and attempts to consent the participant, while the third member of the group observes and makes notes. Following this all three discuss the experience (you can swap over roles as many times as you like). The aim of the exercise is to experience both obtaining consent from participants and what it feels like to be introduced to a study.

Researcher concerns

When I was completing my PhD I had many concerns about the issue of ethics and consent, but relatively few problems getting people to participate, since most were students I was teaching. In other projects I've worked on (which didn't involve undergraduate participants), I discovered that getting people to participate in research is a lengthy and laborious part of any study, regardless of its size. Researchers know that they should get consent, but they also have the (often conflicting) demand to get the maximum possible numbers of partici-pants recruited into their study. There is a temptation to gloss over the consent process, to hurry it up, or to pressure participants to take part (for example, by promising something you can't deliver). While this can increase your numbers, the downside is you may not be getting a representative group of participants, and you are breaching ethical guidelines. Most journals now require information on VIC, so this aspect of your work should be transparent and honest.

Some researchers worry that explaining research in great detail will dissuade participants or skew results. While some people may be put off, it is sometimes the case that people who refuse do so before you even get round to talking about consent. Whether participants are approached by letter/telephone/or face to face, the study has to be outlined to them first, and it is at this stage that most people will refuse. But don't worry, explaining research and discussing the study can often make participants feel more involved (and therefore more likely to consent).

Implications for participation

In order to get participants to consent, it is customary for the researcher to outline the benefits of doing the research. This could be a direct benefit (payment, a gift or other "reward", course credits) or an indirect benefit (better local services, improved facilities at work or in the community, helping others). It is up to the researcher to be clear about potential benefits, and to avoid exaggerating them, or offering rewards that cannot be delivered. Don't forget, if you are giving a financial reward, many participants receiving state benefits may have to declare cash received—you may instead give vouchers for use in a store to the same value, which can count as a "gift" rather than "pay-ment". Any direct rewards should not be introduced at the start of the consent process, otherwise people may join for the reward, not for the study. On one of my projects I carefully avoided mentioning that we were giving participants shopping vouchers as a "thank you" for completing the study. However, my efforts were undone by a woman shouting "There's a lady in there giving out fivers!" to everyone in the waiting room at the surgery where we were completing the study.

Negative aspects may not be confined to the study itself. If a nega-tive impact may occur after a study (for example, when the work is published), you need to broach this with participants. This is particu-larly true of marginalised groups, or participants who occupy a minority position that makes them easily identifiable. If results may not reflect well on a participant or their community/organisation, consider what that may mean to participants, whether they'll suffer any negative repercussions, and what needs mentioning in your consent form/information sheet (see Chapter 8 for more information).

Exercise: What effects could participation have?

Write your study aim and design at the top of a blank sheet of paper. Along the top, draw three columns and label them before, during and after research. Down the side create three rows entitled participants, researcher and others. Consider for each category what the implications for the people completing the research will be.

On bigger studies, you may wish to seek ethical approval to contact a selection of volunteer participants at random after they've completed their part of the research. In such cases, participants need to be informed of this, and to be told who will be contacting them and why. This is to ensure that the participants were real people, not cases fabricated by a fraudulent researcher and that the experience of completing the research was acceptable to the participant. Researchers also need to be aware that this is part of maintaining good practice in studies, so they don't feel they're being picked on. Used appropriately, this method can ensure good-quality research, and can aid the management of researchers (see Chapter 6).

Debriefing

Once a study has finished, it is the role of the researcher to go over the study, thank participants and check they are happy with (and understand) the research they've just completed (Snowdon, Garcia, & Elbourne, 1998). Debriefing should not be used in place of introducing the research to participants: it is a means of double-checking that people understood the study. This may include (Howitt & Cramer, 2000, p. 25):

- The impressions that the participant had about the study or experiment—what they thought the study was about
- Whether they had any problems in understanding the procedures and questionnaires
- What they saw as affecting their behaviours and answers in the study
- Any specific areas of concern that the researcher has with the study
- A general exchange of information between the researcher and participant.

You may use these pointers in piloting as well as in debriefing (see Chapter 4).

How are participants presented in your work?

Research has traditionally presented the participant's role as ending once they finish whatever task you've set them (completing a questionnaire, participating in a trial, giving an interview and reading through the transcript, etc.). Some participants want no more involvement than this, but many have needs and views that don't fit the traditional format of research. For example, they may call the researcher for help and advice once the study is completed, or want to hear about the study results (possibly even seeing any reports created). Some researchers may also want to keep in contact with participants, particularly if they have become close during the research process (Boynton, 2002).

Whatever the level of participant involvement, when you write your findings you need to consider three issues:

1. That participants are reflected fairly, but accurately
2. That participants' confidentiality/anonymity is maintained
3. That participants are not mocked, endangered, or likely to be harmed by what you say.

When I completed a study on women involved in street prostitution, one working woman we interviewed told us that she'd talked to a journalist at the local paper about being a prostitute. She'd worked on the same patch for two years, without being noticed. The journalist promised to keep her identity secret, but when the story broke the working woman had been described by the distinctive way she did her make-up. Following this she was spat at in the street, physically assaulted, and her local store refused to serve her. Although this is not an example of research, it's clear that participants can be identified and this can have seriously negative repercussions.

While the above three pointers may seem obvious and reasonable, on certain studies they may not be so straightforward. For example, you may try and reflect participants fairly and accurately, but an accurate description may upset or offend some participants. Again, in our research on street prostitution we found that many girls had boyfriends, who we knew were their pimps. We had to be careful to explain this difference without undermining, patronising, or offending participants.

In some cases, protecting participants can be difficult—for

example, in community or case studies people can be locally identified. You also need to consider who you are reporting, what your study is, and who your eventual audience might be. Findings need to be presented clearly and with substantiation, in order to avoid any confusion or misinterpretation. Participants' use of humour or making controversial statements could be ambiguous or problematic, as participants' confidentiality/anonymity could be breached, and people may misunderstand them.

> *I once interviewed a police officer. He gave me some excellent information, but was very sarcastic in his humour. The problem was, I wanted to use some of these quotes but I couldn't since those reading the final report may not have understood he was being ironic, which could have got him into trouble as it wouldn't take much to work out who he was.* (Gus, postgraduate)

Most studies are written up as short reports, projects, theses or conference/peer reviewed papers (see Chapter 8). It may be worth considering additional issues such as how you'll report your findings, who will see the work, where it will appear, and so on. It is worth thinking about what else may happen when your work is made public, and whether this has any bearing on what you produce. While you should not distort your findings, it may be that issues/data/quotes can be edited or removed if they could be detrimental to participants. However, this shouldn't mean that any work can be cut to suit. If work is likely to be controversial then the researcher needs to prepare participants, steering group, community, or organisation—whoever may be affected by the study—for any adverse findings.

Confidentiality and anonymity

In research participants need to be reassured that what they reveal will be treated as "private" (confidentiality) and that they won't be identified through the research (anonymity) (see also NHS Information Authority Privacy Statement, 2002—http://www.nhsia.nhs.uk/def/pages/privacy/asp). This may mean changing people's names in qualitative research, using identification numbers in quantitative studies, or finding other ways of keeping participants' details private. If this is not possible, then participants (and ethics committees) need to be warned before the study progresses. It is important to explain clearly what these two terms mean, since many researchers/practitioners do not have the same understanding of them as participants/patients. If in doubt, ask participants what

interpretation and communication of their research results. Technically, potential mistakes could result from hasty conclusion, overgeneralization, and provincialism (Kahane, 1992). Epistemologically, there are different and even conflicting approaches to research, with no one being considered perfect. As a matter of fact, there have been heated debates about what science is. It is hard to imagine that a researcher would provide a masterful understanding of the research results without an awareness of its epistemological implications.

Epistemology is the knowledge of knowing, or study of studying. Methodology is considered a subfield of epistemology, which is addressed to the logic of research and therefore to the process of theory construction (Lin, 1976). In such a sense, methodology is different from specific research methods, or procedures of "how to" carry out certain research activities. Behavioral and social science researchers are generally required to have an empirical rather than philosophical orientation. In methodological reflections, they are supposed to follow such scientific principles as skepticism, empiricism, logical reasoning, systematic classification, and genuine relation. The understanding of the kind of epistemological issues ranging from objectivity or intersubjectivity to hypotheses testing, however, has much to do with philosophical thinking. Specific research techniques are based on certain general epistemological approaches, and an awareness of the difference will enable us to make full sense of our research findings.

Neuman (1997) summaries the many arguments stemming from a major reevaluation of social science that began in the 1960s in terms of three idealized models as alternatives to social science. The three approaches or paradigms are positivist social science, interpretive social science, and critical social science. Each is associated with different traditions in social theory and diverse research techniques, though most ongoing social science research is based on the first two (ibid.).

The foundation of positivist social science was first laid by the father of sociology, Auguste Comte (1798-1857). This tradition is generally termed logical positivism or empiricism, though varieties have emerged as it has undergone more than a century of evolution. Postpositivism and behaviorism are two of such variants. According to Neuman (1997), positivism sees social science as an "organized method for combining deductive logic with precise empirical observations of individual behavior in order to discover and confirm a set of probabilistic causal laws that can be used to predict general patterns of human activity" (p.63, in italics). Social science has been dominated by the

they think the terms mean and outline how their explanation fits into your study.

> I often remind researchers that in qualitative research it's not exactly accurate to reassure people "nobody will see what you say" when introducing the research and discussing confidentiality. Those involved with transcribing, analysing and coding transcripts will all see what the participant says. It's better to tell them something like "only the research team will see what you say". But check this is okay when you get ethics approval. (Avril, senior lecturer)

Often researchers promise to protect confidentiality and anonymity. A clearer explanation for participants might be: "What you tell us will remain confidential, and we will anonymise whatever you say."

To cut or not to cut?

Again, during the prostitution study someone on the steering group wanted to know whom a particular respondent was, as they didn't agree with what they'd said, and wanted to "discuss" it with them. We cut the particular quote that attracted attention and refused to give more details about the respondent. On the same study we didn't find high use of drugs in working women (contrary to findings in other research). It wasn't that our data was inaccurate or particularly groundbreaking—more that our participants were not necessarily representative of all prostitutes (they were older, had kids to support, and were sober enough to concentrate on in-depth interviews) (Boynton, Bucknor, & Morton, 1998). We emphasised this in the report but we didn't alter the findings—although there was disappointment from some of the steering group members that we didn't link prostitution and drugs more explicitly (Boynton, 2002). The politics of research may mean that certain issues or topics are either missed out, or given greater attention than previously anticipated (see Chapter 3). In such cases priority should be given to the protection and well-being of participants and those related to the study who are likely to suffer any negative repercussions from either cutting or including information in a research report. Edits and alterations are for protecting participants, but throughout research you need to think about balancing this with producing high-quality, accurate findings.

How work is used

In research we produce work that may then be quoted, critiqued or re-evaluated by others. Or we may create work that may have a direct impact on people's lives, without receiving much academic interest. When work becomes "public", there is a chance it may receive interest from the media—or other researchers. Whoever you are talking about your research with, remember that anyone who is not a researcher directly involved in your work should not be told anything that could harm or identify participants. Avoid making the mistakes that some researchers have: that their report or paper protects and reflects participants fairly, only to have it let down by the researcher making comments that are detrimental about the study or the participants (see Ubel, Zell, Miller, Fischer, Peters-Stefani, & Arnold, 1995).

It is important for researchers to consider how participants are treated in research and subsequently reported, because:

- It complies with ethical regulations
- It may encourage the participant or those who know them to assist in future research
- If a researcher upsets participants/groups/individuals it may affect their future career, and also may jeopardise the success of other researchers working in the area in the future.

Anticipating negative events

Depending on the subject of your study, people may become distressed or annoyed by the research, or overly enthusiastic, or not involved enough. In the planning stages of a study, researchers can become aware of potential design problems, areas that may be controversial or awkward, or issues that might cause upset or distress. Many issues can be limited via the research process (see Table 5.12).

In research there will be issues that you'll be aware of from the start, some that emerge during the study, and some unexpected ones you may not have much control over. Your aim is to deal with the first two of these, and limit the third wherever possible. For emerging problems, again, don't keep them to yourself. Tell someone involved with your research, discuss any problems and try and find a solution together—and again, document everything.

TABLE 5.12

Ways to avoid potential problems

❏ During the literature review and study design period, note potential problem areas and discuss them (and how to overcome them) with your colleagues.

❏ Put your study through an ethics committee.

❏ Note, discuss, and overcome problems that emerge during piloting.

❏ Take advice from appropriate outside agencies.

❏ Consider the implications of all parts of the study (from selection and recruitment through to the study itself and beyond).

❏ Be honest. In studies that are controversial, don't skirt the issue, be open, and talk it over with your research team (document these discussions).

Strategies for dealing with problems or complaints

Suppose you've done all your background work, considered all the issues suggested in this chapter, and have talked your research plan through with your colleagues to create a "perfect study". What happens if there are still problems?

Firstly, keep calm. As social and health research involves dealing with people, and people are always unpredictable, it's inevitable that there may be some difficulties. In fact, this doesn't have to be negative. If you have planned for problems, then although it can be distressing if any emerge, you at least have a strategy to deal with them. If you think about your study timescales (see Chapter 3), it's possible to predict key times where problems are most likely to arise and to have a strategy for dealing with them (Table 5.13).

If a participant does complain, firstly find out what the problem is. It may be they are angry with issues related to the research, rather than the research itself.

> *I had a woman complaining, really distressed. But it wasn't about the research—even though it seemed that way. She was in a study on school bullying but she was upset over her son's exclusion. (Barbara, researcher)*

If it's related to another issue, refer to your list of support networks. If it is related to your research, find out exactly what the problem was (for example, the consent process, the research itself, or the

TABLE 5.13

Critical stages in research

Critical stage	Coping strategy
Being approached	Even if you've made it clear, participants will probably want to know why they've been selected and what the work is for. Be ready to explain in detail (see previous sections), and thank people for their time, even if they do not want to take part.
The study topic	Once a person's agreed to participate, you may find that they don't much like what the study involves, or what you're asking them to do. You can reduce the likelihood of this causing distress by explaining the study in great detail, obtaining VIC correctly, and emphasising that participants are free to withdraw at any time, and without it compromising them. If a study is on a sensitive topic, introduce this in a sympathetic yet straightforward way. Don't mislead people in the hope they won't notice that your research is on something more sensitive than you first presented. Actions like this are far more likely to cause upset than being honest from the start.
After taking part	Sometimes people complete a study, only to think about it later and then have concerns or worries (such as what will happen with their answers, or will anybody find out about their participation?). These worries should be addressed when the study is introduced, but you should also ensure that participants take an information sheet about the research to refer to later (which includes a contact number for the lead researcher). You should also provide participants with a list of sources they could go to for help if necessary. If your research is liable to cause distress, a form of support (e.g. counsellors) should be built into the research design/budget.
Hearing about research when it's published	If participants are likely to be distressed by the research results or report, it is important to tackle these worries and concerns prior to publication. If participants are likely to be identified, you should take every possible step to prevent this happening, and talk over with them any worries they might have about any publicity generated by your study. Again, seek support from outside agencies to help participants if you feel it is necessary.

FIGURE 5.3a Example of patient help sheet

INFORMATION LEAFLET

Sometimes completing research raises questions or issues for people. For advice about your health you can speak to your doctor—you may also find information about local health/advice groups displayed at your doctor's surgery. You could also try your local Citizens Advice Bureau, library, or community centre. The telephone directory contains information about advice lines, and details of local advice services, council information, and community and social services. If you have access to the internet, you can get links to advice pages at http://www.helplines.org.uk.

This leaflet contains some telephone numbers for helplines and organisations, which may be useful. If you require additional information about the numbers given in this leaflet, or wish to discuss any issues raised in this research, please contact the research team on 0171 8302374.

These numbers are correct at time of going to press. The advice expressed by the organisations in this leaflet may not reflect the views of the project staff.

- Gay and Lesbian Legal Advice (GLAD) — 0171 8375212
- London Bisexual Helpline — 0181 5697500

MEN (the first two advice lines in this list are for men at risk from, or who have problems with, violence)

- Everyman Project — 0171 7376747
- Men's Advice Line and Enquiries (MALE) — 0181 6449914
- Men's Health Line — 0181 9954448

MENTAL HEALTH
- Careline — 0181 5141177
- Mindinfo Line — 0345 660163
- SANELINE — 0345 678000

OLDER PEOPLE
- Age Concern UK — 0800 009966
- Help the Aged — 0808 8006565
- Counsel and Care Advice for Older People — 0171 4851566

RAPE/SEXUAL ABUSE
- London Rape Crisis Centre — 0171 8371600
- Women's Aid National Helpline — 0345 023468
- Kiran—Asian Women's Aid — 0181 5581986

RELATIONSHIPS
- Relate — 01788 573241
- Marriage Care Helpline (also for those in long-term relationships) — 0345 573921
- Dignity (advice and support on adultery) — 01773 850200

SEXUAL HEALTH/ADVICE
- Institute of Psychosexual Medicine (list of private/NHS doctors) — 0171 151800631
- Sexwise — 0800 282930
- Young people's sexual health helpline — 01438 353434
- Resolve (vaginismus support group—fax) — 0181 8836571
- Endometriosis Helpline — 0171 2222776
- The Sexual Dysfunction Association (advice for men and women) — 0870 7743571

WOMEN
- Women's Health — 0171 2516580
- Women and Girls' Network — 0171 6104345

Figure 5.56 Example of patient help sheet

How to use this information leaflet

This leaflet presents advice sources in alphabetical order. Telephone numbers that start with 0800 are free to call. Those that start 0345 are charged at the local rate. The majority of other numbers in this leaflet are local (London) numbers. Some of these helplines are available 24 hours; others may have special hours of service, so you may need a pen and paper ready when you call the numbers in case you need to take further details.

How to make your call

You do not have to give your name, address or telephone number to the organisation you are calling (unless you want to). If you do not want to be identified you can dial 141 before dialling the main number. 0800 numbers will not show on your telephone bill.

Don't have a telephone?

If you do not have access to a telephone, or find it difficult to use the telephone you can write to most of the organisations listed in this leaflet. The researcher can give you details of contact addresses.

Not enough advice?

If you feel you need a more specialised helpline you could try a group that most closely matches your question and ask if they have an alternative service to suit your needs. The researchers also have additional information on other advicelines.

Can you help?

You may know of an organisation we have not included. If so, please pass this information on to the researcher so we can help others.

ALCOHOL
- Alcohol Advisory Service — 0171 5305900
- Drinkline — 0800 9178282

BEREAVEMENT
- CRUSE Bereavement Line — 0345 585565
- National Association of Bereavement Services — 0171 2471080
- Lesbian and Gay Bereavement Helpline — 0181 4558894
- Cot Death Helpline — 0171 2351721
- Stillbirth & NeoNatal Death Society (SANDS) — 0171 4365881
- Jewish Bereavement Counselling Service — 0181 3490839

CARERS
- Carers National Association (CarersLine) — 0345 5733369

CONTRACEPTION
- Brook Advisory Centres (under 25s only) — 0800 0185023
- Family Planning Association — 0171 8374044
- Pregnancy Advisory Service — 0171 6378962

CRIME
- Crimestoppers — 0800 555111
- Victim Support — 0845 3030900

DEPRESSION
- Samaritans — 0345 909090

DISABILITY
- Association to aid the sexual and personal relationships of people with a disability — 0171 6078851

DRUGS
- Mainliners — 0207 5825226
- SMART project — 0208 6779541

HEALTH
- NHS Healthline — 0800 665544
- Patients Association Helpline — 0181 4238999
- National Waiting List Helpline — 0181 9831133
- Medical Advisory Service General Medical Helpline — 0181 9949874

HEALTH
- Medical Advisory Service General Medical Helpline — 0181 9949874

HIV/AIDS
- Blackliners — 0171 7385274
- National AIDS Helpline — 0800 567123
- Positiveline — 0800 616212
- Positively Women — 0171 7130222
- Terrence Higgins Trust Helpline — 0171 2421010

LESBIAN, GAY & BISEXUAL
- London Lesbian and Gay Switchboard — 0171 8377324
- London Lesbian Line — 0171 2516911
- London Friend (Lesbian & Gay Helpline) — 0171 8373337
- Irish Gay Helpline — 0181 2082855
- Jewish Lesbian and Gay Helpline — 0171 7063123

researcher). Apologise straight away and tell the person what you will do to fix the issue (e.g. withdraw them from the research, talk to the researcher in question). If necessary take the person's details and get back to them later detailing how their complaint has been dealt with. An example of a patient help sheet is shown in Figure 5.3, based on one I used in a past project. The sheet was designed to be printed on both sides and folded in three—obviously the advice sources would need to be tailored to your particular project, as well as being checked and updated. A "quick guide to dealing with complaints" is given in Table 5.14.

TABLE 5.14

Quick guide to dealing with complaints

❑ Never keep complaints to yourself; let others in your team/department know.

❑ Keep records of complaints made and how they were dealt with.

❑ Be aware of your complaints procedure, and plan strategies on how to deal with them before they arise.

❑ Accept responsibility if you are at fault.

❑ State to the complainant that you recognise the problem, that you are sorry for their distress, and tell them what you are going to do next to put the problem right.

❑ Find out exactly what the problem is and what the participant wants done about it.

❑ Remember you can only act on participant complaints—if their friends/relatives don't like them being in your research they need to deal with the participant, not you.

The participant who won't accept it's over

So far this research has outlined how to approach people about your study, consent them into research, and deal with any problems or complaints people might have. However, some problems can emerge because participants enjoy being in your research. A few years ago I worked on a study where I had to interview older people, many of whom were housebound. Some of these patients received few visitors and had no friends or family to support them. My research visit became a highlight for them (which meant lots of tea and cake for me, but left me feeling sad I couldn't do anything to end their loneliness and isolation). One gentleman was a retired army captain who was utterly charming, and completely isolated. He didn't understand that my role as researcher gave rise to my three visits to him to find out about his care. He thought I had become his advocate, and put my name down as his next of kin on several forms. The result was that each time he had a fall or other health problem, social services would call me. He also would phone me regularly begging for a visit as he was alone. I felt dreadful, and didn't know what to do. My "objective researcher head" told me I should ignore his calls, but my heart went out to a lovely man who had a whole life story to tell, but nobody in his life to share it with.

Exercise: Talking about research

This task helps explore how you deal with questions about your research. Work in pairs on the following three scenarios. Discuss each case before moving on to the next. Make notes on how you feel, what you did and what you said. You may also like to create other scenarios on research situations you've encountered. Remember to discuss the scenarios together before you play them out, and stop if either of you finds it uncomfortable.

Case 1: You've approached an elderly patient in a study and asked them to participate. They refused. Later you are confronted by their son/daughter asking about putting their relative in your study as they think it may help. (Here one of you plays the researcher; the other is the son/daughter.)

Case 2: A participant you have interviewed in a study on teenagers' attitudes to exams keeps calling you and asking you for careers advice and help with their homework. They have been calling evenings and weekends, and you are now getting at least three calls per week from them. (Here one of you plays the researcher; the other is the persistent teenager.)

Case 3: You are doing an interview with a participant; halfway through they become angry and aggressive about the questions you are asking. You believe you warned them at the start that some questions were sensitive, and they had consented with this knowledge. You also told them they could leave at any time. You remind the participant about this but they become angry and abusive, and won't leave! You begin to feel irritated and uncomfortable. (Here one of you plays the irate participant; the other is the researcher.)

Within your research, consider who your participants are: some may not understand or accept when research is "over" (Lipson, Stern, May, Morse, & Thorne, 1997, p. 8) particularly when they've been involved in a study over time. You need to train yourself (and your research team) to cope with this and make endings as clear and pain-free as possible. You may also want to consider the way researchers feel in these situations, since often they may become attached to participants and find it hard to say "goodbye" at the end of a project (Boynton, 2002).

Modern manners

When you are completing research, the role and well-being of the participant is not constrained to the moments when they are involved in the study. You need to think about how you represent yourself, your research, and your participants at all times. A researcher follow-ing ethical procedures in a study, and then making fun of participants after they have left, or making damaging remarks about them after a study is published, can undo a good project. People are giving up their time to participate in your research, and that (along with what-ever information they share with you) ought to be repaid with respect. Remember the famous slogan from the Second World War, "Careless talk costs lives"? You can apply that to the research process. It's unlikely your conversations about research would cost someone their life, but a tactless word in the wrong place could certainly com-promise someone's dignity, their right to confidentiality, and your reputation as a researcher. This means it's better to keep work-related discussions within the workplace.

> *My friend and I are both researchers, and we were at a party recently when I heard her telling some guests about a person she interviewed. The participant had had a stroke and kept swearing and using the wrong words in the interview. I guess it made for quite a funny story, but I couldn't help feeling uncomfortable that this was somebody being made fun of, and having their confidence broken.* (Rochelle, postgraduate researcher)

In the past, research was set up with a clear hierarchy (Danziger, 1990). The researchers (or scientists) were at the top of the tree, setting the agendas and delivering results or diagnoses (Rosaldo, 1989). Many of these behaviours advanced the careers of the scientists, but did little to help their participants (Lewontin, 1993; Cherry, 1995a); in some cases their actions damaged people's physical or psychological well-being (Howitt & Owusu-Bempah, 1994). Such authoritarian approaches are now frowned upon, but that's not to say that researchers can't act inappropriately. The fact that you are running a study that interests you (or at least pays your bills) doesn't mean you have the right to force people to be in your research or treat them like commodities. There are a few simple checks you can make on your approaches to participants (and those around them—friends, family, co-workers, etc.) to ensure you do not cause distress (Table 5.15).

Think about who your participants are: Not just in terms of whether they fit your research design, but what their lives are like, what they do in their spare time, and what they might think about you and your research. Considering people as individuals with their own lives, not as your participants, may enable you to treat people respectfully.

Exercise: Walking in someone else's shoes

In a group of four, think of an issue that's not particularly emotive, but is interesting, and devise a list of five open-ended questions about that topic. Split into pairs and interview each other, audiotape the interviews with each person asking the other the same set of questions (you can take it in turns—one person is interviewer and one runs through all the questions before swapping). Transcribe each of the interviews (each person transcribes the interview where they were the interviewer). Following this, each person works through the interview they've transcribed, looking for themes and ideas. Discuss the four interviews in the original group. Review the transcripts and see how closely they match the interview experience of both the interviewer and the interviewee. Talk about the themes you picked up on and what quotes drew your attention. Did the group members select similar or different themes—and where was there agreement? How did the interviewees feel about the way they were represented, and how their words were fitted into different themes? Did they agree or not? Extensions on this exercise include writing a short piece about the outcomes, themes, etc.—either using one transcript or drawing on all four. The purpose of this exercise is to look at the variety of themes that may emerge in an interview, and how people interpret interviews in different ways. More import-antly, you want to explore from the perspective of the interviewees what it felt like to be interviewed—and how participants might feel seeing their words as a script, and seeing that script manipulated and cut for the purpose of research.

two comprehensive papers that you will have to write: The theory paper and the research paper. For the master's and undergraduate students, there is usually no such requirement. But the various forms of term papers (also commonly called research papers) they write, including any kind of research report, provide similar opportunities for the honors and master's students to lay the groundwork for their thesis project.

If some of the papers, especially the comprehensive papers and the reports of projects for the research courses, are carefully planned and well written, they may serve as an advanced basis for your thesis or dissertation. The theory paper and the like usually deal with literature review and theoretical framing, which could possibly be revised, updated and used in the thesis/dissertation for your hypotheses formulation. The research paper and other research reports could serve as some pilot project(s) to your thesis/dissertation research, with the methods being tested and preliminary results obtained. Once you have proved yourself on the right track of inquiry, the ideas and contents of such papers could be directly incorporated into various parts of your thesis or dissertation. Even if you found that the topic for your paper(s) turned out not to be the right one for your thesis or dissertation, you could avoid further delay by rethinking your subject. In any case, a planned, systematic attempt is desired, and pursuing your study in that organized manner would save you a considerable amount of time.

The proposal

The proposal for your thesis/dissertation research is sometimes also called your study plan. But here we distinguish between the two, with the study plan focusing on pre-thesis/dissertation studies, which have been discussed above. The proposal is specifically concerned with your thesis or dissertation. When you get to the proposal stage, you probably have completed most or all of your coursework. If you have never thought about your thesis/dissertation until you enter this stage, it would be too late for you to get a quick start on your research project. Since the thesis or dissertation is a culminating and synthesizing activity based on your prior study, it is to your advantage to plan your study as a whole from a very early stage.

Formally engaging in the preparation of your thesis/dissertation proposal, however, marks a new start in your student career. Now you have a chance to put together all your ideas that you think are important and relevant to your current

empiricist/positivist tradition, which has been defined by the validation or falsification of operationalized research hypotheses by quantitative methods, especially those with sampling and statistical procedures. For decades, this paradigm is deemed *the* scientific approach with all the optimism of logical positivism. Yet recently positivism has been criticized, for reasons such as reducing people to numbers. In the field of social work, for example, the profession is said to have been lured away from its own foundation of practice wisdom, and therefore has not entirely succeeded in developing its own value base, theories and methods. Emphasizing the rigor of detached objectivity, positivism held little regard for subjective constructs such as morality, spirituality, and cultural or personal belief systems (Goldstein, 1990). The profession's original mission of serving humanity was split with method, and intuition and common-sense ways of understanding were discredited (ibid.).

As positivism gradually becomes a pejorative label, the value of several other research paradigms are recognized, ranging from hermeneutics, phenomenology, constructionism, to ethnomethodology. These methods, along with cognitive, idealist, and subjectivist approaches, are given the general name "interpretive social science," or "qualitative research" (Neuman, 1997). According to Neuman, the interpretive approach is "the systematic analysis of socially meaningful action through the direct detailed observation of people in natural settings in order to arrive at understandings and interpretations of how people create and maintain their social worlds" (ibid., p.68, in italics). The interpretive approach is associated with symbolic interactionism, which can be traced to the work of sociologist Max Weber (1864-1920). Its orientation, unlike the positivist approach, is practical rather than instrumental. It emphasizes the meaning of social action, not just the external or observable behavior of people (Neuman, 1997). This has become an alternative approach to positivism.

Critical social science is related to conflict theory in sociology, which can be traced to the work of Karl Marx (1818-1883). The variants of this approach includes dialectical materialism, class analysis, feminist perspective, radicalism, and critical theory. As Neuman (1997) narrates, the critical approach defines social science as a "critical process of inquiry that goes beyond surface illusions to uncover the real structures in the material world in order to help people change conditions and build a better world for themselves" (p.74, in italics). This approach is being widely used by feminists and other scholars in such fields as social work. It should not be simply equated with any kind of critical view held by or against anybody.

TABLE 5.15

Six sure-fire ways to annoy participants

Getting names or titles wrong	If you are unsure on how to address a participant, ask what they would like to be called and if unsure on pronunciation, get them to repeat their name to you.
	The researcher called me Daisy from the word go. It would have been polite to call me Mrs Collins, but she never asked. I didn't like being called by my first name by someone younger than my granddaughter. (Participant in trial on Parkinson's disease—name has been changed)
	The researcher got my name wrong every time he called. He must've pronounced it so many different ways. I kept telling him how to say it, but he just replied "Oh your names are all so funny I never know how to say them." (Comfort, participant in study on exercise for African women)
	Last time she came, she called us "you kids" and then "children". We didn't talk to her after that. (Darren, participant in after-school study)
Acting like you own the place	When you visit a participant, either in their home or in a place that is not your office, ensure you are polite and ask permission for things like where you can sit, using their bathroom, etc. Complimenting someone on their home is fine, but make sure you don't seem like you're being nosy (see Gillespie and King, 1998, pp. 49–50).
	He walked in and straightaway acted like he owned the place, he threw his coat over my chair and plonked his computer down on my table. I didn't want him to put it there, but before I could say he'd already done it. (Joe, participant in care at home study)
	After my Caesarean the researcher came over and sat on my bed. She didn't ask if she could, and she bumped down so hard it really hurt me. (Michelle, participant in a birthing experience project)
Forgetting your introductions, or giving the wrong impression	Remember that as well as introducing the research, you need to explain who you are, and why you are doing the research (your qualifications may be mentioned here). Don't forget to say who you are, and don't mislead participants in the research.
	He came and interviewed me at work and asked me about workload. I said I was exhausted and wanted to know what I could do about it. He said "I can't help you, I'm not a doctor" but it said he was on his name badge and on his letter. I didn't know what to believe after that. My boss said he was a PhD, but I don't know why that meant he couldn't answer my question. (Jenny, participant in workplace stress evaluation)

Not making people feel valued	People are giving up their time for your study, often voluntarily. You should do your utmost to make them feel appreciated.
	I did the questionnaire, and she took it back. She didn't even say thank you. She collected them in and said to us "You can go now." (Alex, participant in another student's project)
Having unclear roles and boundaries	Make it clear to participants what you can and can't do. Explain your role and what it qualifies you for. Don't make promises you cannot deliver.
	Last week a researcher came and she promised she'd help me fill in my benefit forms. This week she calls and says she's not allowed to. By who? It's only a silly form. I'd do it myself but it's hard to follow and she said she'd do it for me. I'm missing out on money while I wait for her. (Michael, participant in a back-to-work evaluation)
Being very busy	If participants have given time to you, then you need to give time back to them. This means having time built into your research to allow for this, and having referral services if participants will require more support. It also means clarifying your roles and boundaries (see above).
	I enjoyed doing the research and I wanted to know more about being a psychologist, but the lady who I did the questions with said "I haven't time for that now." I'd spent a whole hour telling her things she wanted to know and she couldn't spare me five minutes. I think she just thought I was too thick to understand. (Ginny, participant in survey of gym activity)

Celebrating difference

A few years ago I was working in a department where a large-scale project was underway about staff at a nearby factory. Many of the workers didn't speak English as a first language, and it had been suggested that interpreters or peer researchers be used to identify the views of people in this group. One of the researchers on the study said *"That's all I need. We're over budget and overworked and now I've got to get translators in. It's just too much trouble: it isn't going to happen."* And it didn't. Which meant a group of staff at the factory were not interviewed, and the research findings weren't representative of all staff.

Research has moved from the researcher defining who or what was worthy of study and how participants would be described or categorised (which was often patronising at best, prejudicial at worst) to embracing "similarity" (people are the same and share identical rights and needs). We are now beginning to acknowledge "difference", recognising that people aren't the same, nor should they be treated as such (Wilkinson & Kitzinger, 1996). However, not everyone follows this, or knows how to, particularly since dealing with difference can feel embarrassing, awkward, or challenging.

Social and health research is built around people, and people are all built differently. In order to work effectively with participants you need an awareness and understanding of their differences (Howitt & Owusu-Bempah, 1994; Wilkinson & Kitzinger, 1996). Much of the medical and social sciences has been underpinned by theories that are racist, sexist, or homophobic (Burman, 2000), which may mean that you are unaware of how to work with or approach people who are "different" from you. For example:

- Researcher is HIV negative and female; participants are positive and male
- Researcher is disabled; participants are able-bodied
- Participants are white; researcher is Chinese
- Researcher is in her twenties; participants are all aged over 75
- Participants are Muslim; researcher is Jewish
- Researcher is a lesbian; the majority of her participants are straight.

I don't think it's fair to blame researchers when they just start out. A lot of people I meet are young, they've often been to university and they've often not mixed with people all that different from themselves. Meeting those who seem "different" can feel very scary. I think we need to allow people to learn about others and realise this is an essential part of research training—it ought to be central to all health and social science courses too, and part of people's continuing professional development. Where I lose patience is when researchers hang on to prejudices when they should know better, or when they use their ideas and beliefs about their superiority to put down others, or disrespect them in research. (Josh, senior researcher)

In order to complete studies that are both participant- and researcher-friendly, you need to consider difference very carefully. Rather than being a barrier to research, differences should be considered as a natural extension of working with the public. However, differences should be thought about carefully since you don't want to upset either participants or researchers, nor assume everyone is the same (see Equal Opportunities Commission (http://www.eoc.org.uk) and Commission for Racial Equality (http://www.cre.gov.uk) for additional guidance; Table 5.16 gives a checklist for inclusivity in research).

TABLE 5.16

Checklist for inclusivity in research

❏ Use translation services (it is preferable to use such services rather than relatives or friends, who may not be reliable or who could limit or be upset by what the participant says).

❏ Plan research that fits in with participants (for example, that doesn't fall within religious special days, holidays, or cultural celebrations—see http://www.interfaithcalendar.org).

❏ Match researchers to participants (this doesn't mean that women automatically get on with women, or that gay researchers have an affinity with all gay participants—but it can make research feel more comfortable).

❏ Don't assume "sameness" (just because a researcher is black, doesn't mean they can interview all black participants: a black African researcher may not suit an African Caribbean participant group, for example).

❏ Offer choices (of who does the research, how it is presented, and where it gets completed).

❏ Include participants in the planning and dissemination of research, and use peer-researchers where appropriate.

❏ Use participant-friendly methods (not all participants have the same understanding of linear ratings presented in questionnaires; some languages are not written—therefore you need to match your methods to the needs and understanding of your participants).

See also Boynton (2003b)

You may have been taught a "one model fits all" approach to research, meaning you pick the method and participants join in. In practice, this may not always work. The challenge for the twenty-first century is to recognise that it is the participant who largely directs the research process. Before moving on to the next chapter, spend a while considering the examples in Table 5.17, which outline genuine research situations (Boynton & Wood, 1998). There are no right or wrong answers, but it will help you to think about the well-being of participants, and yourself.

Research can be frustrating, and some participants are exasperating or difficult. If you are having particular problems, the next chapter shows how to protect yourself, should you need to.

TABLE 5.17

What would you do?

---

(1) Ruth is a recent graduate, working on a community-based research project evaluating residents' opinions about improvements to a local housing estate. Her job involves visiting all the local residents and asking a series of semi-structured questions. On one visit to a middle-aged couple (Mr and Mrs Jenkins) she is welcomed warmly, and is enjoying hearing their views about where they live. During the course of the interview Mrs Jenkins mentions that they appreciate the improvements, but their neighbours the Singhs do not. Mr Jenkins explains that Mr and Mrs Singh are not able to appreciate the changes to the neighbourhood because of their background, and tells the researcher that "They are not as developed as us, are they love?" What might Ruth do next?

(2) Michael is interviewing young children about their attitudes to sex for a PhD on children, health, and sex education. He has permission from teachers at a local school to conduct informal discussions with eight- to ten-year-olds about basic sex-education issues. However, many of the parents are concerned that as a male researcher Michael should not complete the research. How might Michael overcome these problems?

(3) Lennox is completing a funded research project on elderly patients following an acute admission to hospital. His job is to complete quality of life measures with patients on their return from hospital. After one interview with a 75-year-old man, Lennox is invited to stay for a meal. He has some work to do back at the office, and wants to go out for a drink with friends later, but the man seems lonely and has helped with the research. What are Lennox's options?

(4) Juliet is in the middle of an interview with a male patient in a local day centre. He has been happy for most of the discussion, but towards the end he breaks down and cries. What could she do?

(5) Richard is completing research on housing for the local council. Towards the end of one interview in a person's home he is asked to help them complete their benefit forms. Is it okay for Richard to do this?

(6) Jackie and Elaine are conducting community-based research on teenage girls involved in prostitution. One of the participants whom they have got to know approaches them one night and asks them to help her escape from her "boyfriend", who has beaten her up and threatened to kill her and anyone who helps her. How might Jackie and Elaine feel?

(7) Mohammed is carrying out a number of focus groups with students about gender and sport. After one study has finished a group member says "My girlfriend was in one of your other study groups, what did they have to say?" What would be the best thing Mohammed could do in this situation?

(8) Fiona has been working with men who have heart disease, to examine whether a new patient awareness scheme has been successful. She is in the middle of one section of her interview schedule with a patient that asks about his general well-being. The patient emphasises there is nothing wrong with him, and proceeds to stroke her leg. Fiona is not sure whether the man is joking, and feels uncomfortable but not threatened. How might Fiona deal with this patient?

(9) Jonathan is an outreach worker and is evaluating his health promotion programme. He presents preliminary findings at a conference for psychologists and health professionals, outlining in particular the success of a safer sex campaign aimed at men who have sex with men. Following his presentation a member of the audience asks him a series of questions about gay men and appears to assume Jonathan is gay. Does Jonathan's response depend upon his sexuality?

(10) Pippa is carrying out an observational study on young people involved in selling crack-cocaine. One evening a participant whom she doesn't know well asks if she is interested in guns. He proceeds to place a hand-gun on the table in front of Pippa and tells her "It's loaded." Following this, he asks Pippa to deliver a package to his friend. Pippa is going to visit this friend the next day as part of her research. How might she respond to this incident?

Researcher well-being 6

The previous chapter covered issues around protecting participants. Researcher safety and well-being are equally important, but tend to get far less coverage in academic literature and training. This chapter will cover the well-being of researchers, addressing:

- General safety issues (at the start, during, and at the end of research)
- Going out and about
- Violence and risk
- Bullying and harassment.

Where's the risk?

Evidence shows that people working with the public are at risk (Kidd & Stark, 1992; Owen, 1992; Wyatt & Watt, 1995), and although guidelines exist for those working in different communities (Kendra & George, 2001; Nadwairski, 1992; Royal College of Psychiatrists, 1998), there is little formal guidance for health and social scientists. True, "health and safety" is covered in workplace guidance, but it tends to focus more on dangerous substances or equipment than risks to researchers from people or places (see for example p. 13 of the 2001 Department of Health *Research Governance Framework*). Clear guidelines for social science researchers are currently notable by their absence (Williams, Dunlap, Johnson, & Hamid, 1992). Risks to researchers vary in severity, but can (and do) include physical assault, theft, verbal abuse, and emotional distress (Nadwairski, 1992; Williams *et al.*, 1992). The guides that exist on researcher safety (Paterson, Gregory, & Thorne, 1999) tend to be aimed at researchers working in highly dangerous environments (Broadhead, 2001; Williams *et al.*, 1992). These studies can provide useful a useful background, but this chapter goes further by offering guidance to researchers working in community settings, or places (such as universities) assumed to be "safe" (Wood, 1999).

Why does this problem exist?

It is unclear why this lack of training and support exists, but one explanation could be that managers assume staff are already trained in research skills, and therefore have an awareness of safety. This may be because the researchers are qualified health professionals or recent graduates. Yet experience of community work or a degree in the social sciences does not guarantee an awareness of safety (Boynton, Catt, & Wood, 2001). Because there is a lack of systematic research and clear formal guidelines, safety policies are often implicit, and may be driven by false generalisations and stereotypes (for example, research with young men is "dangerous", while working with older people is "safe"). If managers do not check on their staff's training needs, it may be that staff are unaware that they can ask for support, or may even feel they cannot report problems. It's often junior members of a research team or lone workers that do most of the "data" collection, and they may feel pressured to endure potentially distressing situations for fear of looking like they can't do their job, or that they aren't working "hard enough".

> My first RA [research assistant] job was on a study of diabetes. I had to monitor patients who were in a trial for a new drug. My task was to ask them questions about their physical and emotional health. Because diabetes affects sexual functioning, I had to ask them questions about sex. I didn't mind asking the questions but many of the men would wink or leer at me or pat my leg as they gave their answer. I hated that. It was almost as though they were proving they had no sexual problems in their reaction. I felt I had to endure it though, since my boss was a total tyrant and if you didn't complete an interview she always threatened you with dismissal. (Name and details kept anonymous)

Alternatively, some researchers report a "macho culture" at work which means that researchers appear to compete on risky issues, sharing "horror stories" of dangerous situations they have encountered. In some cases managers hold this attitude, making it virtually impossible for staff to ask for help. It may also be that staff feel they are already in a minority due to their ethnicity or sexuality, and do not want to draw further attention to themselves by reporting a problem. Indeed, evidence suggests that the harassment of researchers from minority groups places them at risk within their organisation as well as the research environment (Reay, 1998; Wood, 1999).

Researchers have needs for support in training in a number of key areas. For those working "in the field" (defined here as any area where they encounter the public) there are issues of safety during travel, visiting homes or public places, interpersonal communication with participants, and encountering others (non-participants) through the course of research. Ways of dealing with these situations effectively are covered in the "General safety issues" and "Violence and risk" sections of this chapter.

The "risk" may not be "out there"

Some researchers are not troubled working with participants, but have their safety compromised by a lack of support from others (again, this is particularly true of junior researchers who are often the least skilled but placed in highly demanding research situations). This is addressed in the "Bullying and harassment" section of this chapter. Staff need training and support to enable them to ask sensitive questions, assist participants, and cope with their own emotions after completing interviews. In addition, many researchers lack awareness about "difference" in participants, and require educating to ensure they do not compromise their safety by unwittingly distressing or offending participants. Managing participants, opening and closing interviews, and showing the research has "ended" also require support and training (Boynton, 2002). Even when data is being collated and analysed, the risks to researchers are not over—particularly where qualitative work is concerned and researchers have to listen to or read accounts that may cause distress (Gregory, Russell, & Phillips, 1997; Hadjistavropoulos & Smythe, 2001). Therefore many of the strategies outlined in this chapter ought to apply to those coding or analysing qualitative or quantitative data that might be upsetting or stressful.

As mentioned above, junior researchers are particularly likely to be placed in situations that could be very dangerous (e.g. working in unknown communities, with unknown participants), and it may be assumed by more senior researchers/managers that staff will somehow cope with the demands placed on them by such work practices (Boynton, Greenhalgh, & Wood, 2004). The safety and well-being of researchers is currently not addressed on most undergraduate courses, and many postgraduate courses also do not train researchers

Of no doubt, the introduction of scientific methods in social science research was a great historical advancement. Logical empiricism/positivism has offered much for social science researchers to learn, and contributed significantly to the progress of social and behavioral sciences. In light of its drawbacks, however, the humanistic tradition in human inquiry needs to be restored, and the importance of the other approaches must be recognized. In the field of social work, for instance, an alternative approach is proposed with the combination of practice wisdom, the humanities, and the contributions of the emerging interpretive human sciences, with the merit of practice wisdom and the reflection of the practitioner being underscored (Goldstein, 1990; Schon, 1983). In terms of research, the importance and the art of original discovery in science is highly appreciated in light of initial thinking and plausibility, just as that of justification, validation, and acceptability (Orcutt, 1990). A heuristic approach to research is actively advocated (ibid.). In addition, theory is distinguished between generative and normative. All such recent advancement in the epistemology of social and behavioral science research establishes the significance of exploratory, hypothesis-developing studies, which emphasize the heuristic interpretation of the meaning of all important information rather than the justification of some individual arguments. The validation or falsification of the consequent hypotheses can be treated accordingly as the function of future inquiry.

The above discussions offer us at least two lessons. First, whenever possible, a multi-paradigm approach, or a pluralism of approaches, should be adopted. This "triangulation" in research design has been discussed earlier in this book. Different approaches will complement one another and may help avoid the major drawbacks of each method. In interpreting the empirical results, you should not simply play with the numbers. Additional information may be very useful for enriching the meaning of your findings. Second, in positivist social science the researcher is always required to be conservative in interpreting data (Lin, 1976). This is important to a validational study under the positivist framework. With an alternative approach, however, heuristic exploration is encouraged, which is not necessarily "conservative" in nature.

In sum, a clear epistemological as well as methodological understanding is a necessary quality of a good research worker. In the "bio-psycho-social" field the testing of a research hypothesis is closely tied with the use of inferential statistics. With a broader view of human research activities, however, you may consider that descriptive results also render a kind of empirical evidence.

in basic safety awareness. This chapter will outline safety skills for researchers at all stages of a study (before, during, and after research). It will provide links to training materials, and will give tips and strategies for keeping safe and well (physically and psychologically). In addition, the chapter will address the well-being and security of participants—including issues of voluntary informed consent, representing participants fairly, and implications for researchers and participants for completing a study.

It's not pleasant to have to talk about safety issues in relation to research. If you have only carried out research on student participants, chances are it won't have occurred to you that there are issues about safety. Maybe, though, you have also experienced safety problems here (more on this later). We spend a great deal of time in research worrying about the well-being of our participants—and it is right that we do this. But we seem far less inclined to worry about our researchers—and that is a problem (see Chapter 3, on staff roles and responsibilities, for more information). Most people we come into contact with are fine, but some are not. It may be that they are physically or psychologically ill, meaning they react to a researcher in a way that is inappropriate or distressing. Alternatively the researcher may make some *faux pas* or seem inappropriate to the participant, resulting in an argument or unpleasant atmosphere. And sometimes participants are fine, but those we encounter on the way to meet them are a risk to us.

Whose responsibility is it?

This chapter sets out some general pointers on safety, from the responsibilities of an organisation, through to managers, and finally the responsibilities of the researcher. It is the aim of this chapter not to make you frightened to do your job, but rather to enable you to work safely. Following the guidelines here cannot guarantee you won't encounter risky situations in your research, but it can greatly improve the way you deal with them. It is not the aim of this chapter to teach you self-defence skills. If you feel you require this training, ask your manager to organise safety training for you. Before thinking about safety of yourself or your staff, it's worth thinking in more detail about why safety issues are overlooked. Reasons include the following.

- People believe abuse of researchers doesn't happen
- Researchers who have had an abusive experience are ignored or dismissed
- Researchers are reluctant to report problem encounters

- Researchers are blamed by others (managers, etc.) for causing the incident
- Researchers blame themselves for causing the incident
- Researchers can see no point in complaining; they don't feel they'll be supported. (See the anonymous quote above and the one below.)

> When I started in my new job I asked the head of department about their safety procedures. I was going to work in the community with patients with severe mental illness and I wanted to know I was being protected. He said "We don't have a safety policy, just use your common sense." He then added "Well I've never heard of a fatality, so it's not like you need to worry." I didn't feel reassured at all. (Sue, community research coordinator)

The fact that it hasn't happened to you or your staff yet doesn't mean that researchers aren't put at risk, and that problems aren't happening. You can take steps to minimise risk, but should be open to dealing with problems as they arise.

General safety issues

At start of the research

Researcher safety should be considered when a study is being designed (see Chapter 2), and the topic of the project should be noted in terms of additional researcher needs (counselling, the need for injections, etc.). Bids should reflect costs to support researchers (for example, buying and paying for mobile phones, travel allowances that permit the use of emergency taxis or drivers), plus costs for extra staff training in self-defence or assertiveness if required.

Many departments have safety protocols, but these may be linked to dealing with hazardous substances rather than to practical problems in social science research. If your department, university or organisation doesn't have a safety policy for staff working with the public, request that one be created and implemented. Any departmental protocols should be regularly discussed and updated as necessary. Departments should be aware of the need to offer training to staff regarding handling confrontational situations, basic self-defence and awareness of "difference"—again, if these aren't forthcoming, you may want to request their implementation. You may find there are local groups or charities offering training in assertiveness, handling confrontational situations, self-defence, or equal opportunities. Although these courses can be seen as helping with your career development, if your job is placing you in any risk, support and training ought to be given as standard, not as a benefit to you. Managers should be prepared to check regularly on their staff's well-being, as part of project management.

Think about using a "safety buddy". This is a co-worker who will be told what your movements are. Your research manager could fulfil this role, but if not, you need to know which staff member is whose "safety buddy" and check that they are keeping watch on each other. If you are the project manager or a lone worker you need to find a colleague or friend who can fulfil this role.

During research
Making contact with participants

This is covered in greater detail in Chapter 5, but there are specific issues about participant contact that also relate to safety and well-being of both participants and researchers. As we have seen, many researchers contact participants via letter and/or telephone call. Such letters require careful consideration as to the nature of the research and the way in which the researchers are presented. Some researchers may prefer to use their first name/initial and surname with their job title, and the term "Mr" or "Ms". Participants have the right to know the gender of the person who may be coming to see them (as it may have a bearing on whether they wish to participate). However, terms such as "Miss" carry connotations (such as youth, femininity, and inexperience) that may lead to certain participants acting inappropriately. Keeping the researcher's name and details to a professional minimum can help avoid this. When a researcher is making an appointment, if information is available about the participant, the researcher should be aware of it. This may include the participant's needs (they may have visual or hearing problems, or have learning difficulties). There may also be issues that may affect the researcher (the participant having a history of violence, being on medication, etc.). While this shouldn't be a reason for excluding a person (unless they are too unwell to be in a study), researchers need to know as much as possible about whom they are going to see—particularly if it could compromise safety. Familiarise yourself with the geographical area prior to visiting it. On a departmental level, staff should offer advice about any particular areas that may be dangerous, hard to access, or not well served by public transport.

On securing a participant to a study, researchers should create clear databases with participant details, and also keep a record of where they are going and whom they are seeing (see Chapter 7). These secure files should be accessible to only those staff directly involved in a project, and may be used to locate participants when required, and researchers in an emergency.

Going to visit participants

When you have an appointment with a participant you should notify a contact person (usually a co-worker on your project) that you are going to do a research interview with Mrs/Mr So-and-So, and give an approximate estimate of the amount of time you will be gone. If you're going to be doing a number of interviews in a day, then tell your "safety buddy" whom you are interviewing, and the approximate time you'll be with each participant. If you are likely to spend a long time with participants, or require a flexible schedule, then agree a check-in time that suits you. It is useful to carry a local map or A–Z with you, and be aware of the times of the local buses and trains so you can get to and from participants' homes—and safely back to yours. You can use services such as www.streetmap.co.uk to find exact addresses. These print as one page, so you can carry that with you instead of a book. Plan your route, and walk in a confident and purposeful manner when travelling to see participants.

> I work out at the start of each day where I need to go, and then I mark each page of my A–Z with Post-it notes with the address, phone number and name of the person I'm going to see. That way if I get lost I can call the person and follow their directions on my map. (Sam, assistant researcher)

If you are working in the community you should carry a mobile phone with you. Ensure it's always fully charged. If you feel it is necessary, a personal safety alarm can also be carried. Don't feel that this is something that only female researchers require: male researchers may also find a personal alarm helpful. If you carry either a phone or an alarm, ensure that these are kept within easy reach; you don't want to be fumbling in your bag in an emergency.

Clothing

Be aware of what you are wearing. Evidence suggests it's worth dressing "appropriately" in the study setting, although what that means is up for discussion. Some researchers who do participant observation dress in a similar manner to their participants. However, most researchers won't be carrying out research in this way, and so dressing like your participants may actually cause offence. I'm reminded of a student who wanted to do some research on women involved in prostitution and showed me a suspender set and sexy corset she had brought to "fit in". Apart from being astonished at her naivety, I was concerned that the working women she met would be offended by someone who, rather than looking like she fitted in, looked like she was being sarcastic. She ended up not doing the planned research, much to our relief! Think about the impact different outfits might have, for example t-shirt and jeans, a business suit, or a very short skirt. Consider who your participants are, and what you are asking. I once had an assistant who turned up for a study on sexual problems wearing a t-shirt with a Playboy bunny motif on it. Clearly this could be interpreted by participants either as a sexual message or as being unfeeling about participants' problems (particularly when combined with the research topic).

Men should be aware of the research situation when deciding whether to wear ties (a clip-on tie could always be worn if necessary), and women should be careful about wearing necklines that could be grabbed by participants. Wear comfortable clothing and shoes, and check you can walk briskly or run in this outfit if need be. You need to strike a balance between looking smart and being safe. If you need to travel through a dangerous area to get to and from an interview, consider carrying trainers with you to change into for walking. Care should also be taken when deciding to wear jewellery (obvious or expensive jewellery or watches could place the researcher at risk while they are travelling to see participants, or possibly within the interview setting). If you need to carry equipment with you to interviews, ensure you don't overburden yourself with heavy, restrictive items. Be aware that carrying laptops, etc. could make you a target for robbery—so take steps to transport your equipment in a safe manner (for example, use a rucksack designed for laptops rather than a traditional laptop case).

Going out and about

Researchers spend a great deal of time outside the office, either visiting other researchers or people on their study team, or going to see participants. For that reason, most researchers end up carrying part of their office around with them. A good idea is to invest in a strong bag, preferably a rucksack, where you can keep your work (although if you are carrying valuable materials you may need to consider whether a rucksack is the safest way of doing this). You may also want to carry maps, tissues, handwipes, deodorant, or other research necessities if you will spend most of your time outside your office.

> *The first thing I learned as a new researcher was my clothes were all wrong. I wore strappy sandals, and after my first interview my feet were blistered and I could hardly walk. I quickly learned I needed some smart walking shoes, and now I spend most of my time in trainers. I also learned the hard way that researchers need to anticipate everything, so the first time I was caught in a rainstorm I realised it was a good idea to carry a fold-up umbrella in my bag too.* (Suki, senior lecturer)

Arrival

Pay attention to your surroundings, and stay alert when you are travelling to and arriving at an interview. If you travel to visit a participant by car you should remember where you parked, and try to park as close to the participant's home as possible. Make sure you keep your petrol tank filled, and have money for parking tickets or travel charges. Double-check you have the correct address, and if in doubt do not go inside. As you enter the participant's home or research venue, check where the exits are, and note other rooms within the participant's home. Note if there are any other people in the building and be aware of their behaviour too. If you feel uncomfortable or threatened, make your excuses and leave.

During the interview/visit

Sit near the exit, and be able to reach it. It's not enough to see it; you have to be able to reach it. Consider whether to accept food or drink from the participant (some researchers have a rule to accept no food or drink, while others decide on a case-by-case basis). Be aware of your own body language and that of your participant.

Exercise: What do you look like?

The aim of this exercise is for you to watch how you behave in research situations. Work in a group of three. One person is the interviewer, another the interviewee, and the third videotapes the interview. As a group, think of a topic to ask questions about. The interviewee and the third person then work out how the interviewee will react to the questions (without the interviewer knowing). The interviewee should respond in a way that challenges the interviewer—being bored, rude, vague, or generally unhelpful. The interviewer should do their best to get answers. You can repeat this so you all have a go, changing the topic and the behaviour of the interviewee. Following this, play the interviews back, focusing your attention on the interviewer. How is s/he coping? Is she looking unhappy, stressed or fidgeting? Talk about how it felt to be an interviewer, and discuss whether it shows in your body language. The interviewee can comment on how the interviewer's various reactions made them feel too. In doing this you may be able to highlight behaviours that may be inflammatory to participants, and also identify to yourself various postures or expressions that suggest you are getting stressed. You can then be aware of those when carrying out interviews—and be ready to end or amend your interview if you start to feel or act distressed or worried.

Practise, and be prepared to use, strategies for fending off difficult/personal questions from participants—be clear of your role and boundaries as a researcher (see Table 5.17 in Chapter 5 for scenarios). Anticipate reactions to questions from participants—be aware of the reactions certain questions may evoke. Be aware of how much personal information you are prepared to give. Remember that while you are obligated to respect your participants' confidentiality, they may not be aware of respecting yours. Pay attention to your use of humour, jokes, etc.—it may upset participants or give the wrong impression (see Chapter 5).

Closing an interview

Have a list of referral services and support groups to give all participants (see Chapter 5, Figure 5.3). Explain whether or not you'll be coming to see them again. Thank them for their help. Be aware of personal contact—shake hands if you feel comfortable with this but do not initiate touching unless you feel it will be welcomed and you feel comfortable with it. When leaving with a participant, go to the door with them. Face them as you are leaving, and do not turn your back until the door is closed. Be aware about offering extra help to participants. If it's a one-off favour you feel comfortable with (e.g. posting a letter for a house-bound person), then use your judgement. It's not that you can't be helpful, but some participants may misunderstand your visit, which may mean they expect more help from you in the future, or if you are going to interview them again they may give you a different reaction because they like you, not because of how they feel about the issue you are researching.

> *I have a 10-minute rule. If something is going to take only 10 minutes from my day I'll usually do it. I've returned library books, posted letters, or made people toast and tea. If it's a bigger task I always give the person a referral to someone who can help them—be that social services, their GP or another support group.* (Jaz, research nurse)

> *I once complained to the social services on behalf of a participant. All was fine until his benefit was cut. It was nothing to do with me, or the issue I'd complained to social services about. But the patient did blame me, called to my boss and got me into a whole load of trouble. We sorted it out, but my boss explained in future it was better to support the participant, rather than act for them.* (Rachel, research assistant)

Additional pointers

Have policies and procedures in place so you can detach from work. This isn't to say you have to be "detached" during your job: in many cases I think researchers should get involved in their work (see the section "keep on keeping" in Chapter 4). However, if your work is particularly upsetting or stressful, look to ways in which you can switch off, or ask to see a counsellor if you think it will help you. If you are a manager, supervision of your staff should be built into your job description, and theirs. It should also be part of a manager's continuing professional development. Schedule a regular time to check your staff's well-being and appraise their skills to ensure they are not putting themselves at risk through bad practice.

Keep researcher support on a personal, not a project, level. This means if things go wrong, researchers should not be made to feel they are responsible for problems that occur outside their control. Many researchers won't admit to having problems for fear they are going to be labelled as "bad researchers", so make it clear that their well-being is as important as participant well-being, and you'll monitor both as a matter of course. If you are unsure, some colleagues offer management training courses for academic/research supervisors, which may be useful. If you are a junior member of a team (or even if you are senior but need support) then you can request formal supervision and assistance. Supervision isn't about "checking up"—you should be in a place where you can share your fears, feelings, and ideas, and talk over how any problems affect you and their impact on your study.

Violence and risk

Although we don't expect violence from participants in research, there may be occasions when participants act in an aggressive manner. This may be due to them feeling ill or in pain, or due to insecurity (particularly if they feel they are being made to look stupid through research). Feeling anxious, unhappy, disempowered, or having problems with drugs or alcohol can also cause people to behave negatively. While it doesn't excuse the behaviour, it does permit us to predict it. If someone is likely to be upset by the research, they should not be approached—for their own well-being and that of the researcher. If you are likely to work with people who may become violent, training in negotiating skills and/or breakaway techniques can be helpful (McDonnell, Dearden, & Richens, 1991; Shah & De, 1998). But suppose you have performed all these checks: are there other ways of predicting aggressive behaviour? Clues of distress (apart from someone saying so) may include prolonged eye-contact, restless behaviour, or provocative or unpleasant remarks (adapted from Open University *Guidelines on safety and security for associate lecturers*, 2001; http://www.open.ac.uk/ foi.docs/healthC.doc).

In such a situation, it is best to end the interview and remove yourself as soon as you are able. If you have anyone else to help you, go to them. If these options are not immediately open to you, stay calm (deep breathing helps). Make very clear statements (e.g. "I can see you are unhappy, let's end this interview here"). Move slowly and deliberately to an exit, and avoid physical contact with them. Show you are listening to them and taking their concerns on board. They may be angry about another issue, not about you, but while they are acting in a threatening manner it isn't the time to help them solve their difficulties (some might question if this is your role at all). **Never** be persuaded to stay with someone, go to a new venue with them, or to give up your phone. Try not to be prevented from making a telephone call, or trying to get help (see Table 6.1).

Dealing with distress

If a participant, a colleague, or a member of the public becomes upset or angry with you, then the checklist in Table 6.2 may help.

You don't have to become a victim, or take the whole study on your shoulders. Remember your support network. If possible try to have someone in a supervisory or supporting role you can go to, as well as colleagues within your department. They may not be a research expert, but should be someone you can update on your work and well-being. They should also be a person you can trust and who follows the same rules of ethical practice you do. Keep them informed of any issues/difficulties you encounter, as they may be able to support you if you receive any complaints. Maintain links with professional organisations too (remember, though, if you knowingly breach practice or make a serious error your support team/professional body may not be able to protect you).

During the planning phases of your research (see Chapters 2 and 3) consider your participants: certain groups of vulnerable people (such as those with severe mental illness) can represent a risk. Such participants still should be included in research if they are capable of giving consent, but you do need to build additional safety factors into your research and not assume that you can handle difficult situations without training. If you accidentally recruit someone to research who becomes unpleasant or unreasonable, you do not have to deal with them or place yourself at risk. It is better to exclude someone from research who is causing you distress, if you feel they are going to be unpleasant throughout.

> I recruited a guy to my study who started off okay and then started acting very strangely—taking offence at questions and acting in a very paranoid manner. I realised he was probably too ill to be in the research and so explained to him that the questions were over. He spotted I had more to ask and I said "Oh, we only ask women those questions." He took a while to leave, but he did go and he wasn't upset by my ending the research. (Missy, research assistant)

You may also find that if you advertise for participants you end up with a number of calls from people who aren't suited to the research, and who may become difficult or abusive. Again, it is not your role to

Scientific research, indeed, should allow for all forms of human inquiry. And your understanding in this regard would give your quest a great guide.

Effective communication and efficient writing

If you make good reference to your original proposal and other research documentation, it should be no big problem for you to start generating your research report. The organization of the research findings, however, may pose a challenge to you as the results of data analysis may be just overwhelming. The requirement for a "complete" report of all the information is actually unrealistic and often unnecessary. If your data analysis proceeds in an unplanned manner, it is likely that you will end up with a massive quantity of output from which you can only select a tiny bit for detailed reporting. It is advisable that you carefully plan your research project and follow out your research questions and hypotheses. Organizing your research activities as well as report writing around some main themes is a basic strategy for effective and efficient conduct of your analysis and communication of your results. People having a hard time in conducting data analysis and generating research reports often are not familiar or forget about the original thinking in raising the research questions and hypotheses. This is especially the case when data analysts and research associates responsible for drafting the reports are recruited in the middle of a research course. Indeed, the first thing they should do after (or even before) they accept the jobs is to collect all the original research documentation, including the research proposal, trace the course of any change, and make full use of the information.

A tentative outline for the research report will provide data analysis with important guidance. The process and results of data analysis will in turn provide needed feedback for planning and writing a good report. The integration of outlining, drafting, and revising the research report with managing and analyzing the data, therefore, might be considered an optimal or practical approach for many investigators.

Generally speaking, the researcher should address the research questions and hypotheses that justified the initiation of the research project. The researcher should provide the reasons if major revision of the original plan or alteration of the research direction is required. Unexpected findings from data analysis are often the grounds for changing the questions. There are different views, however, as to how the researcher should deal with originally proposed research

TABLE 6.1

Risk assessment for researchers

Area of risk	Issues to be aware of
Buildings	Access from the street/car park to buildings—is it well lit? Are there clear paths, ramps or steps, doors or windows, or any machinery/structural defects that could present a safety problem?
Your property	Keep your bags and belongings in a safe place, even when visiting someone in their home. Ensure you know where your belongings are at all times. Don't take anything valuable with you unless you have to. Managers should be clear about staff safety when staff are responsible for equipment such as mobile phones or laptops.
Well-being	Do you know where fire escapes, the nearest phone or the security office/number is? (If you are directly at risk call 999). Have you had a health check and is this supported in your job? If there are any risks posed to your physical or psychological health, have these been planned for in the project?
Equipment	Are you trained and protected from injury (e.g. needlestick injury, or damage from long-term use of a computer). Have you been trained in the correct use of equipment and been given inoculations if appropriate? If you have to carry equipment for work, has it been checked so you avoid back strain?
People	Anticipate and know how to respond to potential racist/sexist/homophobic remarks or abuse from participants and others. If you are likely to encounter participants who are drunk, on drugs or have severe mental health problems, are you trained in how to deal with them appropriately? Do you know the difference between someone who is ill and someone who is being inappropriate? Do you have the confidence to leave any situation that feels uncomfortable? Are other people around who could come to your assistance should you need it? Are you able to control and leave an interview? Do you have a policy on how to deal with participants who become a nuisance or who won't "let go"? Managers—are you checking your staff are aware of their boundaries and are not promising participants too much or overstepping their role as researcher?

Environment	Are you likely to have to work or travel in adverse weather conditions? Can you plan your route and avoid getting lost? Is there any risk of assault? Have you had or do you require training in self-defence or assertiveness? Do you know the area where you'll be working, or can you find out about it? Are you wearing appropriate clothing? Is there a place of safety you can go to if working in the field?
Lone Working	Can you summon help if necessary? Is the risk posed to you high, medium or low? If possible work in pairs and avoid dangerous buildings/situations. Never allow a person to work in a dangerous situation without training or support. Ensure you record your location, route and expected time of return. Have a check-in system with your buddy. Train and empower staff in raising the alarm if necessary. Get advice from local services (police, council, etc.) on any dangerous locations.
Setup	Have you designed your study to avoid cold-calling? Are researchers equipped with identification badges? Are you regularly checking on the training and emotional needs of researchers?
Other hazards	Have you checked about hazards posed outside of this list (for example handling dangerous substances, etc.?)

TABLE 6.2

Checklist for dealing with distress

❑ Keep calm.

❑ Find out what the problem is (see Chapter 5).

❑ If you need time to find a solution, kindly but firmly ask for space (promise to come back with an answer, and keep your word).

❑ If appropriate get a third party to resolve the problem or support you.

❑ Try not to get angry, sarcastic or aggressive. Try to be positive.

❑ Know your rights.

❑ Put yourself in your participant's place: how would you feel? (See Chapter 5.)

❑ Offload and share with your manager, colleagues or HR department (if appropriate): don't let it become a personal issue that causes you distress.

---

listen to abusive or threatening calls. Make a note of them and report if necessary. You can politely say "I have to go now, I'm putting the phone down" to any caller who is becoming difficult.

Table 6.3 summarises some of the above points.

TABLE 6.3

Points to remember

---

(1) Be polite and professional.
(2) Deal with complaints quickly and calmly.
(3) Refer to others if you need help.
(4) If in doubt, make excuses and end the participant's involvement.
(5) Work with other researchers if possible.
(6) Leave if you feel threatened.

If in doubt . . .

This chapter has covered general safety pointers to help you think about working in a better environment. It may seem that when problems emerge they are very obvious, and possibly very violent. However, many difficulties in research may not be so clear. It may be a general feeling of unease or discomfort. If you are unsure, then leave—you can always repeat the research with someone else, or with the same person at a later stage (once you've got support and have checked they are okay).

If you feel uncertain when arranging research, organise to see participants in your workplace (if possible) or take a colleague with you. Always act on your feelings, don't dismiss them, and don't allow colleagues or managers to make you feel bad for doing so—share your worries with them. Remember to be realistic. There's a difference between being safety-conscious and using safety as an excuse not to have contact with participants.

> *I employed a researcher who looked great on paper, but when it came to doing interviews she refused. She said it wasn't safe to work in the community, even though we had excellent support for our researchers. I couldn't understand it since the job description made it clear, but she saw her role as working in the office with participants coming to her. She left soon after, but it made me realise that not everyone is suited to working with the public, but that safety shouldn't be used as an excuse for not doing what you're hired for! Now I make it clear in the interview exactly what the researcher role is.* (Marek, senior lecturer)

Bullying and harassment

It would be incorrect to suggest that the only problems faced are those of physical violence—participants can be verbally abusive too. Furthermore, it may be that those you work with bully or harass you (see Houghton, 2003; Paice & Firth-Cozens, 2003; Wood, 1999). Researchers may be harassed due to their gender, age, ethnicity, religion, sexuality, or (dis)ability, and may be bullied by managers or colleagues. None of these are acceptable, and the range of the problem within the research world is unknown. The remainder of this chapter tackles bullying and harassment, and what you can do if you feel you are affected.

Everyone has the right to work safely and with dignity. If you are uncertain about your rights, ask your union, or talk to your human resources office. The TUC (Trades Union Congress) has an online guide to safe working standards and guidance on identifying and dealing with harassment (http://www.worksmart.org.uk). Your organisation should also have a statement around bullying, and possibly a staff bullying helpline that you could use. If you are a lone worker there is a list of help sources at the end of this chapter that you can use.

It is also your responsibility to respect other people's feelings and views at work. You may cause offence or distress without being aware of it—although once it is brought to your attention you should be willing to amend your behaviour. Similarly, you should feel you could let others know if their words or actions were upsetting you.

Being bullied or harassed at work—either by participants or by colleagues—can have far-reaching effects, including causing the victim anxiety, stress, illness, absence, and a loss of concentration. It may lead to staff leaving a project, or those managing the study (and their organisation) being held responsible for damages if the victim makes a legal complaint. Managers therefore have the responsibility to offer training to staff to ensure they do not bully others, and to offer clear instructions that can be reasonably expected to be followed.

A one-off negative remark, or general instructions that you don't really like (but that fit your job description) from a manager, does not constitute bullying or harassment. A one-off serious threat of violence is an example of one step too far. And continued, unwanted behaviour that makes you feel vulnerable, offended or upset, and has nothing to do with your work, is unacceptable. Table 6.4 details inappropriate behaviours that you should not have to put up with from your colleagues or your participants (neither should you be displaying them to others).

These behaviours by colleagues are unacceptable and can be challenged by your HR or anti-bullying department. If they are a persistent part of the behaviour of your participants, you may not be able to alter

---

TABLE 6.4

Examples of unacceptable behaviours

Violence (excluding self-defence); unwanted physical contact; sexual assault, touching or comments; shouting, swearing or sarcasm; personal remarks, teasing or name-calling (when it's obviously causing distress); bullying or belittling remarks either behind closed doors or in front of other colleagues (public humiliation); continual unwarranted criticism of performance; unwelcome remarks about sex, a person's body or their appearance (including their dress); unwanted discussion of a person's disability, sexuality or religion; verbal or written harassment (including abusive or offensive emails, telephone messages, letters, or memos); racist or (hetero)sexist "jokes" that aren't welcome; gossip, threats or name-calling over a person's (dis)ability, religion, ethnicity, etc.; intrusion into a person's home life (unwarranted phone calls at home); removing areas of responsibility without prior notice or reason; punishing trivial mistakes and refusing to listen to staff's problems or concerns; ignoring, overlooking or patronising; giving a person a task they can't help but fail at (such as unreasonable workloads/guidelines); posters or other visual material liable to cause offence; alienating or isolating staff.

---

those behaviours, but you should expect to be supported by your manager to work in such an area (or have the right to refuse to work in places where you feel threatened). It is against the law to discriminate against people on the basis of their race, gender, or sexual orientation.

Everyone should take responsibility to check that they are acting appropriately to others, and supporting those who may be being bullied. Managers/supervisors need to set an example by treating staff respectfully, offer training, and, if problems occur, deal with them promptly. You should take people's complaints seriously, but treat them in confidence, and don't wait for someone to report a problem to you if you've noticed another's unacceptable behaviour.

What to do about risk and problems

It's not always easy to deal with risky situations at work, from participants or workmates. However, there are some steps you can take to deal with problems more effectively. Get extra support, and talk any worries over with your colleagues or manager. If that doesn't work then you can also talk to friends, or a representative of a bullying support group. Keep a diary—note down when problems occur. If you find that asking a particular question causes inappropriate reactions from participants, or visiting a certain area feels (or is) risky, then talk this over with your manager (see also Chapter 4, on piloting). If you are a manager, encourage your staff to report any difficulties to you regularly—they can use a diary and report back. If you are being bullied at work, or are having problems with participants that your boss is refusing to deal with, then keep a list of incidents as you may need to use it to support any complaints you make about your management/support. Be assertive—if there are problems that are making you unhappy, preventing you doing your job, or affecting your emotional or physical health, then you need to take steps to stop them. It is hard to stand up for yourself if you are being bullied or threatened at work, but there are groups that can help and advise you, and they are listed at the end of this chapter.

> I worked on a project where I was bullied by my manager. They changed my job description, overloaded me with work and set targets I couldn't reach. No support was offered, but they were verbally abusive to me—including shouting and threatening me in meetings. Rather than leaving or complaining (which I should have done) I stayed, working longer hours and getting unhappier. My reasons for staying were that I didn't want a bad reference, and more importantly I felt I owed it to the participants in the

research—I wanted to get their voices heard. In the end, the project finished, and the resulting report (on which the manager had the final edit) didn't represent the participants fully at all. I've always been against workplace bullies, but that experience taught me that it's just not worth staying. It shook my self-esteem and took me ages to relax into my current job and realise I am a good worker. (Anon, lecturer)

This chapter has covered some issues around safety and well-being. It's important to stress that most research positions are not this stressful and if you take steps to protect yourself, hopefully incidents should be reduced. As a manager, you need to check your staff aren't putting themselves at risk, and university lecturers need to monitor students who may, through over-enthusiasm, put themselves in danger by working in community settings they are neither trained nor supported for. The general rule around safety is to keep talking and sharing, ask for help, and don't be a hero. You have the right to work safely, which others should respect.

Useful resources

- *Victim Support*—Tel. 0845 3030900. PO Box 11431, London SW9 6ZH. Website: http://www.victimsupport.org
- *Personal safety*—Contact your local police station for an appointment with a crime prevention officer. Websites: http://www.crimereduction.gov.uk/personalsafety.htm; http://www.crimereduction.gov.uk/stolengoods2.htm
- *Suzy Lamplugh Trust*—a support group for safety issues at work. Website: http://www.suzylamplugh.org/home/index.shtml
- *Success Unlimited*—support and advice against bullying and harassment. Website: http://www.successunlimited.co.uk
- *Malicious phone calls*—BT, Tel. 0800 666700 (they also have an advice leaflet on dealing with malicious or upsetting calls); the BBC's guide to dealing with such calls: http://www.bbc.co.uk/print/crime/support/maliciousphonecalls.shtml
- *Racial, sexual or homophobic harassment*— http://www.racialharassment.org.uk; http://www.antihomophobia.org.uk; http://www.eoc.org.uk/EOCeng/EOCcs/Advice/sexual_harassment.asp
- *Social Research Association*— http://www.the-sra.org.uk/stay%20safe.htm

Once a study's underway 7

Frequently researchers are trained to think about research in an uncomplicated way. An idea is decided upon, how to test it is established, and bingo! The work just happens. However, research is an evolving process, and needs to be approached as such. As many researchers aren't told to anticipate research in its changeable format, they tend to panic when work doesn't go as they planned. Furthermore, research needs to be flexible, given that changes may occur during a study that will affect its eventual outcomes. This chapter therefore covers some of the practical issues for researchers to think about once they've got their work underway, including:

- Entering, monitoring and storing qualitative/quantitative "data"
- How to "clean" data (and why this is important)
- What needs to be collected routinely
- Keeping records
- Data protection.

Recording and collecting participant details

Whether you are completing research that is qualitative or quantitative, you will usually collect demographic data on your participants. Some researchers are given a list of participant names and addresses to use for recruiting (for example, the names of every head teacher and school in a local area may be used to introduce a study to local schools). Evidently these need to be kept private, and any participant names and addresses (particularly home addresses and telephone numbers) should never be stored in the same file as data gained from participants in research.

Participant details databases serve two purposes. Firstly they allow you to keep a record of who is being recruited for your research, and may possibly be used for mail merges or sending out letters (see Chapter 5). Secondly, you may use the database as a means of checking that you recruit the appropriate participants, and keep a record of those who refuse to participate or are unsuitable for a study. In this way you can show later in your study that you weren't biased in who you invited to take part (unless you specifically wanted to be—for example purposively sampling key informants for a study evaluating crime in a housing project).

Sometimes you will be provided with information (for example, a list of patient details from a doctor's list); other times you may have to collect these details yourself. Either way, you will probably end up with a database that looks like that shown in Table 7.1.

It might not be clear how you could use this information, nor why it would be useful, but here's how it would work. Say you wanted to do a study evaluating whether men were making use of an extended surgery service at a local doctor's (since evidence suggests men do not use GPs much during the day). You want to interview men aged 30 to 50 to see whether they would be interested in such a surgery. The GP gives you a list of all patients who fit your search criteria, and you create a database. But it may not be correct, so having extra details may help. P. Jones doesn't tell you whether a person is male or female, so knowing that this person is male means they can be invited to be in your study. Also, having a name, gender and address means you can now write to Mr P. Jones to tell him about your study. You can tell by the date of birth he fits the criteria for the work. The only problem is that Mr Jones doesn't appear to be on the telephone, so if that is your planned method of follow-up, you may need to write to him again, rather than call.

TABLE 7.1

Participant details database

Name (first name or initial + surname)	Gender (if known/ appropriate)	Ethnicity (if known/ appropriate)	Date of Birth (if known/ appropriate)	Address (line 1, line 2, postcode, etc.)	Telephone number
P. Jones	Male	White UK	25-07-1964	24 Robin Lane, Edgeham	Not on phone

As you'll often be contacting a number of people in research, it is worth extending your database to include a number of other categories to help with managing your project (see Table 7.2). The information in Table 7.2 shows that Mr Jones was initially contacted in June, and after two reminders did agree to take part in the evaluation of the surgery opening times. If he had refused, this table would have noted why (common reasons participants give are "too busy", "not interested", "too personal"). It's important to differentiate between someone agreeing to be in a research and making a note (see final column) when their role in the research is finally over. Keeping these records allows the researcher to be aware of what is going on, and it stops Mr Jones being pestered once he's agreed or refused to take part.

TABLE 7.2

Additional database details

Date participant contacted	Reminders sent?	Agreed to take part?	If no, what is reason?	Completed study?
08-06-2002	2	Yes	–	Yes

You can be flexible with these databases: for example, you may want to add a column showing how you sent reminders (how many emails, phone calls, or letters you had to send). It depends on what your study is about. Using these databases can help you keep on top of participant recruitment, and also allow a project to be managed. Project managers should check all their staff's databases regularly to see how recruitment is going and offer support where necessary (see Chapter 6). If participants appear to be regularly refusing for a particular reason, it may be worth re-examining the researcher's recruitment technique.

> For one of my studies I wanted to look at staff satisfaction with a new meal service our company had introduced. We have offices all over the UK and a new catering contract had been brought in. Several of the offices were helpful, but three of them were impossible to pin down. Eventually I started keeping a note on the amount of time I was spending trying to get hold of them just to introduce the study. In one case it took me 32 phone calls before I got to talk to the person I needed, and then he said they wouldn't take part! (Jake, managing director)

hypotheses and the "make-up" ones. Some would insist that the researcher should be loyal to the original hypotheses and stick to whatever the actual results are. Others may allow the making of new hypotheses during data analysis, but consider this legitimate only if the researcher intends to take it as a starting point for new inquiries. Still others may think that the adjustment of the research plan is normal, and adding more hypotheses and testing them on a more informed basis is not only legitimate but desirable. This, however, should in no way mean that the selecting or dismissing of information is simply a matter of judgment. There are two rules of thumb here: (1) information central to the original questions and hypotheses must not be omitted; and (2) new questions and hypotheses created during data analyses can be included in the report, provided that they will either serve the original research purposes or have special significance in their own right to warrant the expansion or alteration of the research scope.

It should be noted that the sole reason for some students as well as more experienced researchers to change their hypotheses or even the whole topic is that the hypotheses did not pass the tests. Some even panic as the deadline approaches while they still have to switch between topics. The expectation to accept only "positive" results may come from some faculty advisors, the research sponsors, publishers, and journal editors (Sjoberg & Nett, 1968). However, this is not a requirement of science. The advisors, sponsors, as well as the researchers themselves, must understand that scientific findings also include negative outcomes. Publishers and journal editors certainly also have a share of responsibility in this. The purpose of research is attained as long as a project is well designed and properly carried out. What count are the quality of work and the objectives in providing new information, knowledge, and understanding, rather than a specific pattern of results. To protect yourself against bad luck (remember, it is usually unwise to argue with your "boss" during the term of your contract), of course, you may not finalize your hypotheses until you see your results. However, again, to pass some sort of statistical tests should not be the whole purpose.

In practice, the power of computer has eliminated the demarcation lines between data exploration and validation (confirmation), between hypothesis making and testing, and between inductive and deductive logics. In the actual process of computer-assisted data analysis, oftentimes a hypothesis is tested even before it gets formulated. Since the computer can provide you with instant tests for almost any tentative "run," you may prefer a trial-and-error strategy to

In my experience, if someone's going to join in, they tell you fairly quickly. Same goes for saying "no". The problem is the people who are hard to get hold of, or the ones who you think are saying yes to your study but clearly don't want to do it. I've learned that in those cases they usually don't finish your study. But the way we run research means you still have to go on chasing them up until they refuse. Sometimes I make that judgement for participants, especially if I feel my time is being wasted, or I am bordering on harassing them with my calls. (Chiara, medical researcher)

If you keep clear records, you can show others linked to your study how you have spent your time, and justify where you have chosen not to pursue a participant. Keeping this information isn't just necessary for your research; it can enlighten you about the research issue itself. A few years ago I was conducting a study on sexual functioning in patients registered with a GP. In order to meet and interview the patients, I had to gain the approval of local GPs to work out of their surgeries. Many of the GPs were interested and agreed to participate; some were unsure but agreed once I'd visited them and outlined the research. But some just wouldn't play ball. Many were impossible to get hold of, and in other cases the receptionists wouldn't put me through to the doctors. As a result of keeping a note of these calls I could track the average number of calls and faxes it took to get an appointment, as well as the reactions to the study, which told me more about the surgery staff's view on sexual problems. Phrases like "our patients don't have sexual problems", and "oh that's just disgusting" supported evidence that GPs have as many problems talking about sex as patients do, and reinforced my belief that our research was both valid and necessary.

Don't forget that you'll need to include contacting participants as part of your study design, and an ethics committee will need to approve the data you are collecting routinely (names, addresses, reasons for refusal, etc.), as well as any additional research data you are keeping. Only collect information that is relevant to your research, store it safely, and keep names and addresses separate from other participant information.

Sampling: inclusion and exclusion

Some studies are designed to access specifically a small group of people, while others attempt to select a random group who are representative of a wider population; still more approaches (such as ethnography or action research) do not begin with a sample group. However, in the planning stages of research it needs to be made clear who you'll be selecting, and why (even if you do not have a specific recruitment plan). This involves listing factors by which participants will be included in the study and reasons for exclusion. Your selection criteria need to be consistent once your study is underway. If you are relying on others to help you recruit and involve participants, the selection criteria need to be clear, easy to follow, and easy to achieve. You may want to put your selection criteria on any posters or recruitment materials to make it clear what participants are wanted for the research. If, for example, you were running a questionnaire study on the success of a new drop-in centre on young men, your inclusion criteria might be men aged between 18 and 35, who attend the centre, and who can read and write in English. Your exclusion criteria would be women, men under 18 or over 35, those who don't use the centre, and who are unable to communicate in English.

Exercise: Who's in or out?

> Select a number of journal papers with different research designs and participants. See if the inclusion/exclusion criteria for participants are made obvious. If not, can you work them out? Does this lack of information detract from your understanding of the study?

In cases where volunteers are used (and selection criteria may not be so specific), reports should still make clear who volunteered, how they were selected, and what characteristics they possessed. Identifying who your participants are, and the basis by which they are selected, will allow people to understand and interpret your findings when your research is published, and will be vital if people are to replicate your study.

Filing

Create a clearly labelled filing system, with any confidential material kept in locked compartments. If you are working on a project where a number of people will have access to files, you need to create a system you all agree upon and stick to it. The research manager/lead researcher should ensure on a regular basis that all files are kept in order. Organise the system that best suits you. Keep the items used most frequently the most easily accessible. Have a regular clean-out so that out-of-date material is moved, but do not throw away material unless everyone on the project agrees it is no longer needed. Tips on filing are given in Table 7.3.

TABLE 7.3	
Tips on filing	
Papers/articles	Keep records of your references, using a package-like reference manager. Put a number on the paper/report/article that corresponds with the code given by your reference management package. Keep your list of references up to date, and indicate if a paper is out on loan to colleagues. You don't need to keep papers in a locked cabinet, but you do need to have a clear filing system for them.
Copies of letters, questionnaires, interview schedules, consent forms, etc.	If you have lots of information to send out, make multiple copies and store. Uncompleted copies do not need to be locked away; any completed forms need to be securely stored (and, in the case of consent forms and questionnaires, need to be kept separate). You can either make enough to last for your study, or replenish when needed. It may help to nominate a person on the project whose task it is to see that this is done.
Records	Travel forms, correspondence, minutes of meetings, and ethics information all need to be stored for the duration of the study. Make copies of your travel and other expense claims, and if you don't have forms to cover this within your organisation, create your own. Keep a project budget file, and liaise with your finance department (if you have one, and when it is appropriate).

Research diaries

Chapter 2 outlined the importance of planning research (using Gantt charts, for example). Planning the timescale of your research permits you to see where you *should be* in your study. However, you should also use a research diary to keep a record of where you *actually are* (as this may differ from your best-laid plans). Many organisations require you to keep a research diary. These are to keep a record of research activity, and it is usually requested that you do not include personal views within them. In this case you would record information on a

TABLE 7.4

General diary records

	Week beginning 27 August
Monday 27th	*Called seven schools to confirm appointments. Data entry and cleaning.*
Tuesday 28th	*School visits and interviewing.*
Wednesday 29th	*School visits and interviewing.*
Thursday 30th	*Data entry and cleaning, writing conference talk.*
Friday 31st	*Education and Exclusion Conference—presentation.*

daily or weekly basis, and make a note of what activities you carried out (see Blaxter, Hughes, & Tight, 2001, pp. 48–51; Robson, 1993, pp. 254–255). An example from a research diary in this format (for a study on access to education) is shown in Table 7.4.

However, some researchers use their diaries slightly differently, as a record of activity, as well as a safety backup. Therefore the same diary could include the name of the contact person visited at the school, the address and phone number of the school, and the precise times of the visits. This would allow a person to be traced if necessary. Another way in which research diaries can be used is as a reflective exercise as opposed to a practical record. In such cases the diary may look something like the example show in Table 7.5.

How do I know what type of research diary I should use?

If you have to keep a diary, then fit it to the format specified by your organisation. You may want to keep two different sorts of diaries—a desk or computer diary that details your tasks and your whereabouts, and another diary recording your thoughts and feelings about your work. If you intend to do the latter, you need to clarify its purpose. Many people on long-term studies, or those working for PhDs, find keeping a personal diary helpful as it's a guide to their continued development. However, you need to clarify who has ownership of this diary, particularly if you're working as a team. If your personal diary is just for you, then you can say what you like. But if it is going to be used as part of your study, and seen by others, you may wish to consider whether what you write is compromising participant or colleague confidentiality.

TABLE 7.5

Example of more detailed and reflexive diary

	Week beginning 27 August
Monday 27th	*Called seven schools to confirm appointments. Three of them I'd called before and one of the secretaries was really difficult with me. I was really angry as it wasn't up to her to decide whether the research happens, but managed to stay calm. Have arranged to do school visits and interview some of the children over the next month, which I'm really relieved about since we're falling behind on our recruitment and it's stressing me out.*
Thursday 30th	*Spent last two days interviewing in schools. The children were happy to join in, and the teachers seemed happy to have me. One of the teachers confided that she thinks the current after-school club is working really well, and for some of the children with behavioural problems it has really made a difference. Interviewed key staff about their views about accessing education and got loads of really useful feedback about their ideas.*
Friday 31st	*Education and Exclusion Conference—presentation. I was really nervous about giving my paper, particularly as it was the first time I'd talked about interim data. Had a few questions from the audience, and they weren't too bad. Could answer them anyway! Met a lady running a similar project in Leeds, who promised to send me some information about her project. She's working mostly with kids in youth groups so not quite the same area, but helpful nevertheless. Saw Kathy who I'd not seen since university, so that was a great surprise. She's now working on training researchers and asked me if I'd come and do a talk on working with excluded teenagers. Felt it was a really positive day.*

Those of you used to quantitative or experimental research may find it strange to use a research diary where you discuss more than just dates, tasks, and appointments. However, those who have used such diaries find that they can really enrich research, particularly if you're working on a long-term study, or are completing a project for an undergraduate or postgraduate qualification. They can also be useful when one is managing researchers to aid discussions between researchers and managers (see Chapters 3 and 6).

Once you get your study underway

Once your research begins—whether you are using qualitative or quantitative methods (or a combination)—you can take steps to ensure that the "data" collection phase is made easier. Consider entering data/transcribing interviews in "real time". Some researchers focus on collecting all their "data" before entering or transcribing it. For smaller studies this may not be a problem, but even small studies build up information that can quickly become unwieldy. Therefore, as you collect your data, enter it into your database and clean it as part of this process. Get interviews transcribed as soon after the interview as possible. Build time into your research schedule to allow for data entry/ transcription, and cleaning. Keep records on cases that have been entered and cleaned so you can keep up to date with your progress.

> *Never forget to save and backup your work. Keep extra copies on disk as well as on your computer and print records too. I speak from bitter experience after losing a whole load of project data. It nearly lost me my job. Save as you go along: at the end of a paragraph for qualitative work, the end of a line of data for quantitative. Then save and backup your databases, files or documents. That way, even if you do lose some work, it won't be everything the project is depending on.* (Akram, statistician)

Remember, in research it's likely that you'll have a number of databases or files: one for participant records and research progress (see earlier in this chapter), and one (or more) databases/files for your research outcomes (for example, interview transcripts, field notes, or questionnaire answers). Sometimes you may create different databases with information about the same participants (for example, one database for their questionnaire answers from a health survey, a second one for their health notes from their GP records). In this case you can link the files, so ensure you use the correct unique identifier (participant number) to allow you to do this (otherwise you'll link the files but mismatch the person's answers and records).

> *Don't think of statisticians as optional extras. I used to consult with a statistician if I had to, and only then to talk about stats. But I've found that involving statisticians from the planning and design stage of the research can help direct the data we complete and enhance the quality of the study.* (Rufus, lecturer)

Keeping clean

Many researchers are careful to complete a literature review, pilot and check their questionnaire/interview schedule, etc. They may also be scrupulous in setting up a database and getting help from others to check it. However, many people feel that if they put data in carefully, it will be okay. Even if we're really careful, mistakes can occur—and mistakes in your data can affect the quality of the research you are producing and the accuracy of your findings. Ways of keeping quantitative data clean and of checking qualitative data are listed in Tables 7.6 and 7.7.

TABLE 7.6

Ways of keeping quantitative data clean

- ❏ Be as careful and accurate as possible when entering data into a database.
- ❏ If possible, get a colleague to work with you (e.g. read out answers from questionnaires to put into a database, or double-enter the data). Some statistical packages permit you to include a warning message or tone for double data entry. That way, if someone enters data that contradicts the previous answer you'll be notified and can check that the correct data is coded.
- ❏ Take breaks. Fatigue causes mistakes. It isn't an effective way of entering data if you spend hours putting it in, but most of it has to be changed.
- ❏ Double-check your questionnaire against the data you have entered. You can either do this with every questionnaire, or by picking a random sample and checking how accurately the data in the database matches the answers on the questionnaire.
- ❏ Run frequencies on all of your questions. Are there any cases missing? Are there numbers there that don't seem right? (For example, on a questionnaire when participants can only give answers in the range of 1–5, are there any numbers outside that group in your database?) Finding these errors from printing frequencies means you can go back and alter them.
- ❏ Create codes for missing data. This allows you to locate errors quickly. Therefore if participants refused to answer or couldn't answer a question, or answered only part of the study, you can build in codes to account for this. Remember to make them distinct, so they cannot be confused with numbers elsewhere in the database.
- ❏ For questionnaires that have sections that should add up, ensure the answers tally.
- ❏ When answers are missing/don't add up, it can take time to locate incorrect answers. Therefore it's better to check your database regularly to ensure that when errors arise it doesn't take too much work to find them.
- ❏ Make a note each time you clean your data, and where you've got up to in participants' responses. That way, when you find errors, but you know that entries from participant 1 to whatever are clean and correct, you've a better idea of where to locate your problem.

See also Fielding (2001), Robson (1993, pp. 314–317), and a checklist for "respecting your data" at http://www.uiowa.edu/~soc/datarespect/data training_frm.html

TABLE 7.7

Ways of checking qualitative data

❑ Listen to your tape through before you start transcribing. Make notes of main themes and points if you think it will help remind you.

❑ Develop your style of transcribing. Some people listen to a short segment, go back and transcribe. Others transcribe straight from the tape. Try to use the best quality taping equipment your project can afford, as it greatly improves the clarity of tapes and therefore aids transcribing.

❑ Once you've got a tape transcribed, read through the transcript while listening to the tape to check accuracy. Note any errors and correct them.

❑ Ensure you've also checked that you have accurately reflected pauses, interruptions, laughter, sarcasm, emphasised words, etc.

❑ If you cannot hear, you may need help from someone else to listen (someone you can trust to protect the anonymity of participants).

❑ It is helpful to make notes during interviews so that if a tape is inaudible you'll have clues that might help you work out what's being said.

❑ If you're not sure where to put emphasis or whether to transcribe the interview, again, ask a colleague for their views.

❑ Where someone else is transcribing, double-check their accuracy, and ensure that confidentiality is respected.

❑ If you didn't hear an answer, or you didn't make sense of it, you should indicate this in your transcript (how much of the tape is inaudible, and the reason why—the participant or interviewer is mumbling, or there is a problem with the tape, etc.).

See also Denscombe (1998, p. 138); Mason (1996)

What information should I collect routinely?

If you are used to getting participants who volunteer for your study, or reading papers that describe who completed a study (as opposed to who was excluded), you may not be used to the idea of collecting other information about participants. Imagine for a moment that you are completing a survey of patients who are being admitted to a hospital ward. You want to study people admitted for a certain form of treatment. You would note who agreed to take part in your research, and who refused. But you may also have other exclusion criteria (for example, patients on the ward being admitted for other treatments/procedures, or patients over or under a certain age)—you would also need to note this. Therefore, if you are selecting people for research, you may want to collect routine data on everyone approached (e.g. age, gender, date of birth, postcode, address, ethnicity) (see Chapter 5 for more on this). If you plan to collect routine data, you will need ethical approval for this (see Chapters 3 and 5).

Information gathered from routine collection can give a clearer portrait of your participants and account for any biases/discrepancies in the number of people in the study (for example, more men, more white people, or more younger people took part). It doesn't automatically mean there's a problem with your study, but in recording and reporting this information you can suggest the reasons for your participant demographics. Again, the data collection issue should be discussed in the planning phase (see the section on participant details above).

In some cases you cannot collect this information. For example, if you ask for volunteers from a college group by using a poster as advertising, you can't then record the details of all other students who didn't take part—all you can do is describe whether your participants are representative of students generally. You can also find out why participants did volunteer, as this may mark them out as being more or less representative of the population they come from.

Data protection

In 1998 in the UK the Data Protection Act was passed in order to ensure good and ethical practice in the storage and maintenance of the control and contents of any records held on computer or paper (this can include notes, questionnaire and interview data, photographs, and audio or video recordings). If you're based outside the UK, you may wish to identify the data protection laws for your country or state. If you are based within an organisation or university, your workplace may already have guidelines on how it expects you to conform with the data protection act and what information requires registration, so it is worth familiarising yourself with these local instructions, as well as the act itself. The act is mainly concerned with preventing data from being misused; obtained under false pretences; collected, entered, or reported inaccurately; or not being kept securely. This means you should store any information about participants (and project staff) in a safe place, password-protect your computer, store files separately, and ensure the privacy and accuracy of your data. The act is concerned that only those directly related to research have access to the data, store it securely, and use it appropriately—meaning they have consent from participants to do so, have informed the ethics committee of any changes to the storage or collection of data, and do not keep information for longer than is necessary. This applies throughout the stages of research, not just during data collection. When it is appropriate to destroy data, this should be witnessed, and done appropriately (for example, sensitive forms should be shredded). If you have any questions about data protection, you can contact:

The Office of the Data Protection Commissioner
Wycliffe House
Water Lane
Wilmslow
Cheshire, SK9 5AF
Telephone: 01625 535777

See also http://www.informationcommissioner.gov.uk

Readers from non-UK countries should consult their local/national data protection laws.

Recycling and waste

Research can be really wasteful. Table 7.8 identifies some key areas where you can save resources, as well as helping others.

Changes: flexibility in research

Inevitably there will be changes in any study you work on. It may be that the research design needs modifying, perhaps a staff member leaves, or maybe the participants in the research are difficult to recruit. It is important to approach research with the expectation that it will change (particularly if it's a long-term study); rather than this being a problem, it is a feature of research. The trick is to be flexible. If, during the early stages of a study (see Chapters 2 and 3), you have planned for alterations, and built-in time for unforeseen issues within your project, your study should be easier to complete.

This chapter has outlined basic skills for managing, creating and cleaning data, but does not teach qualitative or quantitative analysis because there are already a number of excellent texts for this (see Chapter 1 for more details).

So what about when all the planning's done, participants have been seen, and data entered, stored and analysed? What next? The last chapter covers what to do when you want to write up or present your research.

the traditional linear process model of hypothesis formulation and then hypothesis testing. This, however, should not lead you to the denial of the importance of preset hypotheses. Just like any project that needs a plan, the key questions and hypotheses set useful guidelines for conducting data analysis.

"A perfectly designed, carefully executed, and brilliantly analyzed study will be altogether worthless unless you are able to communicate your findings to others" (Babbie, 1995, p.A14). For the purpose of effective communication, guidelines for reporting analyses include (ibid.): sufficient detail to permit replication of the analysis on the part of the reader of the report; putting tables, charts and figures near the text discussing them; and being explicit and specific in drawing conclusions. Specific writing skills are numerous; and a common advice is that there is no single correct way to write. Different terms may be used to express the same idea, though there may be some subtle differences in nuance. For instance, you may talk about issues, problems, or questions. You may discuss your aim or intent in terms of purposes, goals, or objectives. You can present your assumptions and/or hypotheses. You can justify your research by giving a rationale or clarifying its meaning or importance. And you can have a conceptual framework, theoretical framework, or research framework. Generally speaking, research "questions" need be more articulate than "issues" and "problems." Research "intent" or "purposes" are used at the most general level while "objectives" should be very specific and measurable. "Assumptions" can be general statements, yet "hypotheses" should be subject to empirical testing. The rationale may include the meaning and importance of the research, but you are expected to clearly state the reasons and needs for conducting the research. And finally, "conceptual framework" is a more modest term than "theoretical framework," while "research framework" may include both, or emphasize more on methodology.

It should be noted that the advancement of computer technology has greatly changed the way people write. Being used to various powerful word processing programs, one can hardly imagine continuing to write using traditional paper-and-pen method. Not everybody, however, knows how to make full use of the computer software. One must constantly explore the many advantages of the computer-assisted writing techniques as computer technology develops explosively. The invention of the windows and similar programs has opened up many opportunities to save time and increase research productivity. Not only can you now edit several chapters and documents at the same time, including copying and moving contents between the files, but also you can directly import

TABLE 7.8

Key recycling areas

Resource	Recycling
Paper	Reuse unwanted paper as scrap, or collect for recycling. Don't forget to check it first, though. Any printing containing participant details or personal information should be shredded.
Computers	You can either get parts from old computers recycled, or share old computers with developing countries/projects (see http://www.computer-aid.org; you can apply for a computer through this site too).
Envelopes and packaging	For routine or general post you can re-use some envelopes/ packaging. Remember to use clean envelopes for important business and participant letters.
Books and articles	If you have books or papers that are interesting but outdated, some charities can use them for training in developing countries (http://www.bookaid.org/cms.cgi/site/index.htm).
Printer cartridges	Many companies offer a recycling service: you can post back used cartridges (see also Oxfam's site—they collect and recycle toner cartridges; http://www.oxfam.org.uk/what-you-can-do/recycle/index.htm).
Stamps	Some charities reuse stamps, so if you get lots of correspondence it's worth saving your stamps and passing them on (for example, the Royal National Institute for the Blind: http://www.rnib.org.uk/xpedio/groups/public/documents/publicwebsite/public_frstamps.hesp).
Lighting and heating	If you can, use energy-efficient heating/lighting in your offices. Turn off lights, etc. after use (see http://www.est.org.uk/myhome for more ideas).

End results and reporting findings 8

This book has covered many of the issues that affect research. A final area worthy of discussing is: what do you do with all that data once you have it? As soon as you embark on any study you are already committed to producing something with your work. This may be a dissertation or a student project, an internal report for your organisation, a local community evaluation, or perhaps a national or international project resulting in reports and/or papers in peer-reviewed journals. Frequently in the rush to produce outcomes, evidence, or findings, we forget to consider exactly how we are going to report these findings—or leave this task to the last minute. Chapters 2 and 3 outlined the importance of thinking about research in a holistic format, and it is worth considering your end outcomes as part of this (which is why those chapters emphasised the importance of writing up your research pretty much from the outset). This chapter outlines the following:

- Why you should do something with your work
- Considering the impact your work will have
- What are you producing?
- Who are your outcomes aimed at?
- Is more than one report necessary?
- Places to disseminate information
- Different formats for sharing research outcomes including papers/ reports, videos, information packs/sheets, etc.
- Writing styles and tips for writing—papers/reports/journal articles
- Conference presentations—how to give papers (including symposia), posters, and workshops
- Giving and receiving feedback
- Peer review and how it works
- Dealing with the media

- Dissemination—who pays?
- Who is responsible for research dissemination?

Some researchers never publish their work. This may be because the study they are working on isn't suitable for publication. Other work is not published due to any number of factors ranging from work being badly written to missing the window of opportunity by letting work become outdated. The aim of this chapter is to help you think about when and where to publish/publicise your work, and how to go about it. The chapter will also invite you to consider the impact of any publicity on participants and researchers, so that your work is not harmful to others.

Why you should do something with your work

I believe that when you have been funded to complete research, and/ or have taken up the time of participants (and others) for a study, you need to produce something from it. This may be anything from a short report to an academic paper, and it should always reach the people who need to know about it. Research is wasted if it ends up on a shelf somewhere, or is written in a way that doesn't make people want to read or hear your message. However, you also need to be realistic about what you want to publish, and where. A final-year project won't require a press release or wide-scale dissemination, and a local community study shouldn't be written up as an internal memo without other dissemination. This chapter talks you through the different options available for writing up and disseminating your findings, so that your work is never wasted.

Considering the impact your work will have

Before writing up and/or publicising your research, be aware of what may happen when the information becomes public. When my colleagues and I completed the research on women and prostitution, we prepared a report, which was due to have a public launch with members of the community, stakeholders (police, social services, probation, and working women), and the press present. However, as the research was being finalised we learned that a charity was about to open a refuge nearby for young people at risk from prostitution. As our report was largely qualitative, and in places could be seen as controversial, we felt that it might attract attention and possibly jeopardise the refuge. We therefore opted for a low-key launch, and disseminated only the executive summary. The main report was circulated to key stakeholders at a later stage (Boynton, 2002).

If your research has findings that are likely to upset or cause problems for participants or the wider community, you need to address this from the outset of the research, or as soon as any problems emerge. If the publication of research could cause problems, or breach issues of confidentiality and anonymity, you need to consider hiding participant identities, using pseudonyms, and presenting the research in a way that doesn't attract unnecessary attention (see Chapter 5). Don't assume that a small-scale report or a paper in a journal may not reach the attention of others. Think about the impact your research will have on your participants and those associated with them (friends, family, colleagues, care providers, etc.), the local community or population that the participants represent, and your reputation.

What are you producing?

This chapter will cover different ways of presenting research, ranging from traditional formats (peer-reviewed papers or conference presentations) to other mediums of expression. When you propose your original research idea, you can begin thinking about how you are going to present it. Many funding bodies will specify what they want, but you should consider who needs to hear about your work and how best to reach them. Be aware of the requirements of the organisation funding your work. Some charities or funding bodies prefer a full report, others an executive summary, and still others will accept a publication in a peer-reviewed journal. Many require interim reports as well as an end paper, and the way research should be presented is often specified. Again, check this from the outset and set up any documents in the appropriate format to save having to convert written work at a later date.

Who are your outcomes aimed at?

Your audience will partly determine how you produce your work. If you are writing for a peer-reviewed journal, you need to write in an academic style while fulfilling the criteria for the journal (see later in this chapter). If you are summarising findings for younger people, you may want to write in a way that isn't patronising, but is appropriate to read. Older people or those with visual difficulties may require a report with larger print. If you are dealing with an audience with visual or hearing problems you may need to produce reports using Braille or on audiotape, and if participants speak different languages, translations of copies will need to be produced. Again, using the guide for producing participant information (Chapter 5) can help you decide on how your research needs to be reported, and the formats it should take. If you are aware of who your target audience is, you can produce work that suits it. Remember, translations or tapes can add to the cost of a study. This is not a reason to exclude them, but they should be included in a study budget.

Is more than one report necessary?

One of my main criticisms of how research is taught is that it's over-simplified. We're taught to think of one method versus another, rather than the best method to suit a study or multi-method approaches. By the same token, we tend to think of the final result of our research as being one thing—a paper, a book, or a presentation. While this may work for certain types of research (e.g. an undergraduate dissertation), for many studies you need to consider who needs to hear about your research, and how to reach them. In our research on intermediate care for older people, we produced several publications aimed at different audiences affected by our research. The first piece of work we produced was a report (Boston, Boynton, & Hood, 1999) that was sent to the funding body and key stakeholders who were involved in providing care for older people. Following this we presented the results to the staff on the GP bed unit we were evaluating. This face-to-face session permitted us to discuss our findings, talk about the way the research was perceived by the staff and patients, and consider the impact on the unit following the publication of the research. We produced a leaflet for the patients attending the unit to explain that we had completed an evaluation, and what we had found— copies were available on the ward for patients and carers. Finally we had two papers accepted for peer-reviewed journals (Boston, Boynton, & Hood, 2001a, 2001b). While you are writing up your research (as part of an ongoing process; see Chapters 2 and 3), it is also worth considering who needs to know about your outcomes, and begin creating appropriate publications (for example, a report alongside a flyer).

Places to disseminate information

Chapter 5 outlined how you can publicise a study in order to get participants, and you can use a similar format when it comes to disseminating the results of your work. It is good research etiquette to return to those who assisted with your research to inform them of your findings, and thank them again for their help (for example, staff at a play centre where you're completing an observational study of children's sharing behaviours). Frequently it is the junior researcher that has the most to do with those who are helping with a study, but since they often leave before the research is written up, those helping the researcher never hear any more about it—which can lead to them feeling rejected and made use of. It is the task of those managing studies to note who key individuals/groups are, and ensure they receive information about the research (the costs for this should be built into your budget).

You can produce reports, short papers, or flyers, and make them available to participants and others. You may want to send participants copies of your report, but only do so if appropriate—meaning that you've budgeted for this, your participants will appreciate and be able to follow your publication, and you were given ethical clearance to collect participant names and addresses.

Be realistic: the more participants or other people you'll need to send information to, the shorter your reports/summaries need to be. Produce short documents to accompany larger reports, as most people want to hear the key findings and what will happen with the results, rather than the whole study. Once you've created a short summary, you may want to use local or national media (newspapers, television, or radio) to share your findings, or perhaps make them available through your website. It is useful to mirror the way you recruited participants here—if you contacted them through local services, provide those services with a poster or short summary of the research for people to read, or perhaps if you recruited people through a radio show, you could go back to that programme with an update on your findings (see Chapter 5 for more on this). When it comes to dissemination, you should send information to anyone who could benefit from hearing about your work, and cover all bases.

It's hard to keep things under control sometimes when you're excited about your research. It's easy to feel you've thought up the best-ever study in the world if things have worked out well for you, and your research has gone smoothly. But it may not be worthy of the attention you'd like. Your work should get attention because it has the potential to help others, or add to our understanding of an issue, not just because you'd like some publicity. (Drew, professor)

Different formats for sharing research

As mentioned above, the common formats for producing research are reports (often with two versions, a longer report and a shorter executive summary—two or three pages that outline the research method, main outcomes, and recommendations). Posters, flyers, summary sheets, or papers for peer-reviewed journals are other common research by-products. However, you can afford to think more creatively when it comes to describing your research. In 1998 the report of the Director of Public Health in Wales (Lechyd Morgannwg Health) produced what was described as a report "that you actually wanted to read, that showed you how ill health really affected people's lives, that told it as it was—warts and all, that you would keep, use, share and enjoy". The book was called *Bethan's story/Stori Bethan*, was written in English and Welsh, and had ten chapters focusing on issues affecting teenage Bethan and her family (for example, Bethan gets pregnant, her great-gran Flo has problems associated with old age). Each chapter outlined the story of someone in Bethan's family and then linked it to general health issues relevant to Wales. If you aren't confined by regulations set out by funding bodies or your organisation, the possibilities for sharing research are endless. People have successfully shared their results through drama (plays or films), dance, poetry, stories, painting, photography, drawing, and song (see Norris, 1997).

Exercise: Thinking creatively about findings

Pick a journal article that interests you and consider how you would present it if you were asked to do so in the following ways:

- a film or play
- a dance
- an art exhibition
- a poem
- an interactive CD.

Consider your reactions to each format. How does it make you feel? Does the suggestion make you laugh, feel uneasy, believe it's impossible, think it's not scientific, or even think it has nothing to do with research? Make a note of your feelings and discuss them with colleagues. Perhaps you are right and a poem may not be the best way of sharing research, but maybe your view about how research should be disseminated is limiting you. Think about the paper you have chosen and who it is aimed at (apart from other academics/researchers). How do you think participants might like to hear about the findings? Do you think they'd prefer to read a paper, or would a video be more interesting and accessible to them?

On a piece of paper, draw three columns. Write the five items from the list above in the first column, in the second write "pros", and in the third write "cons". By looking at each medium in relation to a study, and its audience, you can train yourself to think around different ways of sharing research and select a format that would suit your audience—and make your work as interesting as possible.

Even if you don't present all your results in an artistic format, it doesn't mean you can't borrow from the creative or visual arts to illustrate your work. For example, you may use photographs to accompany a talk, or perhaps re-enact some interviews to show people more about your research. It is particularly important to consider wider ways of dissemination if we want to increase participant involvement, make research more user-friendly, and draw on the skills of consumers, who may want to report research in traditional formats, or may have more creative ways of thinking about work.

A few years ago I went to a Consumers in NHS research conference, where over lunch there was a "soapbox session" where delegates could speak for five minutes on a topic of their choice. Those from academic backgrounds got up with an overhead projector and did a mini-presentation, using slides, statistics, and figures. Those who hadn't been indoctrinated in this format produced far more interesting talks. One pair re-enacted a telephone conversation between a lay researcher and project manager to show where researchers can make assumptions about consumer involvement (for example, having meetings at awkward times). Another woman used a painting to talk about living with a stroke, while a third read a short letter from a child carer. This is not to say the academic-style presentations weren't good, only that they are just one way of presenting our findings.

Ultimately we want to transmit information in a way that is meaningful and can lead to an increase in knowledge or a change in policy or behaviour. Therefore think about who you are aiming the research at, and think how they may want to hear about your work (ask a selection of potential audience members if you wish). You should always aim to get research published in a peer-review setting if appropriate, but don't forget that there are numerous other ways you can tell people about your work. Alternatively, you may see parallels between your research and the arts, in which case you can share this information by reviewing materials that others may use as a teaching resource (for example, a film about mental illness). You can find out more on how to do this at University College London's Medical Humanities Resource Database: http://www.mhrd.ucl.ac.uk.

Writing styles and presentation tips

Research papers
Research papers tend to follow a similar format, requiring an abstract, introduction, method, results, discussion and conclusion, and usually range in length from 2000 to 5000 words. However, not all papers lend themselves to this format, and some may be written with the results and discussion combined, or have recommendations instead of conclusions. Some journals allow for a more flexible approach, with sections for researchers to write their observations and experiences, or about the process of research. These tend to be shorter papers than those based on research. Some journals also carry letters pages where you can respond to previous articles or make suggestions, and sections for book or research reviews (if you want to write book reviews contact the reviews editor at the journal that interests you. They can put you on their mailing list and send you books appropriate to your specialty for review. It's a great way of getting a free book!) Decide on the format that best suits what you want to say, and select a journal that supports this.

I found that my writing skills were really helped by two things. Firstly, I started writing papers for journals. They weren't always accepted, but the comments I got back from reviewers helped me improve my writing. I also contributed book reviews and wrote letters to journals. Again, they weren't all published, but it got me used to writing to different formulas. Secondly, I began reviewing for a number of journals. Seeing how other people write and present their work flagged up what good writing looked like, and how not to do it. Many journals are crying out for reviewers with knowledge in different fields, so my advice is contact the editors of journals you like and offer your services. Sometimes you can do this via their website. It'll improve your writing no end. (Ahmed, senior lecturer)

You can determine the format of your paper by the method you have chosen, and the journal you are aiming for. If you want to get your paper published, you need firstly to complete a search. Although there is always going to be pressure to aim for the "higher ranked" journals, you should also consider the best journal to place your work. A study around nursing and patient care may be better read and appreciated in a nursing journal than a social science one. Once you've worked out your audience and a selection of possible journals, read them through to see whether your work will fit their format. Often there are several journals dealing with the same issue from different perspectives. For example, one journal dealing with organisational issues may only accept papers based on research, while another may be keener on hearing from researchers completing policy-based reviews. Decide on the journal that suits your research and has an audience you wish to target. Then follow the guidelines for contributors (these are usually on the back pages of a journal). These guidelines clearly state what is required from you—ranging from font sizes and format of references to length of articles. The most common reason for having a paper rejected is that these guidelines have not been followed (Stern, 1997). Set up your document according to the guidelines specified by the journal you're aiming for, but before you send it out, make sure you check it thoroughly for spelling and grammar, and get colleagues to read it through and check it for any inaccuracies or areas that are unclear. Setting your paper up according to a journal's format doesn't guarantee its acceptance, but it will make it more likely to be read. You can find out more about the process of peer review later in this chapter.

the results of data analysis into the texts. This saves a lot of typing, checking, and also chance of making mistakes. The specific steps for importing data analysis results into your chapters include: (1) save the output of a computational (mostly statistical) program in an ASCII or DOS file, and download it to your PC in that format if the analysis was carried out on a mainframe; (2) run your word processor and read the output file for editing; (3) the contents of the output file may appear in a mess and you need to reformat them by switching to another font and make it smaller (e.g., 9 dpi courier); (4) open the document that contains your research report in another window, and move the cursor to where you want certain analysis results to appear; (5) switch back to the previous window and cut the part of the analysis output that you need; (6) switch back again to your research report file, and paste what you took from the output file; and (7) reformat this imported part into a table, chart, or something else by adding an appropriate title, deleting unnecessary spaces and adding a "hard return" at the end of each line, reranking the numbers if needed, adding some lines, notes, etc.

You may repeat these steps from finishing one part to another. And you can import the results from the output file to more than one text files, especially if you saved the chapters of your research report into different files. The word processing software nowadays, such as WordPerfect or Microsoft Word, usually has the capacity allowing a number of windows to be open at the same time. If you are using Windows or similar user interface you do not even have to close you statistical program (e.g. SPSS) while you are compiling your report in a word processor. This gives the researcher great convenience and makes data analysis and report generation a truly integral process. You may not only switch between different chapters and documents but also jump into an analysis and bring the results right back into your text any time you want. This could happen while you are writing your report in New York and running your data analysis in Los Angeles or even in Hong Kong, if you know how to remote login via Telnet and transfer data through FTP. This is amazing indeed, and as a current researcher you cannot afford not to make use of the rapidly developing computer and information technology.

Eventually, however, it is the human brain rather than the computer that produces such a writing product as a research report. Many traditional writing techniques, therefore, seem never to be outdated. When writing the first draft, for example, a common experience is to jot down your thoughts and notes of reading freely. Just like a computer that needs hard and floppy disks in addition

TABLE 8.1

Structure of a report/dissertation/project

(Table created with J. Nicholls, CHIME, UCL)

Section of report	What it should contain
Title	The ideal title length is about 12–15 words (see Parrott, 1999, p. 57). The title should interest and engage the reader, use active words, and accurately reflect the study.
Acknowledgements	Not all reports require this section: check with your course guidelines. However, if acknowledgements are permitted you should list who has helped you with your research (for example in supervision of your work, or assistance with data collection or analysis).
Contents page	States the sections of the report (as outlined in this table), and the pages where these sections may be found. Ensure the sections and page numbers match. You may need to include a separate contents page for tables / diagrams.
Abstract	This is a summary containing a brief account of the content, purpose and theoretical background of the study. The ideal length for this section is between 100 and 150 words. Think of the abstract as a way of "selling" your report, particularly as most research archives contain abstracts so others can decide whether to read them (see also Parrott, 1999, pp. 59–60).
Introduction	You now "set the scene" for your reader, by describing relevant past research. Begin with a clear indication about the question that your research is attempting to answer. Describe the area in a broad way and then become more specific. You need to state your aims and objectives at the end of this section, and make sure these are clear and specific (even if you are using action research or ethnography, you should still clearly outline the area that you plan to investigate). Don't overload these—you should have one clear aim, and a few easily achieved objectives. Illustrate how you considered possible methodological approaches, and justify your selected one.

Method (participants, design, materials, procedure)	This is where you tell the reader what you did and how you did it. You should provide enough detail so that another person reading this section could easily replicate your study should they wish to.
Results	You state or explain what you found out from your research in this section—either in tables reporting results from analysis, or from the outcomes of qualitative work. If you are completing a quantitative study, there should be no discussion of results here—just an account of your findings. If you have completed a qualitative study you may wish to combine the results/discussion sections for a more flexible approach.
Discussion	In this section you draw together all the areas mentioned so far in the report, and evaluate and interpret your findings in the light of what occurred in your study. Explain what the possible contributions from your study are: has it helped to answer the original question/hypothesis, and what conclusions or theories can be drawn from the work (American Psychological Association, 1994)?
Conclusion	You revisit and briefly list the main outcomes of your research. You may also wish to make policy or research recommendations here.
References	All works cited in your text should be included here, using an approved referencing format (e.g. Harvard or Vancouver).
Appendices	Relevant information referred to in the text may be included here (for example, a copy of the questionnaire used in your study).

Dissertations and theses

Dissertations usually follow the same format as papers, but tend to be far longer. As with journals, your institution will have specific guidelines on how to present your dissertation and limits on words and content. These should be followed to the letter. Table 8.1 details the contents of a report; Table 8.2 lists writing resources.

TABLE 8.2
Resources for writing (collated by Trish Greenhalgh and Jill Russell, Open Learning Unit, University College London)

- Making academic writing more readable: http://www.aston.ac.uk/lis/studentinfo/studyskills
- Effective use of English and academic writing: http://www3.open.ac.uk/learners-guide/learning-skills/english/pages/index.asp
- Using English for academic writing: http://www.uefap.co.uk/writing

Theses are slightly different, as they cover research but are set out in chapters rather than sections (method, results, etc.). You should follow your institutional guidelines for format. Your supervisor will advise you on the content and layout of your thesis, and it is important that you check your work thoroughly for spelling and grammatical errors, and get friends or colleagues to read drafts to check that the work is logical and interesting (Phillips & Pugh, 2000).

> *The trick I was taught during my PhD was to set out files for each chapter early on. I wrote bits in different chapters as they came along. I got the literature review out of the way early on, but kept coming back to it, adding and changing. I also got a folder and set out each chapter in it. That way I could watch my thesis building over time.* (Ceris, post-doctorate researcher)

Conference presentations

Research can be presented at conferences while it is in progress (a good way to get support and feedback on your ideas) or once your work is completed. If you are part of a project team, you should discuss who will present the work (see Chapter 2). Staff should take turns at sharing presentations in order to have experience of conferences and networking. Junior researchers can present work, and should be encouraged to do so as part of their career development. However, this should be discussed with the grant holder or supervisor first, to ensure there is funding to permit them to go to a conference, and there is something to present. You can find out about forthcoming conferences through adverts in publications relating to your subject, in journals, or at the website http://www.papersinvited.com (you can also advertise your conferences there). If you are unsure how to present at conferences, or even if you're an experienced speaker, ask for training. Many colleges, charities, and organisations offer training in presentation skills that is worth taking.

Posters

Many conferences have a space for research posters. These may be used to describe research in progress, or to summarise completed studies. Posters are normally left up for the duration of a conference, but there will also be a set time during the conference where posters are viewed. At this time the presenter stands with their poster, and talks to passing delegates about their work. Not everyone likes giving posters, and some don't see them as important as oral presentations, but I think posters are a great way of selling your work—and networking. After all, you can chat about your work to people at your leisure, rather than having to give a formal presentation. That said, if your poster isn't set out correctly, you might end up wasting time, and putting people off rather than attracting them.

If your work is accepted for a poster presentation, the conference organisers will tell you the size specifications for the poster (this will be the size of poster board you'll be given). You should keep your work to these sizes, since there may not be room for an outsize poster. If you have the money for it in your budget, you could get a professional poster company to make your poster for you (if you send them your work on disk they'll format it for you). This is particularly worthwhile if you're going to use the same poster at a number of conferences. Many universities and research organisations have a media department that can produce posters for you, and offer you advice on how to create an effective poster. Remember that if you are having to take your poster to a conference you need to be able to transport it, so make it suitable for rolling or flat-packing.

Your poster should look exciting and interesting, the print should be a good size, and you shouldn't overload it with text. Think of your poster as an eye-catching advert. Use a snappy title, and keep it bold, so that viewers will see it and want to come and talk to you. A poster is not a board where you can place a copy of a paper (although I've seen it done a lot). Too much text is off-putting, and people won't read it. Pictures, illustrations, and short text are much more inviting (see Griffiths, 2003).

> *I always write a short summary, two sides of A4, that gives the title as shown on the poster, my name, and contact address and email. I then summarise the research, give details, and references to any papers that may be relevant. Sometimes I take copies of published papers with me if relevant, as I can hand those out to interested people. The bonus of having a summary is you can leave them by the poster so people can pick them up throughout the conference, although remember to be assertive. If I see some-one walking towards my poster I say "hi", introduce myself and ask them if they're interested in my research. Sometimes people need a little persuasion to talk about your work, but this approach rarely fails.* (Adele, lecturer)

You may find the following guide helpful (adapted from Wilson & Hutchinson, 1997, p. 79).

Poster checklist

1. Less is better. Don't try to say too much
2. Bigger is better. Don't crowd your exhibit
3. Put the most important message at eye level
4. Write to one person (often a stranger) using active verbs
5. Use short sentences, short paragraphs, and short words
6. Write headlines with brief, colourful nouns and vigorous active verbs
7. Five times as many viewers read headlines as read text copy
8. Headlines with 10 or fewer words get more readers than those with more
9. Headlines that promise the reader a benefit, contain news, or offer helpful information attract above-average readership
10. Use the largest type possible. Headlines must be read from across the room. Text must be seen from three to five feet away
11. Avoid using all capital letters to present text
12. Keep columns three to four inches wide. Longer lines are harder to read
13. Darker (blue or green) type on lighter (white or cream) background is easier to read than white type on a dark background

14. Use colour for emphasis, but limit colours to one or two
15. Help your readers with arrows, bullets, or other marks
16. Set a key paragraph in boldface type for attention
17. Use subheads every two to three inches
18. Photos are better than drawings
19. Write a caption for every graph or illustration. People read text under illustrations
20. If you present unrelated ideas, number them and put them in a list.

Resources for poster design and presentation
The following websites provide poster design templates (collated by Jeanette Murphy, CHIME, UCL).

- Washington NASA Space Grant Consortium (gives tips from getting started to layout): http://www.waspacegrant.org/posterdesign.html
- Cincinnati Children's Hospital (guide on layout and delivering a poster): search for "posters" at http://www.cincinnati childrens.org
- A list of templates for posters can be downloaded at: http://www.owlnet.rice.edu/~cainproj/templates.html

Conference papers and symposia
Your other option at a conference is to give an oral presentation. These normally range from 10 to 20 minutes, with time for questions. Your role is to explain your research in an interesting way. Many people chose to use overheads or PowerPoint slides, or similar visual aids to accompany their talk. The trick with overheads is to keep them to an absolute minimum, and keep them related to your talk. Being overloaded with slides hampers many presentations. In a 15-minute presentation you should aim for having no more than five to ten slides. Any more will distract the audience, and take time for you to go through. If you are using an overhead projector, tear the acetates before presenting, as there's nothing more off-putting (or time-consuming) than someone tearing their way through their talk. As with posters, keep your slides clear, with a good-sized font that can be read from the back of the room, and with a minimum of fonts and colours. You can also prepare a summary sheet or paper to accompany your talk, which you can refer to in your presentation and give to those who require further information. There are many useful guides on giving presentations, which are well worth reading, as they can give you tips on what to include in your talk, as well as handling nerves and questions (Levy, 1997; Mandel, 1987).

Part of any presentation is working the room, and you may find that the following pointers can improve any paper or talk you give (adapted from Midmer, 2003, p. 121):

- Keep lectures [talks] short
- If a lot of content has to be worked through, encourage questions at any time
- Remember less can be more: provide content in handouts, not [talks]
- Use different backgrounds and colours on slides to keep interest high
- Use images to add punch and emphasis, but beware of making it "too cute"
- Try building progressive slides or adding animation
- Scan in different backgrounds, such as nature scenes or photographs, to personalise slides
- Collect appropriate cartoons and intersperse with text. Noisy, laughing groups often work more effectively than sombre, quiet groups
- With overheads, place a clear transparency over the top and use coloured markers to highlight points when presenting. This will help focus attention and help retain knowledge
- Use a flip chart and make a note of key discussion items during [talks] and case presentations
- Writing keeps the presenter moving—another way to keep interest high.

The main thing people worry about in terms of oral presentations is speaking in public. The very thought makes many people feel nervous or anxious. Remember, it is not a test, and you do not have to give a talk from memory. If you are very nervous, you can tell your audience this—they'll be on your side. People get nervous because they think they'll make a mistake, blush or look embarrassed, not be able to answer questions, or receive a hostile response from the audience (more on how to deal with criticism later). You can limit these fears by practising your talk, matching your talk to an appropriate audience, and anticipating difficult questions.

Levy (1997, p. 149) suggests you also try the following before giving a paper.

1. Decide in general terms what you are going to say
2. Write out a rough script, then reduce it to what is essential, and what is desirable if you have time

3. Choose which visual aids you are going to use: flip chart, writing board, overhead projector, slides, video, PowerPoint
4. Prepare your visual aids
5. Choose the venue (if this is down to you).

At least one week before, you should do the following.

1. Rehearse your presentation several times, with the visual aids
2. Time your presentation carefully
3. Decide if there is anything you need to leave out
4. Get some feedback from someone you trust
5. Act on their recommendations and make appropriate changes.

> *I often ask for feedback after a conference. Even if it isn't always positive, it is usually helpful—and can relate to anything from your tone of voice to the colour of your slides. Sometimes the feedback tells you something you'd have never noticed—for example, I had my email listed on my slide, but it was written incorrectly. Luckily someone spotted it and told me so I could change it.* (Magda, conference organiser)

A symposium works in a similar way to an oral paper, in that it's a series of papers arranged under a linking theme. You, or perhaps a colleague, proposes a theme, and introduces and summarises the papers. If you have colleagues working in related areas it is often worth proposing a symposium rather than individual papers. Don't forget, it is worth ensuring as symposium organiser that the papers link, run to time, and are well rehearsed.

Workshops

These tend to run over one to two hours, and are based around a key theme, idea, or piece of research. Although there may be an element of an oral presentation within a workshop (for example, setting the scene at the start), the main aim is to encourage discussion between conference delegates, problem solve, or teach a new skill. The aim of these sessions is to facilitate discussion, so as coordinator you need to be able to help group members to talk, support everyone, and ensure all voices are heard (Elwyn, Greenhalgh, & Macfarlane, 2001). You'll need clear aims and objectives, and a summary at the end of the session. Some workshops work better by breaking up delegates into small groups, bringing them back to a main group at intervals to discuss (this can be highly beneficial if you get a large group).

Propose a workshop if you have something you want to teach, or you want to liaise with colleagues who you feel might be able to help you with an issue. Successful workshops I've participated in are how to learn to use repertory grid techniques, how to improve access to health care for young men, and how to write for journals. These workshops were beneficial because they had a clear goal, were solution-focused, and were hosted by experts who could give practical advice to delegates. If you are attending a conference and workshops are offered, they are well worth attending.

Giving and receiving feedback

When you present work, in a paper, report launch, conference, or elsewhere, you should be prepared to answer questions about your work. This may be in the form of questions after a presentation (for example, at a conference, or from the press or public following a report launch), or by email or telephone (e.g. when someone's read your work and wants to know more). Again, many people find this process stressful, particularly if the questions seem to be hostile or difficult. If you are contacted by email or letter, your response is easier since you can spend time thinking over your reply. Corresponding by email can be particularly useful since you may strike up a new research relationship to add to your network (see Chapters 2 and 3). If you receive a letter or email that seems particularly hostile, or requires a great deal of work from you, you can discard it. If someone dislikes your work, there are appropriate ways to challenge it—abusive letters to you aren't one of them (see Chapter 6 for more on this). If your work is criticised within a journal, you have a right to reply, but do so through the journal rather than directly to those who have written the critique of you.

Dealing with questions following an oral presentation or launch may be more difficult, since you'll be required to think quickly (see Quinn, 1994) and respond to previously unknown points, in front of people whose opinion you may value. If it's a difficult question, and one you feel you cannot answer, then explain that you'd need to go back to the data, but you will take the questioner's details and send them a reply if they wish. If you feel it is a question you don't follow because it has been asked badly, then reply to the questioner "It sounds like you are asking me _____: is that right?" If so, you can go on and answer the question; if not, they can rephrase for you. If you are going to present anything that may seem controversial or upsetting, it's important to point this out before you begin your talk, and give people the chance to leave if they are likely to be offended. If they stay and complain about your talk, you will be in your rights to say you did explain what it would be about. Most questions are not difficult, and it's important to stay relaxed and answer clearly. If someone is hostile towards you, then it is better not to get drawn into a row. But you don't have to accept an insult passively: if you feel brave enough, you may say that they are being rude or unpleasant—again, such bullying needs to be stamped out.

> I saw a guy give a talk once and he wasn't the best speaker ever. He was clearly very nervous, and his talk wasn't very dynamic, but the topic itself was interesting. At the end the chairperson asked if there were questions and a guy got up and his opening line was "That was the worst presentation I've ever seen." I don't remember what his actual question was. It was very interesting what happened in the audience, who really took against the questioner. It made me realise that a hostile questioner will always look stupid, not big like they think they will. (Don, lecturer)

It is not the aim of this chapter to scare you out of presenting. For the most part you'll find presentations should go smoothly if you've rehearsed them, and negative reactions are rare. However, since they are the thing people often fear, anticipating them and considering ways to cope will hopefully make you feel empowered when it's time to give your talk.

The following "strategies of responding to criticism" are adapted from Hupcey (1997), p. 150.

Strategy I: Correction of the original work—Used when the criticism is right/correct, or justified
Method
1. Clarify the issue
2. Evaluate within own work/results
3. If the point is correct, agree with and thank the questioner.

Strategy II: Justification of the original work—Used when there is a general attack on the research
Method
1. Read the commentary and identify the issues
2. Place the issues within a higher conceptual level
3. Respond to the greater issues in the context of the criticism.

to its RAM, you need to expedite your thinking by promptly unloading your short-term memory and using the external equipment to store, edit, and organize large quantities of information.

The golden rule for writing is that you write only when you really have something to say. Writing demands broad knowledge. The writing of a research report especially requires that you know what you are doing. Writing attitude is also very important. Although you are encouraged to write freely on your first draft, taking it as your final draft will sometimes make you more serious and you may thus make faster progress. Don't be blocked by a desire for perfection, however. Do the best you can, and always do something to keep progressing and writing. You should know that a successful author is probably not someone who can produce a book overnight, but someone who can write something each day or each week. Some general readings on composition written by language professors would help with many technical details (e.g., Veit, 1990). Those guides may not really help much in conducting and understanding research, yet they are useful references for writing papers and reports. Of course, if you are already good at writing and you can keep producing something, probably you are the one who should teach yourself and even write a guide for others.

All in all, research seems to be a creative business. It is not just the application of the techniques you have learned from the research methods classes. Simply following the procedures will lead you to certain results and findings. But extraordinary efforts must be guided by innovative ideas and insights. The experiential approach of learning by doing will equip you with unique skills and insights that are needed for high quality work.

Wrapping up the project

After your data analysis as well as presentation of results have addressed all your research questions and hypotheses, it is time for you to draw conclusions and explain them. Investigators may use the concluding part of a research report to summarize the major findings by recapitulating the important results of the data analysis. Some would further ponder the results in an attempt to arrive at some overall conclusions by taking the findings as a whole. In a more adventurous effort, certain generalizations may be made based on the particular research project. This is seldom considered legitimate by methodologists as they require the researchers to strictly confine themselves within the range supported by their

Strategy III: Diffusion of the criticism—Used when there is a global attack on the research topic, method, results, and the author must respond as with a commentary response

Method

1. Select an issue or topical area that was mentioned
2. Agree or disagree with the observation
3. Thank the questioner for her or his important observation
4. Discuss the issue, extending it beyond where the questioner has taken it.

Strategy IV: Counterattack—Used when the author needs to justify their own approach/results by selecting errors or poor examples from other research

Method

1. Identify the concerns
2. Sort the literature into those who agree and disagree with your research
3. Construct an argument to support your research by pointing out the errors, biases, or poor examples in the other research, including that conducted by the criticiser.

Strategy V: Choosing to ignore the criticism—Used when responding to criticism would result in a worthless debate or a continued personal attack on the author

Method

1. Identify the issues and fully understand the concerns
2. If you decide these issues have no scientific basis and that by your responding the issues would escalate, you may deliberately choose not to respond.

If you are asked to be a reviewer, you'll be given a guide on what criteria are required, and can use this to direct your comments. As mentioned above, being a reviewer can help improve your writing skills, but it can also help with the way you give and respond to feedback.

If you are called upon to give feedback you may find the following pointers helpful (summarised from Elwyn (2001), pp. 69–71).

• Make time for feedback

- Use a set order with priority given to the individual
- Avoid scoring points
- Be constructive
- Make observations, not assumptions
- Give reactions, not judgements
- Give specific examples, not general impressions
- Concentrate on what is possible and most important
- Use questions, not suggestions
- Don't be overwhelming.

Peer review and how it works

If you submit a paper to a journal or conference, it will be subjected to peer review. This means it will be sent to two to four people with expertise in the area of your research, or who are serving on the conference committee. If there is a call for papers for a journal or conference, you'll usually be told your paper has been accepted for review, and when you'll hear whether it will be chosen for the journal/conference. If you submit to a journal without there being a call for papers, you will get a letter saying your paper has been accepted for review, and how long you can expect to wait before you hear a result. As mentioned above, if you have not fulfilled the criteria for submission, you may be rejected without your paper being read. When you get feedback, it could take several forms: A rejection, an acceptance with minor or major revisions (this is the usual response), or an outright acceptance (very rare, but fantastic when it happens!). With conferences you may be asked to present your work in a different format to that which you proposed (for example, a poster instead of a paper). With journal papers you'll be given a time limit to return corrections.

If you feel that your paper hasn't been read properly, or has been unfairly reviewed, you can appeal with the editor—pointing out where any irregularities lie in the reviewers' comments. Don't feel that comments you receive from reviewers have to be followed to the letter—they are usually suggestions for change. If, however, they are not possible, or do not fit with the aim of your paper, then you'll need to indicate this in a letter to the editor when you return your draft.

Getting feedback can be stressful. Sometimes reviewers hide behind an anonymous review to be downright unpleasant. I'm not in favour of this academic bullying, and feel that reviews should, where possible, be open—we should know who is writing them (see also

Morrow-Brown, 2003). After all, if they're confident to make negative or personal remarks, they should be equally confident to put their name to them.

It is recognised that getting a bad review can be hurtful, and even put people off writing in the future (Stern, 1997). Therefore if you receive an upsetting review, you should draw this to the attention of the editor—the same goes for lengthy delays or lack of feedback in the reviewing process. It is particularly important where junior or lay researchers are involved, since academic discussions may seem even more brutal to these groups.

Peer reviews should point out errors, omissions, and lack of clarity in work. They should also provide solutions and offer additional references or ideas for improving the work. Anything that goes beyond this, and is particularly abusive about the chosen method or the researchers, should not be accepted unless the researcher has breached ethical standards relating to participants and deserves harsh criticism.

Dealing with the media

Before you take your research story to the press, first consider whether you want publicity. Getting press interest can help promote your research and transmit findings to a wide audience (Boynton, 2003d; White, Evans, Mihill, & Tysoe, 1993). It can invite negative publicity on occasion, or sometimes, frustratingly, no attention at all. You can get press interest in the following ways—you send out a press release about your research, the press contacts you after your work is presented at a conference or appears in a journal, or your name is associated with a general research area and journalists contact you about that issue. If you want to have press interest, keep it in perspective. There's no point in sending out a press release for a final-year project, or a national release if you have completed a small-scale, local project that will have little or no national interest. Therefore if you are considering publicising the outcomes of your research, keep it in perspective. Local media for a local story that's needed to reach your immediate community; a national release for a study of national interest.

> When I want to send out details of my research to the media, I don't write releases myself. I'm really bad at doing them. Instead I get our press office to do it, as they're really skilled. They help me decide the key issues that need flagging up, and help me

deal with the media enquiries when they come in. (Jung Lee, research manager)

If you have to write a press release, you'll need to check the following: design, distribution, timing, and composition (White *et al.*, 1993, p. 75). This means that an appropriately designed release is sent to the right people at the right time (for example, just before a conference or when a paper is due to be published—after this the "story" ceases to be "news"). Your release should cover the five Ws (who, when, what, where, why), and you should write it in a way that is concise but snappy. Always provide a contact number for the key researcher who will be talking to the press, and ensure they are around to do these interviews. You will find that people in your media office are highly skilled in writing releases, so where possible get them to advise or help you, since it saves time and gives the release a better chance of hitting the headlines.

If you are going to talk about your research, it is a good idea to set aside time when you can tell journalists you'll be available. You may want to do a press launch where journalists are invited to hear the results of research, but this is only really necessary for large-scale projects. For smaller-scale projects a press release will suffice. If you've not dealt with journalists before, it is a good idea to receive training in dealing with the media, to ensure you can speak confidently and deliver a key message clearly. Universities, professional bodies, charities, and organisations offer media training, and it is worth doing a course (see also Boynton, 2003d; Kutner & Beresin, 1999; Shortland & Gregory, 1991; Stauffer, 1994; White *et al.*, 1993).

Having decided to talk to the press about your research, the tips in Table 8.3 may be helpful (see also Boynton, 2003d; White *et al.*, 1993).

Dissemination—who pays?

Depending on the scale and purpose of your research, you need to incorporate the cost of disseminating information. This may include attending conferences, or producing, copying, and distributing reports or papers. For smaller studies these costs may be lower, but shouldn't be left to the end of the research before they are considered. For any research involving participants, some form of feedback should be offered—be that a summary sheet about the research or a copy of the final outcomes. In addition, pay attention to who is working on your project. Many conferences require payment in advance for

TABLE 8.3

Media checklist

- ☐ Always take advice from your media support department, and use them for backup whenever you are uncertain.
- ☐ Work out with the reporter what is required, what they want to know, and what their deadline is.
- ☐ If you need time to think of your answer, request this and call the journalist back in half an hour or so.
- ☐ If you have any release or research summary you can send them, offer this as it may help build their story.
- ☐ Give them details of your background, where you work, and what you do. I often find journalists refer to me as a therapist, or a psychiatrist, because "psychologist" is a misunderstood title—I remind them I'm a research psychologist in order to clarify things. If possible, place your details on a website, or a résumé that you can send out on request.
- ☐ Keep your answers short and simple, without jargon, and without "talking down".
- ☐ If you are talking about an issue that is controversial or debated, then explain this. If a topic is up for discussion, you shouldn't imply that your view is the only one.
- ☐ You can ask to see a copy of the story they are working on, but in most cases this doesn't happen. This is why it is important that your press release is clear and correct: many journalists will work from this, and may not even talk to you.
- ☐ Find out what they want you for—is it a quote for a paper, or a television or radio show? If it's for a show, ask whether you'll be the only contributor or whether it will be a discussion (you don't want to end up in an unexpected debate).
- ☐ Ask who'll be interviewing you if you are going to do a programme, and also request the questions you'll be asked.
- ☐ If you need to travel to get there, ask if they can provide this.
- ☐ Find out how long you'll be needed for.
- ☐ Be positive: use questions as keys to advertise your own work and what you want to say.
- ☐ Have an agenda—say at the start what you want to talk about, and return to it.
- ☐ Make your key points at the start, and summarise at the close of the interview if possible.
- ☐ Keep to the point and be assertive; don't let the interviewer go off the point or draw you into an argument. Repeat your answers calmly.
- ☐ Don't use jargon or complicated terms—everyday language is fine.
- ☐ Try and think of some key soundbites or headlines that summarise what you want to say and try and get them into your interview.
- ☐ Make a note of what you want to say, and anticipate the question(s) you really don't want to be asked—just in case they are.
- ☐ You will usually be edited unless it's a live interview. That means that whether it's a programme, newspaper, or magazine, you need to get your key message in at the start and keep repeating it.

registration, along with the costs of accommodation and travel. This may not be suitable for all, as the quote below illustrates.

> *I'm currently employed as a lay researcher on a large-scale research project on mental health service users. I enjoy the work and was really pleased when our head of department asked me if I'd like to help present some preliminary findings at a conference. I agreed, but since then it's been really bad. When I registered they wanted payment up front. The way it seems to work is that I have to pay and it gets paid back from my department, but I didn't have the money for that. My department didn't have the facilities to pay for me upfront, so my boss had to, which I could tell she didn't like and I hated having to ask her. It got worse when we had to arrange travel. They wanted me to book online, and it asked for my credit card details. I don't have a credit card. I have a bank account but again I didn't have enough money to pay upfront for my fare. So my boss had to get a colleague to pay that for me. I know they get the money back but I felt like I was begging.* (P.J., community researcher)

Therefore, when designing a study, it is important to consider the needs of your staff. If conferences or travel will be part of the research, and the staff you are likely to be employing may not have the resources to pay for them, you need to discuss with your finance department how this can be managed. Many lay researchers or junior staff members may not have extra savings or facilities to fund extras like travel. Therefore enable them with travel cards or by paying for their costs (see also Griffiths, 2002). Do not expect them to have to do so upfront, particularly if this could lead to embarrassment for them. Again, these costs should be planned at the start of a study, not when researchers are in place.

Who is responsible for research dissemination?

Chapter 2 outlined the different positions held by researchers within a study. If you are the sole researcher then it is down to you to decide when and how your research should be disseminated. If, however, you are part of a team, the spokesperson for the research needs to be discussed alongside the issue of authorship. It is usually the grant holder that talks about the study, although the lead researcher may share the discussions with the media, writing of reports, or preparing a press release, since they'll have been closer to the data. What isn't acceptable in research is talking about findings publicly before research has been published (unless it's work in progress), or making claims beyond the data. Many professional bodies have specific guidelines on what you can and cannot say in reports or dealings with the press, and it is worth familiarising yourself with those. Finally, when sharing research, keep it relevant, and focus on the community that most need to hear it. Don't forget you need to keep the needs and dignity of participants uppermost in your mind, and make sure you don't get so carried away in a presentation or conversation that you compromise their right to confidentiality (Lipson, 1997).

We need to share our research for a number of reasons. It tells people what we found out, contributes to knowledge, and can inform policy or enlighten us about research practice. If you find that your study reveals unexpected or disappointing results, or your work doesn't happen the way you expected, you can still write about this so other researchers can avoid similar problems (a bit like I've done with this book). Think of sharing information as a way of increasing your skills, your networks, and your knowledge.

Endnote 9

I hope you've enjoyed reading this book, and have found it useful. Research is an ever-changing and ongoing entity, and I have found myself learning more about it as I've gone along. Since there is so much to discuss about research, you may want to share your questions and solutions with others after reading this book. You can do so in the forums on our website: http://www.psypress.co.uk/boynton.

These discussion forums are there for you to ask questions, share experiences, or offer advice. They are not a replacement for ongoing research management, or ethical approval for research, and may not reflect the views of all researchers. It is advisable that you read this book through before posting a message, since questions asking for advice covered in this book will not be included. Please respect others' views and learning experiences when posting on this board. Abusive or offensive postings will be removed.

1 Methods

Not sure what method to use for your research? Have you ever used the "wrong" method by mistake? Don't know where to begin? Post your questions and views here.

2 Computer packages to help with research

Having trouble understanding or using a research database, or do you have one to recommend? Been on a good training course? Share your experiences here.

3 Planning research

Running into logistical problems, or maybe you have some ideas of good practice you'd like to talk about?

4 Managing your research

Do you have ideas about how to keep research on track, or have you found it slipping out of your control? Tell us about your experiences.

5 Working effectively with participants

Are your participants driving you to distraction? Or do you have some tips on how to manage people effectively?

6 Researcher safety and well-being

Do you feel at risk at work, or is your research making you feel uncomfortable? Do you have examples of good practice within your research organisation?

7 Managing and cleaning your data

Dirty data mounting up? Share tips on keeping it under control here.

8 Qualitative/quantitative analysis

Are you finding it difficult to analyse your "data", or do you have ideas on how to improve data analysis? Post your ideas here.

9 Presenting and reporting data

Want to present your findings in the best way possible? Share your hints and tips here.

10 Recommend resources

Is there a research book, paper, website, conference, or other resource you've found helpful? Don't reinvent the wheel: recommend research materials here!

Finally, it's vital to remember that research is a learning experience as well as a means of finding answers to issues. Therefore it's important to acknowledge, discuss, and share your experiences as you develop your skills as a researcher. To that end, I leave you with a few pointers to help your day-to-day survival:

- Keep things in perspective
- Ask for help if you need it
- Share and/or delegate wherever possible
- Think about planning your work; do as much as you can at the start as this will save your time and energy later
- Don't let research take over your life—take regular holidays and breaks.

I have learned so much through completing research, and even more through writing this book. During the course of this book's writing certain research issues have received lots of attention in the press—for example, research governance, ethics, and declaring conflict of interest in studies. There have been changes in the way that health and social care has been structured, as well as a greater awareness of the need to offer researchers proper training. The role of the consumer or lay researcher has also gained ground and support, and many projects now require consumer involvement in their planning stages.

I anticipate that there will be more changes in the years ahead, and I look forward to learning a great deal more from the feedback you give me about this book, and your own research stories. I've enjoyed compiling this book, and am aware that there are always issues that could have been missed out—such is the case with research. So feel free to contribute to the message boards (http://www.psypress.co.uk/boynton), or contact me with your comments and ideas at info@drpetra.co.uk.

data. As a starting point for new inquiry, however, such generalizations can be valuable by serving as new research hypotheses and stimulating theoretical exploration. Indeed, inference from the results to the theoretical structure is a necessary condition for theoretical development.

Oftentimes the concluding part of a research report will also include some discussions about the research project and its findings. The researcher may discuss the implications of the findings to theory development, practical application, and/or policy making. It should be noted that it is often value issues that become the focus of argument. In writing the research proposal as well as the research report, you may be advised to make sure that no one will be hurt and no important political group will be offended. In other words, try to be analytical rather than critical as much as you can. For the sake of your project, these are helpful instructions indeed. Nevertheless, as a matter of science as well as justice, the social researcher can hardly keep "neutral" for ever. Specifically, the emergence of critical social science is posing a greater and greater challenge to the traditional positivist point of view. It is left with you, the researcher and author, therefore, to choose your own path and wrap up your research project.

The researcher should provide an adequate assessment of the significance of the results no matter what others may say about them. Although overstatement can be a problem, the researcher's expertise and experience should be respected. Like other aspects of life the research community also needs to maintain its norms and standards by gate-keeping and criticism. These measures certainly help to improve research work and to maintain academic/professional standards. However, judgment made by others could be more arbitrary than that made by people deeply involved in the research project. To make the different views complement each other, a thorough understanding as well as effective communication is needed.

No study is perfect. The shortcomings and limitations of the particular project should be pointed out in the discussion. This will help to clarify not only the conditions of the findings but also potential directions for future research. An inherent task of any research project is to elicit more theoretical questions and find new research problems. Probably due to the nature of research, social science will never achieve its ultimate end. Even for a perfectly executed statistical test, for example, there are always the Type I and Type II errors associated with its result. The process of research is actually often imperfect. Although our sampling strategy tends to deviate from the simple random logic, we seldom adjust for the practical complication beyond weighting for some

References

American Psychological Association (1994). *Publication manual of the American Psychological Association* (4th ed.). Washington, DC: APA.

Banyard, P., & Hunt, N. (2002). Reporting research: Something missing? *The Psychologist, 13*(2), 63–71.

Benson, A., & Blackman, D. (2003). Can research methods ever be interesting? *Active Learning in Higher Education, 4*(1), 39–55.

Blaxter, L., Hughes, C., & Tight, M. (2001). *How to research* (2nd ed.). Buckingham, UK: Open University Press.

Boote, J., Telford, R., & Cooper, C. (2002). Consumer involvement in health research: A review and research agenda. *Health Policy, 61*(2), 213–236.

Boston, N., Boynton, P. M., & Hood, S. (1999). *An evaluation of a GP ward in an inner city area*. Kensington & Chelsea and Westminster Health Authority, London; NHS R&D.

Boston, N., Boynton, P. M., & Hood, S. (2001a). An inner city GP unit versus conventional care for elderly patients: Prospective comparison of health functioning, use of services and patient satisfaction. *International Journal of Family Practice, 18*(2), 141–148.

Boston, N., Boynton, P. M., & Hood, S. (2001b). GP use and views of an inner city GP unit. *British Journal of General Practice, 51*, Feb., 139.

Bowling, A. (1997). *Research methods in health: Investigating health and health services*. Buckingham, UK: Open University Press.

Boynton, P. M. (1998). People should participate in, not be subjects of, research. *British Medical Journal, 317*, 1521.

Boynton, P. M. (2002). Life on the streets: The experiences of community researchers in a study of prostitution. *Journal of Community and Applied Social Psychology, 12*(1), 1–12.

Boynton, P. M. (2003a). Keeping sex secret: The hidden aspects of sex-research. *Radical Statistics*, special issue, *Sexuality and Radical Research*, 42–57.

Boynton, P. M. (2003b). "I'm just a girl who can't say no"? Women, consent and sex research. *Journal of Sex and Marital Therapy, 29*(s), 23–32.

Boynton, P. M. (2003c). How to get the best advice from academics. *PsychTalk, 41*, October, 24–28.

Boynton, P. M. (2003d). Never trust a journalist? A woman's guide to working in the media. *Psychology of Women Section Review, 5*(1), spring, 15–25.

Boynton, P. M., Bucknor, N., & Morton, J. (1998). *Somebody's daughters, somebody's sisters: A reflection of Wolverhampton working women's lives*. Birmingham, UK: Aston University.

Boynton, P. M., & Catt, S. (2002). Selling yourself in the psychology job market. *PsychTalk*, spring, 6–12.

Boynton, P. M., Catt, S., & Wood, G. (2001). Overcoming overuse of undergraduates in research. *The Psychologist*, Jan., 14(1).

Boynton, P. M., Greenhalgh, T., & Wood, G. (2004). A hands-on guide to questionnaire research. Reaching beyond the white middle classes. *British Medical Journal*, 328, 1433–1436.

Boynton, P. M., & Wood, G. (1998). (Un)Learning difficulties: Workshop on sensitive topics in psychological research, *British Psychological Society Regional (West Midlands) Conference*, Aston University, Birmingham, April.

British Psychological Society (2000). *Code of conduct, ethical principles and guidelines.* Leicester, UK: BPS.

Broadhead, R. S. (2001). Hustlers in drug-related AIDS prevention: Ethnographers, outreach workers, injection drug users. *Addiction Research and Theory*, 9(6), 545–556.

Bulmer, M. (2001). The ethics of social research. In N. Gilbert (Ed.), *Researching social life* (2nd ed.). Thousand Oaks, CA: Sage.

Burman, E. (2000). Method, measurement and madness. In L. Holzman & J. Marss (Eds.), *Postmodern psychologies, societal practice and political life*. London: Routledge.

Carr, B. J. (2001). Making the best of consumer participation. *Journal of Qualitative Clinical Practice*, 21, 37–39.

Carter, Y. (1997). Writing a research proposal and getting funded. In Y. Carter & C. Thomas (Eds.), *Research Methods in Primary Care*. Oxford, UK: Radcliffe Medical Press.

Cherry, F. (1995a). *The "stubborn particulars" of social psychology: Essays on the research process.* London: Routledge.

Cherry, F. (1995b). Are you a "real" scientist? *The "stubborn particulars" of social psychology: Essays on the research process*. London: Routledge.

Cooper, H. M. (1989). *Integrating research: A guide for literature reviews.* Thousand Oaks, CA: Sage.

Cresswell, J. W. (2002). *Research design: Qualitative, quantitative, and mixed methods approaches* (2nd ed.). Thousand Oaks, CA: Sage.

Danziger, K. (1990). *Constructing the subject: Historical origins of psychological research.* Cambridge, UK: Cambridge University Press.

Denscombe, M. (1998). *The good research guide: For small-scale social research projects.* Buckingham, UK: Open University Press.

Department of Health (2001). *Research Governance Framework for Health and Social Care.* London: Department of Health.

Dickerson, F. B. (1998). Strategies that foster empowerment. *Cognitive and Behavioural Practice*, 5(2), 255–275.

Dickson, D. (1998). UK contract staff need help, says report. *Nature*, 395(6703), 631.

Drenth, J. P. H. (1998). Multiple authorship: The contribution of senior authors. *Journal of the American Medical Association*, 280(3), 219–221.

Elwyn, G. (2001). Facilitation. In G. Elwyn, T. Greenhalgh, & F. Macfarlane (eds.), *Groups: A guide to small group work in healthcare, management, education and research*. Abingdon, UK: Radcliffe Medical Press.

Elwyn, G., Greenhalgh, T., & Macfarlane, F. (2001). *Groups: A guide to small group work in healthcare, management, education and research*. Abingdon, UK: Radcliffe Medical Press.

Fielding, J. (2001). Coding and managing data. In N. Gilbert (Ed.), *Researching Social Life* (2nd ed.). Thousand Oaks, CA: Sage.

Galvan, J. L. (1999). *Writing literature reviews: A guide for students of the social and behavioral sciences.* Los Angeles, Pyrczak Publishing.

Game, A., & West, M. A. (2002). Principles of publishing. *The Psychologist*, 15(3), 126–127.

Gillespie, H., & King, S. (1998). *The lonely doctor's survival guide*. London: Chelsea and Westminster Hospital Trust.

Greenhalgh, T. (2001). *How to read a paper: The basics of evidence based medicine* (2nd ed.). London: BMA Books.

Greenhalgh, T., & Donald, A. (2000). *Evidence based health care workbook: understanding research; for individual and group learning*. London: BMJ Books.

Gregory, D., Russell, C. K., & Phillips, L. R. (1997). Beyond textual perfection: Transcribers as vulnerable persons. *Qualitative Health Research, 7*(2), 294–300.

Griffiths, M. (2002). How to get conference funding if your department won't pay! *PsyPag Quarterly*, September.

Griffiths, M. (2003). Tips on giving poster presentations. *British Medical Journal, 326* (Student ed.), 46.

Hadjistavropoulos, T., & Smythe, W. E. (2001). Elements of risk in qualitative research. *Ethics and Behavior, 11*(2), 163–174.

Haivas, I. (2003). Doctors' well-being. *British Medical Journal, 326*, 718.

Hart, C. (1998). *Doing a literature review: Releasing the social science research imagination*. Thousand Oaks, CA: Sage.

Have a Job, Give a Damn Project (2003). *Get ahead: How to be more successful at work*. London. Have a Job, Give a Damn Project.

Hoen, W. P., Walvort, H. C., & Overbeke, J. P. M. (1998). What are the factors determining authorship and the order of the authors' names? *Journal of the American Medical Association, 280*(3), 217–218.

Hopkin, K. (1998). How to wow a study section: A grantsmanship lesson. *Scientist, 12*(5), 11–12.

Houghton, A. (2003). Tips on what to do if you are being bullied. *British Medical Journal, 326* (Student ed.), 130.

Howitt, D. (1991). Tribulations of real-world psychologists. *Concerning psychology: Psychology applied to social issues*. Milton Keynes, UK: Open University Press.

Howitt, D., & Cramer, D. (2000). *First steps in research and statistics: A practical workbook for psychology students*. London: Routledge.

Howitt, D., & Owusu-Bempah, K. (1994). *The racism of psychology*. London: Harvester Wheatsheaf.

Hupcey, J. E. (1997). Responding to criticism. In J. M. Morse (Ed.), *Completing a qualitative project: Details and Dialogue*. Thousand Oaks, CA: Sage.

Involve (2003). *Involving the public in NHS, public health and social care research: Briefing notes for researchers*. Eastleigh, UK: Involve.

Kendall, M., & Carter, Y. (1997). Research ethics committees. In Y. Carter & C. Thomas (Eds.), *Research methods in primary care*. Oxford, UK: Radcliffe Medical Press.

Kendra, M. A., & George, V. D. (2001). Defining risk in home visiting. *Public Health Nursing, 18*(2) 128–137.

Kidd, D., & Stark, C. (1992). Violence and junior doctors working in psychiatry. *Psychiatric Bulletin, 16*, 144–145.

Kutner, L., & Beresin, E. V. (1999). Media training for psychiatry residents. *Academic Psychiatry, 23*(4), 227–232.

Levy, M. (1997). *Presentation tips and techniques*. Ely, UK: Wyvern Crest Publications.

Lewontin, R. C. (1993). *The doctrine of DNA: Biology as ideology*. London: Penguin.

Lipson, J. G. (1997). The politics of publishing: Protecting participants' confidentiality. In J. M. Morse (Ed.), *Completing a qualitative project: Details and dialogue*. Thousand Oaks, CA: Sage.

Lipson, J. G., Stern, P. N., May, K. A., Morse, J. M., & Thorne, S. (1997). On terminating a project. In J.M. Morse (Ed.), *Completing a qualitative project: Details and dialogue*. Thousand Oaks, CA: Sage.

Mandel, S. (1987). *Effective presentation skills*. London: Kogan Page.

Mason, J. (1996). Sorting, organising and indexing qualitative data. In *Qualitative researching*. Thousand Oaks, CA: Sage.

McDonnell, A., Dearden, B., & Richens, A. (1991). Staff training in the management of violence and aggression. Setting up a training system. *Mental Handicap, 19*, June, 73–76.

Meretrix, M. (2001). *Turning pro: A guide to sex work for the ambitious and the intrigued*. Emeryville, CA: Greenery Press.

Midmer, D. (2003). Presentation magic. *BMJ Career Focus, 326*, 120.

Morrow-Brown, H. (2003). Peer review should not be anonymous. *British Medical Journal, 326*, 824.

Morse, J. M. (1997). *Completing a qualitative project: Details and dialogue*. Thousand Oaks, CA: Sage.

Nadwairski, J. A. (1992). Inner-city safety for home care providers. *Journal of Nursing Administration, 22*(9), 42–47.

NHS (2001). *Public Engagement Toolkit*. Durham: Northern and Yorkshire Region NHS Executive.

NHS (2002). *Toolkit for producing patient information*. London: Department of Health.

Norris, J. R. (1997). Meaning through form: Alternative modes of knowledge representation. In J. M. Morse (Ed.), *Completing a qualitative project: Details and dialogue*. Thousand Oaks, CA: Sage.

Owen, J. (1992). Death threats to psychiatrists. *Psychiatric Bulletin, 16*, 142–144.

Paasche-Orlow, M. K., Taylor, H. A., & Brancati, F. L. (2003). Readability standards for informed-consent forms as compared with actual readability. *New England Journal of Medicine, 348*(8), 721–726.

Paice, E., & Firth-Cozens, J. (2003). Who's a bully then? *British Medical Journal, 326* (Student ed.), 127.

Parkinson, M. (1994). *Interviews made easy: How to gain the psychological advantage*. London: Kogan Page.

Parrott, L. (1999) *How to write psychology papers* (2nd ed.). London: Longman.

Paterson, B. L., Gregory, D., & Thorne, S. (1999). A protocol for researcher safety. *Qualitative Health Research, 9*(2), 259–269.

Phillips, E. M., & Pugh, D. S. (2000). *How to get a PhD: A handbook for students and their supervisors* (3rd ed.). Buckingham, UK: Open University Press.

Plain English Campaign (2001). *How to write medical information in plain English*. Available online at http://www.plainenglish.co.uk.

Quinn, P. (1994). *How to think on your feet*. London: Kogan Page.

Reay, D. (1998). Surviving in dangerous places: Working-class women, women's studies and higher education. *Women's Studies International Forum, 21*(1), 11–19.

Reif-Lehrer, L. (1995). *Grant application writer's handbook*. Boston: Jones & Bartlett.

Report to the Director of Public Health (1998). *Bethan's Story/Stori Bethan*. Swansea, UK: Lechyd Morgannwg Health.

Rhodes, P., Nocon, A., Booth, M., Chowdrey, M. Y., Fabian, A., Lambert, N., Mohammed, F., & Walgrove, F. (2002). A service users' research advisory group from the perspectives of both service users and researchers. *Health and Social Care in the Community, 10*(5), 402–409.

Robson, C. (1993). *Real world research: A resource for social scientists and practitioner-researchers*. Oxford, UK: Blackwell.

Rosaldo, D. (1989). *Culture and truth: The remaking of social analysis*. London: Routledge.

Schepers, J. S., Sadler, E. J., & Raun, W. R.

(2000). Grantsmanship hints. *Agronomy Journal, 92*(1), 1–5.

Shah, A., & De, T. (1998). The effect of an educational intervention package about aggressive behaviour directed at the nursing staff on a continuing care psychogeriatric ward. *International Journal of Geriatric Medicine, 13*(1), 35–40.

Shelton, N., Laoire, C., Fielding, S., Harvey, D. C., Pelling, M., & Duke-Williams, O. (2001). Working at the coalface: Contract staff, academic initiation and the RAE. *Area, 33*(4), 434–439.

Shortland, M., & Gregory, J. (1991). *Communicating science: A handbook.* London: Longman.

Slife, B. D., & Williams, R. N. (1995). *What's behind the research? Discovering the hidden assumptions in the behavioural sciences.* Thousand Oaks, CA: Sage.

Snowdon, C., Garcia, J., & Elbourne, D. (1998). Reactions of participants to the results of a randomised controlled trial: Exploratory study. *British Medical Journal, 317,* 4 July, 21–26.

Stauffer, D. (1994). *Mediasmart: How to handle a reporter by a reporter.* Minneapolis, MN: MinneApple Press.

Stern, P. N. (1997). Strategies for overcoming the rage of rejection. The case of the qualitative researcher. In J. M. Morse (Ed.), *Completing a qualitative project: Details and dialogue.* Thousand Oaks, CA: Sage.

Tallon, D., Chard, J., & Dieppe, P. (2000). Consumer involvement in research is essential. *British Medical Journal, 320,* 380–381.

Terre Blanche, M., & Durrheim, K. (1999). *Research in practice: Applied methods for the social sciences.* Cape Town, South Africa: University of Cape Town Press.

The Royal College of Psychiatrists (1998). *Management of imminent violence: Clinical practice guidelines.* Blackmore, Dorset, UK: The Royal College of Psychiatrists.

Ubel, P. A., Zell, M. M., Miller, D. J., Fischer, G. S., Peters-Stefani, D., & Arnold, R. M. (1995). Elevator talk: Observational study of inappropriate comments in a public space. *American Journal of Medicine, 99,* 190–194.

White, D. (2003). Consumer and community participation: A reassessment of process, impact and value. In G. L. Albrecht, R. Fitzpatrick, & S. C. Scrimshaw, (Eds.), *The Handbook of Social Studies in Health and Medicine.* Thousand Oaks, CA: Sage.

White, S., Evans, P., Mihill, C., & Tysoe, M. (1993). *Hitting the headlines: A practical guide to the media.* Leicester, UK: BPS Books.

Wilcox, L. J. (1998). Authorship: The coin of the realm, the source of complaints. *Journal of the American Medical Association, 280*(3), 216–217.

Wilkinson, S., & Kitzinger, C. (1996). *Representing the other: A feminism and psychology reader.* Thousand Oaks, CA: Sage.

Williams, T., Dunlap, E., Johnson, B. D., & Hamid, A. (1992). Personal safety in dangerous places. *Journal of Contemporary Ethnography, 21*(3), 343–374.

Wilson, H. S., & Hutchinson, S. A. (1997). Presenting qualitative research up close: Visual literacy in poster presentations. In J. M. Morse (Ed.), *Completing a qualitative project: Details and dialogue.* Thousand Oaks, CA: Sage.

Wood, G. W. (1999). Review of a protocol for researcher safety. *Psychology of Women Section Review, 2*(1), 64.

Woolgar, S. (1996). Psychology, qualitative methods and the ideas of science. In J. T. E. Richardson (Ed.), *Handbook of qualitative research methods for psychology and the social sciences.* Leicester, UK: BPS Books.

Wyatt, J. P., & Watt, M. (1995). Violence towards junior doctors in accident and emergency departments. *Journal of Accident and Emergency Medicine, 12*(1), 40–42.

Yate, M. J. (1992). *Great answers to tough interview questions: How to get the job you want* (3rd ed.). London: Kogan Page.

Author index

American Psychological Association, 163
Arnold, R. M., 103
Atkinson, P., 8, 9

Banyard, P., 3
Benson, A., 16
Beresin, E. V., 175
Blackman, D., 16
Blaxter, L., 68
Blaxter, L., 27, 63, 145
Boote, J., 47
Booth, M., 51
Boston, N., 5, 156
Bowling, A., 27
Boynton, P. M., 3, 4, 5, 33, 46, 47, 48–49, 71, 72, 100, 102, 109, 116, 120, 121, 155, 156, 174, 175
Brancati, F. L., 97
British Psychological Society, 58, 72, 88
Broadhead., R. S., 119
Bucknor, N., 3, 102
Bulmer, M., 91
Burman, E., 9, 114

Carr, B. J., 47
Carter, Y., 36, 58
Catt, S., 5, 46, 47, 48–49, 71, 120
Chamberlain, K., 8
Chard, J., 47
Cherry, F., 10, 111
Chowdrey, M. Y., 51
Cooper, C., 47
Cooper, H. M., 23

Cramer, D., 9, 88, 91, 99
Cresswell, J. W., 27
Cryer, P., 8

Danziger, K., 110
De, T., 130
Dearden, B., 130
Delamont, S., 8, 9
Denscombe, M., 8, 20, 27, 149
Dickson, D., 46
Dieppe, P., 47
Donald, A., 52
Drenth, J. P. H., 57
Duke-Williams, O., 46
Dunlap, E., 119
Durrheim, K., 16

Economy, P., 8
Elbourne, D., 99
Elwyn, G., 52, 169, 172
Evans, P., 174, 175

Fabian, A., 51
Fielding, J., 148
Fielding, S., 46
Firth-Cozens, J., 135
Fischer, G. S., 103

Galvan, J. L., 23
Game, A., 53
Garcia, J., 99
George, V. D, 119
Graham, L., 9
Greenhalgh, T., 24, 52, 121, 164, 169
Gregory, D., 119, 121

Gregory, J., 175
Griffiths, M., 166, 177

Hadjistavropoulos, T., 121
Haivas, I., 67
Hamid, A., 119
Hart, C., 23, 25
Harvey, D. C., 46
Have a Job, Give a Damn Project, 51
Heiman, G. A., 8
Hoen, W. P., 57
Hood, S., 5, 156
Hopkin, K., 36
Houghton, A., 135
Howitt, D., 3, 9, 88, 91, 99, 111, 114
Hughes, C., 27, 63, 145
Hunt, N., 3
Hupcey, J. E., 171
Hutchinson, S. A., 166

Involve (formerly Consumers in NHS Research), 4, 47, 50

Johnson, B. D., 119
Judd, C. M., 8

Kendall, M., 58
Kendra, M., 119
Kidd, D., 119
Kidder, L. H., 8
Kitzinger, C., 114
Kutner, L., 175

Lambert, N., 51
Laoire, C., 46
Ledbetter, D., 9
Levy, M., 167, 168
Lewontin, R. C., 111
Lipson, J. G., 109, 178

McDonnell, A., 130
Macfarlane, E., 52, 169
Mandel, S., 167
Mason, J., 8, 149
May, K. A., 109
Mental Health Foundation, 69
Meretrix, M., 69
Midmer, D., 168
Mihill, C., 174, 175
Miller, D. J., 103
Mohammed, F., 51
Morrow-Brown, H., 174
Morse, J. M., 109
Morton, J., 3, 102
Murray, M., 8

Nadwairski, J. A., 119
Nelson, B., 8
Nicholls, J., 162
NHS, 2001, 27
NHS, 2002, 74
NHS Information Authority Privacy Statement, 2002, 101
Nocon, A., 51
Norris, J. R., 27, 158

Overbeke, J. P. M., 57
Owen, J., 119
Owusu-Bempah, K., 111, 114

Paasche-Orlow, M. K., 97
Paice, E., 135

Parker, I., 9, 10
Parker, R. C., 10
Parkinson, M., 47
Parrott, L., 162
Parry, O., 8, 9
Paterson, B. L., 119
Pelling, M., 46
Peters-Stefani, D., 103
Phillips, E. M., 8
Phillips, L. R., 121
Plain English Campaign, 74, 87
Powell, K., 8
Pugh, D. S., 8

Quinn, P., 170

Race, P., 8
Raun, W. R., 36
Reay, D., 121
Reif-Lehrer, L., 36
Report to the Director of Public Health, 158
Rhodes, P., 51
Richardson, J. T. E., 8
Richens, A., 130
Robson, C., 4, 17, 27, 35, 63, 145, 148
Rosaldo, D., 110
Royal College of Psychiatrists, 119
Russell, C. K., 121
Russell, J., 164

Sadler, E. J., 36
Sapienza, A. M., 9
Schepers, J. S., 36
Shah, A., 130
Shelton, N., 46
Shortland, M., 175
Slife, B. D., 5, 19

Smith, R., 8
Smythe, W. E., 121
Snowdon, C., 99
Stark, C., 119
Stauffer, D., 175
Stern, P. N., 109, 161, 174

Tallon, D., 47
Taylor, H. A., 97
Telford, R., 47
Terre Blanche, M., 16
Thomas, S. A., 10
Thorne, S., 109, 119
Tight, M., 27, 63, 145
Trades Union Congress (TUC), 135
Tysoe, M., 174, 175

Ubel, P. A., 103

Walgrove, F., 51
Walvort, H. C., 57
Wang, W., 10
Watt, M., 119
West, M. A., 53
White, D., 47
White, S., 174, 175
Wilcox, L. J., 53
Wilkinson, S., 114
Williams, R. N., 5, 19
Williams, T., 119
Wilson, H. S., 166
Wood, G. W., 5, 71, 116, 120, 121, 135
Woolgar, S., 5, 19
Wyatt, J. P., 119

Yate, M.J., 47

Zagumny, M. J., 9
Zell, M. M., 103

Subject index

Entries for main headings that have subheadings represent introductory/general aspects of topic.

Entries for figures/tables appear in **bold**. Entries for exercises/researchers' experiences appear in *italic*.

Book titles appear in *italic*.

Accommodation/travel expenses, 175, 177
Accountability, staff, 39, 53, **54–55**, 56–57, *see also* Responsibility
Acknowledgments, 157, 162
Action research, **28**
Adaptability, *see* Flexibility
Addressing participants, 78, *see also* Interviews/visits; Letters of introduction; Telephone introductions
Advice/counselling, for participants, 73
Aggression, participant, 122, 130, 131, **134**, *see also* Risk; Safety; Well-being
Anonymity, participant, *see* Confidentiality/anonymity, participant
Ansaphones, 80, 83, **84**
Applications, job, 46–47, **48–49**
Archives, research, **25**
Art, *see* Creativity
Assertiveness training/negotiation skills, 33
Authoritarianism, researcher, *see* Manners

Authorship guidelines, **53**, 56, 57

Bethan's story/Stori Bethan, 158
Book reviews, writing, 160, 172–173
Boredom, *see* Motivation, researcher
Braille, for blind participants, 5, 73
Breakaway techniques, 130
Buddies, safety, 124
Budgets/funding, 19, 35–36
accommodation/travel, 175, 177
checklist, **37**
mistakes to avoid, **7**, 36
researchers' experiences, *35, 37*
resources, **36**
Bullying/harassment, **7**
by co-workers, 120, 121, 135–137, 171, 173
dealing with, 137–138
by participants, 121, 135
researchers' experiences, *120, 137–138, 171*
unacceptable behaviours, **136**

Career development/training/appraisal, 39
Case studies, **28**
participants, 75–76
Changes, *see* Flexibility
Closing/terminating interviews, 5, 108–109
Clothing, appropriate, 126
Cochrane Database of Systematic Reviews, **25**
Coercion, avoiding, 91, 93, 95, 98, *see also* Voluntary informed consent
Cold calling, 80
Collaboration, 33–35, **34**, *see also* Delegation
Commission for Racial Equality, 115
Communicating with your staff, **8**
Community
studies, 3, 4, 5, **7**, 71
support, 39
Complaints, participant, strategies for avoiding, **104**, **105**, **108**, *see also* Problems
Comprehension/piloting exercise, research questions, *64*

disproportionate stratification when calculating the errors. Also, different patterns of missing data for different variables will make a uniform treatment very difficult. For all such kinds of reasons, we can never be so sure as to become absolute about our research findings.

A complete research report should include necessary appendices, notes, and a bibliography. The researcher must guard against plagiarism by giving credit to information sources through proper citation. Methodologists and professional writers usually focus on the rules and formats of citation. Some practical issues in preparing the research report have not been adequately addressed. These issues may stem from some very early stages of a research project, such as note-taking in reviewing the literature. When you read an article or a book you often need to take notes as well as jot down your own thoughts. Some confusion will be caused later in writing the research report if you forget to distinguish between your notes of other people's words and your own thoughts. It is important, therefore, to repeatedly put the citations by your notes and quotes while using special symbols, such as brackets, to mark your own thoughts. This way you may avoid turning a technical issue into an ethical problem.

Generally speaking, it is a good idea to keep a record of all the things left over when writing your draft. When you start revising or rewriting the report, you will have a complete checklist to ensure nothing important will be omitted. One thing that you cannot forget about is to check your ethical responsibility in conducting the research project. The confidentiality of individual information, for example, must be observed as you promised the research subjects and as is required by the ethics of social science research.

Finally, wrapping up a project means the completion of the requirements for a research contract; or for a student that will mean the finishing of an academic degree. In finalizing the research report, thesis or dissertation, the intended audience, the purpose of the research, the content, the medium for communication, and the appropriate writing style should be kept in mind. Agency guidelines from the funding source, if any, must be honored. If you are a student, revision often has to be made following the comments and directions of your advisor or committee members. This is especially important when you are required to defend your work before the committee. Taking the suggestions and criticisms before and during the defense positively will provide you with a unique opportunity for improvement, which probably you can find in no other situation. This could be a painful process, though. Sometimes you feel you are so prepared that you are able to produce anything to meet the requirement.

Computer packages, **9**
Research companion
website, 179, 181
Computers/equipment, 39,
40, 41
Conference papers/
symposia, 164–165,
167–169
answering questions from
the audience, 170
nerves over public
speaking, 168
Confidentiality/anonymity,
participant, 101–102
researchers' experiences,
102, 110
test exercise, *94*
Consent, informed, *see*
Voluntary informed
consent
Consumers, research, 47, 50,
55, *see also* Involve;
Participants;
Stakeholders
Coping strategies, *see*
Motivation, researcher
Costs,
accommodation/travel,
175, 177, *see also*
Budgets/funding,
Counselling, for
participants, 73,
106–107
Creativity, in research
presentation, 27, 158
exercise, *159*
Crediting other studies, 22
Critical textwork, **9**
Criticism
response to, 171–172
strategies for dealing with,
104, **105**, **108**
Customers (stakeholders), **7,**
31–32, 32, *see also*
Participants
Cutting/editing reports, 102

Dance, *see* Creativity

Data analysis, 27, 30
Data cleaning, 3, **7**, 147, **148**
Data collection/
management, 3, **7,**
146–147, *see also*
Information;
Results/findings
checking qualitative data,
149
filing, 143, **144**
large datasets, 3, 5
participant details,
139–142
Research companion
website, 179, 180
routine inclusions,
149–150
Data entry, real time, 147
Data protection, 150–151
Data Protection Act (1998),
150
Databases
Current Educational
Research UK, 25
General Practice Research,
25
Medical Humanities
Resources, 160
participant details, 139,
140, 141
Reference Manager, **24**
researchers' experiences,
147
Debriefing participants,
99–100
Declaration of Helsinki, 91
Delegation, importance of,
69, 181
Depression, participant, 5,
108–109
Diaries, research, 144–146,
145, 146, *see also*
Creativity
Difference, *see also* Ethics
celebrating, 114–116, **115,**
116–117
respecting, 121, 123
Disabled access, 73

Discourse analytic research,
9
Dissertations/theses, 164
structure, **162–163**
Distress
participant, 122, 130, 131,
134
researcher, caused by
findings/interviews,
119, 121
Doc Potter's advice site, 69
The doctoral experience, **8**
Drama, *see* Creativity
Dress, appropriate, 126

Economic & Social Research
Council, list of funded
research, 25
Editing reports, 102
Efficiency, 2, **7,** *see also*
Data collection/
management;
Managing research
Ending/terminating
interviews, 5, 108–109
Equal Opportunities
Commission, 115
Equipment, essential, 39, **40,**
41
Ethics, research, 2, 3, **7,**
88–89, **90,** *see also*
Confidentiality;
Difference; Manners
exercise, *59*
and participant
representation, 100–101,
103
researchers' experiences,
59, 88–89
Ethics committees, 5, **7,** 39,
57–60
exercise, *59*
role in complaint/problem
prevention, 104
Ethnography, **29**
Evidence-based medical
information, **25**
Exclusion criteria, *see*

Inclusion/exclusion criteria
Exercises
  checking comprehension/ piloting, *64*
  confidentiality test, *94*
  creative presentation, *159*
  effects of participation, *99*
  ethics, *59*
  inclusion criteria, *143*
  interview appearance/ behaviour, *128*
  introductions, self, *72*
  obtaining informed consent, *97*
  perspectives, participant/ researcher, *111*
  planning/simplicity, *30*
  publicity, *86*
  reasons for doing research, *20*
  researcher skills and abilities checklist, *10–16*
  scoping research question, *22*
  stakeholder analysis, *32*
  talking about research, *109–110*
Expenses, *see* Budgets/ funding
Experimental methodology, **29**

Feedback, giving/receiving, 169, 170–173
  response to criticism, 171–172
  reviewing, 161, 172–174
Filing, 143, **144**
Film, *see* Creativity
Findings, research, *see* Results/findings
First steps in practical statistics, **9**
Flexibility, 4, 5
  managing research, 151
  research questions, 21
  time limits, 73

Focus groups, **28**
Format/presentation of results, 155, 158–160
Forms (VIC), 73, **92**, 95–97, **96**
Funding, *see* Budgets/ funding

Gantt charts, **42**, 144
General Practice Research Database, **25**
Grant holders, **54**
Grey literature, 25
Ground rules for good research, **8**
Guide to Intellectual and Financial Ownership, 57
Guidelines
  authorship, **53**, 56, 57
  humanitarian, *see* Voluntary informed consent; *see also* Ethics,
  safety, absence of, 119, 120–121, 122
Guidelines on Safety and Security for Associate Lecturers, 130

Handbook of qualitative research methods for psychology and the social sciences, **8**
Harassment, *see* Bullying/harassment
Hearing problems, participant, 5, 73
Help sheets, participant, **106–107**, *see also* Information forms
Hierarchies, staff, 39, 53, **54–55**, 56–57
Holidays, importance of, 69, 181
Holocaust Exhibition, Imperial War Museum, 91

How to get a good degree, **8**
How to get a Ph.D., **8**
How to write a great research paper, **9**
How to write health science papers, dissertations, and theses, **9**

Imperial War Museum, Holocaust Exhibition, 91
Incentives, participation, 88, 98–99, *99*
Inclusion/exclusion criteria, 3, 5, 73, 142–143
  exercise, *143*
Inclusivity, **115**, *see also* Difference, celebrating
Information, *see also* Data collection/management
  background/backup, 22–23
  dissemination, 157–158, *see also* Results/findings
  forms, for participants, 73, *see also* Help sheets
  Research companion layout, **7**
  sharing, 2, 154, 178
Informed consent, *see* Voluntary informed consent
Intellectual property rights, research, 7, 39, **53**, 56–57, *see also* Ownership
Intermediate care for older people study, 5
Interpreters/translation services, 5, 73, 83, 114
Interviews/visits, to participants
  acting on intuition/gut feelings, 127, 134–135
  arrival, 127
  bags, 126, 127
  breakaway techniques, 130
  closing, 5, 108–109, 128–129

clothing, wearing
appropriate, 126
distress/aggression,
participant, 121,
130–131, **134**
distress, researcher, 119,
121
during, 127–128
negotiating skills, 130
planning, **29**
researcher appearance/
behaviour exercise, *128*
safety issues, 124–125
supervision, researcher,
129–130
Interviews, for research
posts, 45, 47
Introducing studies (to
participants), 5, *72, see
also* Letters of
introduction; Telephone
introductions
Involve (formerly
Consumers in NHS
Research), 4, 47, 50, 159

Job applications, 46–47,
48–49
Journals, getting papers
accepted, 160–161

Language barriers, 5, 73, 83,
114
Letters of introduction, 73
checklist, **79**
composing, **74, 76**
concerns/worries/problems,
75–76, 78
mail-out strategies, 77–78
names/addresses/titles,
78
practicalities, 76–77
setting out, **77**
Literature searching, **7**
background/backup
information, 22–23
common worries, **24**
dos and don'ts, 25–26

grey literature, 25
methodology/training for,
23, 25
for research methodology,
62–63
ongoing, 61–62
online searches, 23, **25**
researchers' experiences,
23
unpublished studies, 25
using/crediting other
studies, 22
Local research ethics
committees (LRECs), 57
Loneliness
participant, 5, 108–109
researcher, 68

Mail-out strategies, 77–78,
see also Letters of
introduction
Management, staff, **7, 8**, *see
also* Supervision
hierarchies, 7
training, 51
Managing for dummies, **8**
Managing research, *see also*
Data collection/
management
changes/flexibility, 151
filing, 143, **144**
inclusion criteria exercise,
143
recycling, 151, **152**
recruitment, 141, 142
Research companion
website, 179, 181
research diaries, 144–146,
145, 146
sampling inclusion/
exclusion, 142–143
Managing scientists, **9**
Manners, towards
participants, 110–111,
112–113, *see also* Ethics
Measures, reviewing/
selecting, 62–63, *see also*
Methodology

Media, 157, 174–175, *see also*
Publicity; Results/
findings
checklist, **176**
media training, 175
participant representation,
100–101, 103
Medical Humanities
Resource Database
(University College
London), 160
Medline, 23
Methodology, 69
choice, **8**
creative, 27, 158, *159*
literature searching, 23,
25
planning approach, 26–27,
28–29
research, 62—63
Research companion
website, 179, 181
reviewing/selecting, 62–63
Microsoft® Office 2000 for
Windows® for dummies®,
9
MIND, 4
Mistakes, *see* Problems
Motivation, researcher, 7, 61,
66–69
experiences, *68*
strategies, **67**
time off/work sharing, 69,
181
MultiCentre research ethics
committees (MRECs),
57
Music, *see* Creativity

Names/addresses/titles,
participant, 78
National Foundation for
Educational Research,
database of Current
Educational Research
UK, 25
National Research Register
(NRR), 25

National Statistics Online, **25**
Needs
  participants, 5, 32–33, 72–73
  researchers, 5, 32–33, 39
Negotiation skills, 33, 130
Networking, 5, **7**, 33–35, **34**
  and steering groups, 52
NHS Centre for Reviews and Dissemination, 25
Nominal groups, **28**

Observation, **28**
Office equipment, 39, **40**, 41
Open University *Guidelines on safety and security for associate lecturers*, 130
Originality, research, 22, 62
Ovid, 23
Ownership, research
  Guide to Intellectual and Financial, 57
  intellectual property rights, **7**, 39, **53**, 56–57
  stakeholders, 31–32, 32

Painting, *see* Creativity
Participant/s, 3, 4, **7**, 71, 72, *see also* Ethics; Voluntary informed consent
  approaching, 5, 72, *see also* Letters of introduction; Telephone introductions
  bullying by, 121, 135
  case studies/opinions, 75–76
  celebrating differences, 114–116, **115, 116–117**
  closing/terminating sessions, 5, 108–109

complaints, strategies for avoiding, **104, 105, 108**
comprehension/understanding, 95–96
confidentiality/anonymity, 101–102, 110, 178
debriefing, 99–100
definitions, 71–72
distress/aggression, 122, 130, 131, **134**, *see also* Safety; Well-being
exercises in dealing with, *72, 111*
help sheets, **106–107**
implications of research for, 98, *99*, 103
incentives, 88, 98–99, *99*
inclusivity, **115**
manners towards, 110–111, **112–113**
names/addresses/titles, 78
needs, 5, 32–33, 72–73
perspectives, *111*
recording/collecting details, 139–142
recruitment, 141, 142
representation, media/reports, 100–101, 103
Research companion website, 179, 180
researchers' experiences, *75–6, 78, 84*
stereotypes, 120
type/background, 3, 5, 71, 97
Patients, *see* Participants
Peer review, 161, 172–174, *see also* Feedback, giving/receiving
Perspectives, participant/researcher, *111*
Pilot studies, **7**, 27, 61, 63–64, **65, 66**
  exercise, *64*
  timescales, 43

Planning research, **7**, 19, *see also* Budgets/funding; Literature searching
  background/backup information, 22–23
  data analysis, 27, 30
  exercise, *30*
  methodology, 26–27, **28–29**
  networking/collaboration, 33–35, **34**
  participant/researcher needs, 32–33
  purpose/scale, 30–31
  qualitative/quantitative, 26, 27, 30
  requirements of different studies, 19
  Research companion website, 179, 181
  research questions, 20–23
  stakeholder analysis, 31–32, 32
Poetry, *see* Creativity
Posters, 165–167
Practical skills, research, 1, 2
Presentation, results, 155, 158–160, *see also* Publication; Results/findings; Writing styles
Press releases, 174–175, *see also* Media; Publicity
Problems, **7**
  blame attribution, 5
  budgeting, **7**, 36
  participant, 5, 73, **104, 105, 108**, *see also* Help sheets
  schedules, failure to keep to, 43
  telephoning, 83, 84
  timescales, 43
Proofreading, 63
Property rights, research, **7**, 39, **53**, 56–57, *see also* Ownership
Prostitution study, 3–4, 102, 126
  impact, 154–155

PsycINFO, **25**
Public speaking, 168
Publication, research, 39,
160–161 *see also* Media;
Publicity; Results/
findings; Writing skills
Publicity, 85–88, *see also*
Media
exercises, *86, 94, 97,*
109–110
participant representation,
103
press releases, 174–175
pros/cons, *86*, 88
researchers' experiences,
85, 158
sources, **87**
timing, 86
websites, 87
PubMed, 23, **25**

Qualitative health psychology,
8
Qualitative methodology,
3, 4
data analysis, **9**
data checking, **149**
data cleaning, **148**
planning for, 26, 27, 30
Qualitative researching, **8**
Quantitative methodology,
3
data analysis, **9**
planning for, 26, 27, 30
Questionnaires, 4
planning for, **29**, 30
researcher skills and
abilities checklist,
exercise, *10–16*
Questions, research, 20–23,
22

R&D Forum, 57
Randomised controlled
trials (RCTs), **29**
Real-life situations, 4
Real time data entry, 147
Recycling, 151, **152**

Recruitment, participants,
141, 142
Reference Manager
database, **24**
References, formatting, **163**
Replication, research, 22,
62
Reports, *see also* Writing
skills
cutting/editing, 102
structure, **162–163**
Research, 181
archives, **25**
crediting other studies, 22
definition/nature, 16
delegating, 69, 181
experiences, *21, 30–31,*
43–44, 62–63
findings, *see*
Results/findings
getting started, **7**, 16–17
keeping in perspective, 181
objectives, 39, 43–44
planning, *see* Planning
research
problems/mistakes, *see*
Problems
property rights, **7**, 39, **53**,
56–57, *see also*
Ownership
publication, 39, *see also*
Media; Publicity;
Results/findings
questions, 20–23
reasons for doing exercise,
20
replication/originality, 22,
62
safety considerations, *see*
Safety
settings, 3, 5, **7**, 71
starting, **7**, 16–17
studies, managing, *see*
Managing research
staff, *see* Staff/staffing
Research assistants, **54**
Research companion
aims, 17

enjoyment, 16
how different, 2–5
how use, 6
layout, **7**
scope/coverage, 6, **7**,
8
why use, 1–2
Research coordinators/
managers, **54**, 55
Research diaries, 144–146,
145, 146
Research Governance
Framework, 57
Research methods in
psychology, **8**
Research methods in social
relations, **8**
The research student's guide to
success, **8**
Researcher/s, *see*
Staff/staffing
Researchers' experiences, 2
applying for work, *46*
approaching participants,
75–6, 78, 84
budgets/funding, *35, 37*
bullying at work, *120,*
137–138, 171
celebrating differences,
114–115
collaboration/networking,
34, 35
conference presentations,
feedback, *169*
confidentiality/anonymity,
102, 110
costs, accommodation/
travel, *177*
data analysis, *30*
databases, *147*
dealing with participant
distress/aggression,
131
ethics, *59, 88–89*
helping participants,
129
intellectual property
rights, *57*

keeping on top of things, *68*

literature searching, *23*

loneliness, *68*

media press releases, *174–175*

motivational strategies, **67**

posters, *166*

presentation of participants in reports, *101*

problems/complaints/ criticism, *104*

publicity, *85, 158*

recruitment, *141, 142*

replication/originality, *62*

reasons for research, *21*

research measures, *62–63*

research objectives, *43–44*

researcher needs, *32–33*

researcher well-being/ safety, *120, 123, 135*

simplicity, *30–31*

staff, advertising/ selection, *44, 45*

staff roles, *56*

staff training, *52*

statistics, *147*

steering groups, *52*

timescales, *42, 43*

validated/standardised measures, *62*

voluntary informed consent, *93*

writing skills/ presentation, *161, 164, 166*

Resources, research, **8, 9**

websites, **164**, 167, 180

Respect

for difference, 121, 123

for participants, 111, *see also* Ethics

Responsibility, researcher, **7**, *see also* Accountability

for research findings, 177–178

for safety, 122–123

Results/findings, 153–154, *see also* Media; Publicity; Writing styles

accommodation/travel, costs, 175, 177

disseminating information, 157–158

feedback, giving/ receiving, 169, 170–173

format/presentation, 155, 158–160

impact of findings, 154–155

information, importance of sharing, 2, 154, 178

multiple publications, 156–157

peer review, 161, 173–174

publication, 39

Research companion website, 179, 180

responsibility for, 177–178

target audience, 155–156

utilising your work, 154

Reviews, writing, 160, 172–173

Risk, 119–120, 130–31, *see also* Safety; Well-being

assessment, **132–133**

Safety, researcher, 41, *see also* Bullying/harassment; Interviews/visits; Well-being

buddies, 124

risks, 119–120, **132–133**

setting up safe practices, 123–124

staff training needs, 121, 123–124

stereotypes, 120

violence, 130–131

Sampling inclusion/ exclusion, *see* Inclusion/ exclusion criteria

Search engines/research archives, **25**

Secretaries, **55**

Settings, community/ student studies, 3, 5, **7**, 71, 97

Sharing

information, 2, 154, 178

workload, 69, 181

Signing, for deaf participants, 5, 73

Silverplatter, 23

Skills, research

checklist, *10–16*

gap, *see* Training

practical, 1, 2

Social Science Search Engine, **25**

Sponsors, research, *see* Ownership

The SPSS book, **9**

Staff/staffing, research, 39

accountability, 39, 53, **54–55**, 56–57, *see also* Responsibility

advertising/selection, 44–45

applying for posts, 46–47, **48–49**

assertiveness training/ negotiation skills, 33

career development/ training/appraisal, 39

collaboration, 33–35

experiences, *see* Researchers' experiences

interviews, 45, 47

management, *see* Management

needs, 5, 32–33, 39

perspectives, *111*

practical skills, 1, 2

Research companion website, 179, 181

roles/accountability/ hierarchies, 39, 53, **54–55**, 56–57

selection criteria, **45**

short-term contracts, 46

skills and abilities
  checklist, *10–16*
training, *see* Training
  researchers
well-being, *see* Well-being
workloads, 43
Stakeholders, **7**, 31–32, *32*
Standardised measures, 62
Standing Advisory Group
  on Consumer
  Involvement in NHS
  Research, 72
Statistical tests/analysis, 3,
  9, **55**
  researchers' experiences,
  147
Steering groups, 3, 39, 51–53,
  52, **54**
Stereotypes, participant, 120
  see also Safety; Well-
  being
Stories, *see* Creativity
Stress, coping with, 69
Students, using, 3, 5, **7**, 97
Studies, *see also* Research
  community/student
  based, 3, 5, **7**, 71, 97
  unpublished, 25
Subjects, *see* Participants
Supervision, researcher,
  129–130, *see also*
  Management; Training
Supervising the Ph.D., **9**
Symposia, 164–165, 167–169,
  170

Talk, telephone, 79–80
  example of conversation,
  82
Talking about research
  exercise, *109–110*
Target audience, 155–156
Teamwork, 5, 69, 181, *see also*
  Collaboration
Telephones, 79
  ansaphones/voicemail, 83,
  84
  cold calling, 80

example of conversation,
  82
messages, 80
preparation, 81, 83
problems, 83, 84
protocol, 81
talk, 79–80
timing, 80
Terminating interviews, 5,
  108–109
Theses, 164
  structure, **162–163**
Time limits, flexible, 73
Timescales, 39, 41–43
Training researchers, 5, 39
  assessing needs, 13, 50–51,
  50
  on budgets/funding, 35
  literature searching, 23,
  25
  management training,
  51
  media training, 175
  researchers' experiences,
  52
  safety/well-being, 119,
  120–124
  study skills, **8**
Translation services, 5, 73,
  83, 114
Transport, providing for
  participants, 73
Travel costs, researcher, 175,
  177
Triangulation, 27

University settings, 3, 5, **7**,
  97
Unpublished studies, 25

Validated/standardised
  measures, *62*
Violence, participant,
  130–131, *see also* Risk;
  Safety; Well-being
Visual problems,
  participant, 5, 73
Voicemail, 83, **84**

Voluntary informed consent
  (VIC), **7**, 91, *see also*
  Ethics
  avoiding coercion/
  pressure, 91, 93, 95, 98
  checklist, **96**
  comprehension/
  understanding, 95–96
  exercises, *94*, *97*
  forms, 73, **92**, 95–97, **96**
  inability to give consent,
  95
  obtaining, 91–94
  researchers' experiences,
  93
  stepwise guide, **93**
  participant incentives, 88,
  98–99, *99*
  refusal to participate, 3–4,
  95
  researcher concerns, 97–99
Volunteers, *see* Participants

Web of Knowledge, **25**
Web of Science, 23
Websites, **9**, **164**
  applying for research
  posts, 46
  Doc Potter's advice site, 69
  publicity, 87
  Research companion, 179,
  180
  writing skills, 167
Well-being, researcher, **7**, *see
  also* Bullying/
  harassment; Interviews/
  visits
  absence of
  guidelines/training,
  119, 120–121, 122
  awareness/respecting
  difference, 121, 123
  distress caused by
  findings/interviews,
  119, 121
  macho culture, 120
  negotiating skills, 130
  overcautiousness, 135

Research companion
    website, 179, 180
researchers' experiences,
    120, 123, 135
risks, 119–120, 130–31,
    132–133, *see also* Safety
staff training needs, 121,
    123–124
stereotypes, 120
Work, applying for, 46–47,
    48–49
Working from home, 41

Workloads, **7**, 43
    sharing, 69, 181
Workshops, 169–170
Workspace essentials, 39, **40**,
    41
Writing/presentation skills,
    2, *see also* Publication
acknowledgements, 157,
    162
conference papers/
    symposia, 164–165,
    167–169, 170

dissertations/theses, 164
posters, 165–167
references, formatting,
    163
report/dissertation/project
    structure, **162–163**
research papers, 160–161
researchers' experiences,
    161, 164, 166
resources/websites, **9**, **164**,
    167
workshops, 169–170